Social
Theory

Social Theory

JOHN WILSON
Duke University

Prentice-Hall, Inc., Englewood Cliffs, New Jersey 07632

Library of Congress Cataloging in Publication Data

WILSON, JOHN, (DATE)
Social theory.

Bibliography
Includes index.
1. Sociology—Philosophy. 2. Sociology—Methodology.
3. Sociology—Classification. I. Title.
HM24.W548 1983   301'.01   82-16637
ISBN 0-13-819573-0

Acknowledgments for the use of copyrighted material appear on page 231.

Editorial/production supervision
  and interior design: Barbara Kelly Kittle
Cover design: Ray Lundgren
Manufacturing Buyer: John Hall

Printed in the United States of America

10 9 8 7 6 5 4 3 2 1

ISBN 0-13-819573-0

Prentice-Hall International, Inc., *London*
Prentice-Hall of Australia Pty. Limited, *Sydney*
Editora Prentice-Hall do Brasil, Ltda., *Rio de Janeiro*
Prentice-Hall Canada Inc., *Toronto*
Prentice-Hall of India Private Limited, *New Delhi*
Prentice-Hall of Japan, Inc., *Tokyo*
Prentice-Hall of Southeast Asia Pte. Ltd., *Singapore*
Whitehall Books Limited, *Wellington, New Zealand*

Contents

Preface

The sociological perspective enables us to look beyond individual psychology and unique events to the predictable broad patterns and regular occurrences of social life that influence individual destinies. Sociology shares with all other essentially scientific perspectives the assumption that there is order in nature and that it can be discovered, described, and understood. It is the purpose of social theory to guide this process of discovery and comprehension by identifying the units of human action and explaining their relations. Good sociological research without theory is unthinkable.

On the other hand, theorizing cannot be considered in isolation from the many other activities involved in practising sociology. Theory means nothing without research because it is against the results of research that theory must be judged. And this judgment must follow criteria laid down by a community of scholars who look to each other for validation of their work. This is not just "a theory book," then, but a description of the various ways of doing sociology, with special emphasis on how doing sociology is shaped and guided by theory.

There are many ways of classifying soical theories. Some I have avoided because they present a false image of the relation between theoretical thinking and sociological research, and give the wrong reasons why sociologists sometimes disagree about the nature and purpose of their discipline. Included in this category are classifications which focus on the intellectual biographies of "great" sociological thinkers, those which classify theories according to one or more core ideas ("order versus conflict") and those which allocate individual theorists to various categories on the basis of the philosophical assumptions which seem to inform their work. I especially wish to avoid seeming to associate particular theories with particular individuals. The greatness of the classical sociological thinkers lies in their recognition of the fact that there are many paths to sociological truth. Many of the better-known theorists on the contemporary scene have trodden a number of these paths during the course of their career. Conversely, none of the categories of theory described in this book is the intellectual preserve of one individual: each is the result of the work of many sociologists.

The classification scheme I have developed assumes that variations in social theory are caused by variation in the combination of three aspects of the sociological enterprise. Philosophy plays a part because theorizing about social life always rests on certain assumptions about the nature of social reality and how reliable knowledge of that reality is obtained. Research plays a part because sociology is an empirical science in which experimentation and systematic observation play crucial roles in evaluating theories. And the social organization of sociology plays a part because theorizing is carried out by sociologists trained in particular departments, employed in particular institutions and linked to other sociologists by particular networks of communication in ways that affect which theories they think are worthwhile.

The classification scheme has three levels. At the most concrete level substantive theories are distinguished. Theories about social inequality, about race relaltions, about deviance, and so on, address issues of general public concern from a sociological perspective. These are the divisions that might comprise an introductory textbook in sociology. But I classify theories not by the topic they address but by the way they address these topics.

The manner in which a sociological topic is addressed in theory is determined by the research tradition in which the theory is situated. A research tradition is a set of general assumptions about the entities and processes in a domain of study and about the appropriate methods to be used in investigating the problems and constructing theories in that domain. The research tradition will tell the sociologist whether "poverty," "relative deprivation" or "modernization" is a genuine sociological problem at all and, if it is, how theories to explain it should be constructed and tested. There are a number of research traditions within sociology. Sociologists who work within the same research traditions will build the same kind of theory and use the same kind of methods whatever the substantive issue they address.

Research traditions, in turn, can be classified according to the world-view adopted by those working within the tradition. This world-view contains philosophical assumptions about social reality, its constituent parts, their relations, and their methods of change, as well as assumptions about methods of obtaining reliable knowledge of the social world. They are usually taken for granted, Unless we are exposed to a competing world-view, we are barely conscious that we have one. The parts of this book describe the three world-views which have exercised the greatest influence on contemporary sociology. The boundaries between them are by no means as clearly marked as the treatment I have given them might imply. Each world-view has fostered a number of research traditions. I have chosen to describe only those which have attracted a large following among modern sociologists. Positivism is the dominant world-view and has spawned a rich variety of research traditions, of which I have chosen to describe four; but the idealist world-view has proved a strong competitor for positivism and I have described two of its more popular research traditions; realism, a world-view with a history as ancient as the other two, has not gained such a large following in contemporary sociology, and I have chosen to describe only one contemporary research tradition which adheres to realist principles.

The parts of the book can be read in any order. Each part is introduced by a chapter in which the philosophical assumptions contained in the world-view are described. Each of the chapters should provide a feel for the kind of sociology practiced within the research tradition it describes. I have tried to show the research tradition "in operation," providing examples of research and analysis to illustrate the different ways of doing sociology. Each chapter concludes with a review of the more commonly encountered criticisms of the research tradition.

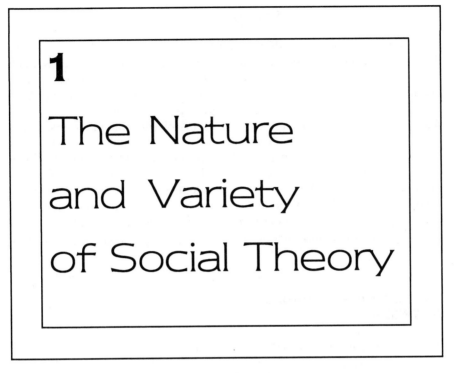

1

The Nature and Variety of Social Theory

Most of us think of theorizing as quite divorced from the business of gathering facts. It seems to require an abstractness of thought remote from the practical activity of empirical research. But theory building is not a separate activity within sociology. Without theory, the empirical researcher would find it impossible to decide what to observe, how to observe it, or what to make of the observations.

Theory tells us what is relevant and problematic about groups of facts. Different theories will assign different relevances to the same group of facts and even, on occasion, uncover new facts. Facts without theory are truly blind (Laudan, 1977:13). A book about theory and about theory differences thus has a direct bearing on the conduct of empirical research. It will tell us why certain facts are seen as significant, why certain questions are asked, and why certain solutions are accepted.

The aim of social theory is to solve problems having to do with social interaction. What is society? What are its constituent parts and how are they related? How do societies retain their unity and continuity while undergoing change? What is the cause of social change? Sociology provides many answers to these questions because it contains many different theories. These theories differ in their characteristic description and explanation of social processes. They reflect the variety of ontological and epistemological commitments it is possible for a social scientist to make.

Ontology has to do with what exists, what is real. Epistemology has to do with knowing, how we can know what is real. Sociology embraces many different kinds of social theory because sociologists disagree on what is real about social interaction and about what counts as reliable sociological knowledge. Some regard human societies as expressions of human consciousness; others think of society in terms of physical processes. Some sociologists think of society as an aggregate of individuals; others think of society as an organic whole giving form and content to individuals. Some see social order resting on consensus; others believe social order depends on coercion. Epistemologically, some sociologists believe that sociology must follow the lead of the natural sciences, some think that the interpretation of meaning is the most appropriate method for sociology, and others apply the dialectical method to obtain knowledge of society's fundamental processes.

THE COMMON PROPERTIES OF THEORY

The coexistence within sociology of different theoretical approaches, each with its own assumptions about social reality and correct method, would seem to rule out any possibility of making statements about theory in general. However, there is a consensus among sociologists on certain fundamental properties of theory. This consensus is sufficient to give this book a common focus. There is agreement that the purpose of theory is to *explain* facts, that theories should be *testable,* and that theorizing is a *process,* with no final resting point.

Theories Explain

A statement is not a theory unless it offers an explanation of facts. A theory must specify the conditions under which some things happen rather than others. There are many statements in sociology that look like theories but fail to qualify because they offer no explanation. Some are empirical generalizations, merely summarizing existing knowledge. The statement "members of higher income groups belong to more social clubs" is an empirical generalization because it is derived from existing knowledge rather than from a general law or principle. If there were a theory which related the extent and variety of voluntary association memberships held by an individual to the amount of resources possessed by the individual, a proposition which would predict this empirical generalization could be derived. What is more important, the more abstract principle could do what an empirical generalization cannot do. It could predict that the poor (who have few resources) would join fewer social clubs. The theory, unlike the empirical generalization, enables us to imagine new facts.

Another statement which resembles a theory but fails to qualify because it offers no explanation is a statistical correlation. If we find that total lifetime earnings correlate with a cluster of variables, such as parental education, amount of schooling, occupation, sex, and race, we cannot claim to have discovered a theory. This multiple correlation is merely a complex description. We know *that* total lifetime earnings are associated with these other factors but we do not know *why*. A theory would tell us why this relationship is necessary.

Finally, a theory is more than a conceptual scheme. Concepts and concepts arranged in a framework or scheme are the beginning of generalization—by the simple act of asserting that two instances are alike, "a class, a concept, is created, a generalization about it is offered" (Stinchcombe, 1978:123). But concepts alone do not explain, for they contain no laws or principles.

All theories, then, explain why social phenomena exist. However, as we shall see, sociologists do not always mean the same thing by explanation. Some sociologists believe that explanation consists of relating variations in one thing to variations in another thing by means of a set of principles that apply in a number of different situations (Collins, 1975:4). Others think of motives and intentions when they explain social actions. A third group looks upon explanation as a process of uncovering the mechanism which necessarily generates social interaction.

Theories Are Testable

Theories are explanatory statements which can be tested empirically. A statement which cannot be tested in any conceivable way is not a theory. In this respect, the theories of sociology are distinguishable from the theories of the layman. Sociologists try to state their preconceptions and their principles of explanation with sufficient precision that they can be rejected if the facts fail to validate them. Whatever disagreements we might find among sociologists, the need to make theories testable is not disputed.

The consensus on the need to have testable theories masks disagreement on what the proper test of a theory is. The relation between theory and the facts which would test it is itself an issue in the debate. All sociologists recognize that facts are "theory-laden." How facts are defined and how they are observed is determined by the very theory that the facts are supposed to test. We see only that which our theory tells us to see. Furthermore, tests of theory always take place against a background of assumptions, themselves guided by theory, about testing procedures. For example, certain theories in sociology must be tested by conducting laboratory experiments. These experiments are supposed to yield the "raw" data to test predictions made by the theory. But these data are not raw if by that we mean that they have no theory in them. Experiments are conducted on the basis of theory-guided assumptions about how people normally behave under stress, how they use motor and cognitive skills, and so on.

It is thus no simple matter to test a theory by seeing if it fits the facts. The distinction between a theoretical statement and a statement which summarizes our observations is not so sharp as might be supposed. Among sociologists, there is no agreement on the implications this has for sociological research. Some sociologists assume that accurate, objective, and unchanging observation statements about social life can be made which are independent of and unchanged by our theoretical speculations about it. Others proceed as if abstract theories can be constructed independent of our factual knowledge about the social world. Another group proceeds on the assumption that their sense of what is real will inevitably shape their theory, just as their sense of theory will be shaped by their knowledge of an existence in the real world. These differences concerning the precise relation between the knowing subject and the known object have important consequences for the tests of validity to which theories are submitted, and they generate considerable argument about the meaning of validity itself.

Theories Are Processes

All sociologists agree that theories are not things but processes. "A theory *gradually* develops by a process of increasingly precise and detailed statement of the initial vague idea" (Shapere, 1977:553). The practice of science, then, is a search for ever-better theories. A better theory will enable us to pose *new problems,* problems not provoked by the old theory. For this reason, the development of theory is not the same as the accumulation of factual knowledge.

Sociologists of all kinds would like their theories to become better and subscribe to the view that the interaction between theory and fact should be a continuous process. But there is little agreement on how progress is achieved or measured. Some sociologists seek to improve their theory by progressively broadening its scope and by making more accurate predictions, thus bringing theory closer to reality. Other sociologists seek to bring social reality into closer line with their theories. They judge theory by how successfully it changes the consciousness and practice of their subjects. And there are sociologists who look to theory to give them a more comprehensive and deeper understanding of the meaning of social interaction.

Whatever the criterion of progress, it is commonly supposed that theories remain in use only as long as they have not been falsified: theories which leave facts unaccounted for, theories which seem to lead nowhere, will be discarded. Upon closer scrutiny of how scientists operate, this supposition turns out to be false. Most theories in sociology are "undetermined" by the facts. They continue in use even though "they can neither be conclusively refuted nor uniquely derived from statements of facts alone" (Hesse, 1978:1).

Why should underdetermined theories retain their popularity? A theory's correspondence with the facts is only one criterion by which a theory's plausibility is judged. Sociological theories rest upon assumptions about the nature of reality and how that reality can be known with certainty. These assumptions influence our opinions about what a good test of theory is. It is indeed important that the theory fit the facts. But it is also important that the theory authentically reflect the assumptions on which it is built. These assumptions suggest what problems are worth stating, and they will indicate the probable solutions to those problems. A sociologist's failure to find such a solution (i.e. where the facts do not fit the theory's predictions) usually leads to only minor modifications in the theory. It is much more likely to stimulate a search for new facts which fit the theory better. In other words, the sociologist is as anxious about the fit between the theory and its ontological and epistemological base as he is about the fit between the theory and the facts.

The history of science has shown that only persistent, gross anomalies between theory and fact will prompt the abandonment of a theory which fits neatly into the scientist's philosophical world view. Short of this, the scientist will continue to use the theory, modifying it in minor ways, searching all the while for facts which will "save" it. It is no surprise, then, that sociology, a relatively young discipline, should play host to a wide variety of theories and theoretical perspectives, each drawing on a different set of assumptions about social reality and how it should be explained, each claiming to best interpret the facts it has identified as significant.

VARIETIES OF SOCIAL THEORY

In describing those characteristics of theory upon which all sociologists would agree, I have had occasion to mention some of the points on which they disagree. It is now appropriate to explore these differences in more detail. In the past, it has been customary to argue that theory differences within sociology reflect in a straightforward manner deep-seated philosophical assumptions about human nature and society (e.g. Martindale, 1981) or to simply use one or two prominent sociologists to epitomize different sociological styles (e.g. Cuzzort and King, 1980). Each approach has its shortcomings. Theory differences rest as much on social factors (e.g. training programs, networks of contacts, reward systems) and political factors (e.g. state support for certain research programs, shifts in electoral strength, social movements) as they do on philosophical differences. The problem with the second approach is that theoretical perspectives are rarely captured very neatly in the work of individual sociologists. Furthermore, several of the most prominent sociologists have either combined different theoretical perspectives or shifted from one to another in the course of their career. In any case, theory differences are not explained by reference to individuals but by reference to the research tradition within which they were trained and work.

A method of conceptualizing theory differences in sociology which captures both the impact of philosophical or metatheoretical arguments and the social factors entering into the formation of theoretical groups has recently been developed in the history of science. The metatheoretical arguments combine with the forces at work in the scientific community which encourage groups of scientists to use one another as trusted assessors of their ideas and work to produce a "paradigm" which characterizes the scientific work in that community or "school." This paradigm specifies (in ways of which the individual scientist is not always fully aware) what are the important and researchable questions, what are the most general explanatory principles, what are the most appropriate models for research, and what are the criteria for the acceptance or rejection of data (Kuhn, 1962).

What is important about a theory, then, is not how well it fits some supposedly neutral world of facts but how well it fits into a paradigm. This paradigm will not only suggest which problems to study but also the probable solutions—or what to do if the solutions are not found. The implication of Kuhn's idea of paradigms is that theories should be categorized according to the paradigm in which they are situated.

The paradigm concept would seem to be a promising tool for the student of social theory in sociology, where theory differences are wide and numerous. However, Kuhn's idea has been criticized for its assertion that a discipline will be dominated at any given time by a single paradigm as well as for its assumption that paradigms are psychologically exclusive (Martins, 1972:16). A modification of Kuhn's theory which renders it especially suitable for sociology has been proposed by Laudan (1977). Instead of using paradigms, Laudan classifies theories according to the "research tradition" in which they are located. Research tradition is a somewhat looser concept than paradigm. The latter suggests a group of scientists following self-consciously an "exemplar" or model experiment, largely unable to speak the same scientific language as scientists using another paradigm. Research tradition is simply "a set of general assumptions about the entities and processes in a domain of study, and about the appropriate methods to be used in investigating the problems and constructing the theories in that domain" (Laudan, 1977:81). This idea is preferable to that of paradigm in that no assumption is made about psychological exclusiveness. "It would be a serious error to assume that a scientist cannot consistently work in more than one research tradition" (Laudan, 1977:103). This formulation is also preferable to that of paradigm in its emphasis on problem formation: research traditions are different because they identify different problems, not because they contain different facts or demand different methods. Finally, the idea of research tradition does not demand that a discipline must be dominated by one theoretical approach, a tolerant approach much more appropriate for the present state of sociology.

A research tradition is not a theory. It is "the expression of a wish or *will* to produce knowledge of a certain kind" (Radnitzky, 1972:201). Each research tradition in a science will spawn a number of testable theories. These specific theories predict certain things about the world of facts but they also make assumptions about the social world for which they give no rationale. The research tradition provides this rationale, furnishing, among other things, the criteria to measure progress in theory development and empirical research. In classifying particular theories within sociology the first question should therefore be: To what research tradition does it belong?

Within sociology there are several research traditions. These can be arranged according to the "foreconceptions" about science and its subject matter which are part of the "world picture" which establishes and warrants the research enterprise (Radnitzky, 1972:202). The world picture (Laudan calls it "the intellectual milieu") furnishes the research tradition with a metaphysic justifying the kind of research carried out within it. Thus it can make sense for a scientist to raise philosophical objections against a particular research tradition (or a theory within it) if it runs counter to his picture of the world (Laudan, 1977:124). In classifying research traditions within sociology the first question should therefore be: To what intellectual milieu does it belong?

In summary, the classification of social theory requires a conceptual scheme with three levels. At the most general level are "world pictures" which provide the intellectual milieu within which science is conducted. Three world pictures can be identified within sociology (Benton, 1977; Bernstein, 1978; Dandeker and Scott, 1979; Fay, 1975; Habermas, 1971; Radnitzky, 1970; Wagner, 1963). Each world picture comprises a meta-theory, a set of rules and procedures for doing science. Each world picture can be interpreted in a variety of ways, yielding a number of distinct research traditions. The coexistence of several research traditions within the same intellectual milieu is "a normal feature of science" (Laudan, 1977:134). Finally, each research tradition generates a number of substantive, empirically testable theories.

The first of the three world pictures or metatheories I call *positivism* because it defines the social world as resembling in structure and process the natural world and because it urges upon sociology a method of investigation identical to that found in the natural sciences. I call the second *idealism* because it defines society as an aspect of consciousness to be analysed in terms of ideas, thoughts, and feelings. I call the third *realism* because it gives ontological priority to a subterranean dimension of invisible but real structures and assigns to sociology the task of uncovering these structures and specifying their effects.

Positivism

Positivists treat the social world—the world of social actors, social groups, and social organizations—as if it were the world of natural phenomena. All that can be known about that world is given to us in experience, and experience always concerns particular events and happenings. Positivists systematically investigate these events and happenings so as to reveal their underlying regularities. Their goal is to formulate the laws which govern the operation of social groups and organizations.

> ...it is assumed that certain objects and processes exist in the physical world, that certain events occur consistently and that certain stable relationships persist: these objects, processes, events and relationships constitute the facts which science has to describe accurately and explain convincingly....These facts are seen as being theoretically neutral. They can, therefore, be expressed in a language which is independent of theory and formulated in a way which simply represents the observable realities of the physical world. Once firmly established, facts remain unaffected by interpretive advances. Indeed, so long as there have been no observational errors, they can undergo no change of content or meaning and they can be used, therefore, to discriminate objectively between theoretical alternatives (Mulkay, 1979:29).

When fully stated, positivist explanations take the form of valid deductive arguments in which the event to be explained is a conclusion drawn from premises which include one or more universal laws. This is called the "nomological" or "covering-law" model of explanation. An event (B) is explained by reference to some prior event (A) *if* there is a universal law which states that always, if events of the same type as A occur, then events of the same type as B follow. Such explanations are confirmed or refuted by their success or failure in generating accurate predictions. When positivists speak of "cause," then, they mean "a necessary part of a combination of conditions which are jointly sufficient to produce an effect" (Benton, 1977:59). To explain something is to expect it because of prior circumstances.

Idealism

Idealists contend that sociologists should be less concerned with the search for universal laws of social behavior and the construction of covering-law explanations and more concerned with understanding the meaning of people's actions. The subject matter of the idealist is the directing, willing, spontaneously acting individual. This is a more realistic picture of human beings, idealists contend, than the rather puppetlike figure imagined by the positivist. Actions must be explained, not by the forces which impel them but by the end for which they are performed. Explanation consists of giving reasons and motives rather than invoking universal laws.

To the idealist, social reality is cognitive: it consists of ideas, thoughts, and other contents of consciousness. "The extreme idealist position would be that the existence of material things is an illusion since they are actually correlates or creations of consciousness" (Dandeker and Scott, 1979:308). This cognitive world cannot obey the laws of physics. Ideas do not occupy space, nor do they have weight. And they cannot be directly seen or heard. The social world is not a natural world upon which experiments are performed but rather a text which must be read and interpreted. Likewise, if social reality is cognitive, actors are not objects but interpreters. Their actions are accounted for not by treating them as objects but by learning what the world means to them and what they are trying to create for themselves in that world.

Realism

Realists seek to transcend the determinism of the positivist and the voluntarism of the idealist. They take from the positivist the idea that people cannot create society as they wish but must obey certain social imperatives. They take from the idealist the notion that society is the creation of human beings and, unlike the world of matter and energy, can be changed by them. They see society as both the ever-present condition and the continually produced outcome of human agency. In their conscious activity, people unconsciously reproduce the social structure which seems to govern them.

> Thus people do not marry to reproduce the nuclear family or work to sustain the capitalist economy. Yet it is nevertheless the unintended consequence ... of their activity (Bhaskar, 1979:44).

Realists do not accept the covering law idea of explanation, nor do they subscribe to the idealist view that explanation consists of the attribution of agency to actors. In the realist world picture, an adequate causal explanation requires the discovery not only of a regular association between social phenomena but also of some mechanism or structure which links them. Scientific theory must be "a description of structures and mechanisms which causally generate the observable phenomena, a description which enables us to explain them" (Keat and Urry, 1975:5). These structures which are not visible "on the surface" are nevertheless real. Realists thus reject the empiricist argument that reality is defined solely in terms of surface appearances. The task of science is to penetrate to this deeper reality and make sense of what appears on the surface.

CONCLUSION

The three parts of this book describe these world pictures and the more influential research traditions which have grown up within them. Each part is introduced by a chapter which spells out the philosophical assumptions underlying the research traditions. Ontological issues are discussed first because they logically precede epistemological issues: the subject of inquiry must be at least tentatively defined before methodological questions can be raised.

Each world picture is a prediction of what successful sociological theory must look like. The research tradition specifies more concretely the means which the sociologist must adopt to reach good theory. Each makes a distinct and competing set of claims about the kinds of material from which to construct propositions about the world.

No single, all-embracing theory has proven adequate to deal with the wide range of problems sociologists identify as theirs. More strikingly, sociology has produced no agreement on the correct theoretical approach or perspective from which to mount the search for such a theory. This is because sociology has always been called upon to serve a number of purposes. Furnishing laws, propositions, and hypotheses has certainly been one purpose, but sociologists have also looked to theory to help them understand society, to critique society, and to point the way to reform. Concomitantly, theory has been seen as capable of doing many different things and as subject to many different kinds of criticism. All this is not a sign of the immaturity of sociology nor an indication that sociology is an impossible undertaking. The diverse theoretical orientations to be found in the discipline are "variously effective for dealing with diverse kinds of, and aspects of, sociological and social problems" (Merton, 1981:1). The abundance and variety of theory is therefore a sign, not of the weakness and ineptitude of sociology, but of its vitality and strength.

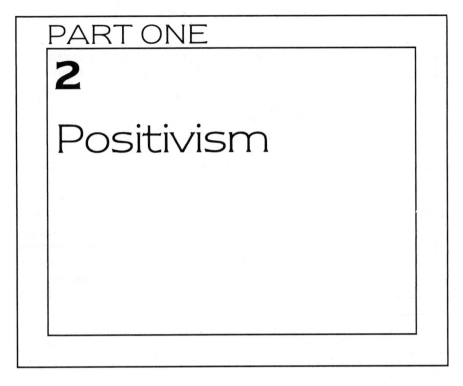

PART ONE

2

Positivism

The philosophy most influential in the development of sociology has been positivism (Collins, 75:27). As a system of thought, positivism assumed the proportions of a religion during the nineteenth century. My concern here is merely to elucidate its function as a metatheory for sociology. Positivist principles guide the work of most sociological researchers and furnish the basis for the more popular and influential textbooks on theory construction and methodology in the field. To the majority of sociologists, the maturation of their discipline depends upon it becoming more positivistic.

The essential tenets of positivism, insofar as it provides a metatheory for sociology, can be stated briefly. First, there are no fundamental differences between the natural and social sciences. The aim of sociology should be to arrive at the formulation of principles that have the same objective status as natural scientific laws. Second, these laws or principles are the means of explaining social events or phenomena. Explanation means bringing together two types of statement: the first is a statement of a general law and the second is a statement that specifies the particular circumstances in which that law has application. The event or phenomenon to be explained is deduced as a necessity from the conjuncture of the two statements. Third, social reality is made known through concepts which refer to what is observable and measurable. The substitution of a precise, formal language of observation for everyday language is essential for carrying out scientific sociology. Fourth, science can only concern itself with what is and how it came to be so. It can say nothing about what ought to be. Science is value-free.

Writings in the philosophy of science in the past two decades have undermined some of the earlier positivists' certainty that they had discovered the correct path to certain knowledge. Doubts have arisen about the logical status of the covering-law method of explanation, about the distinction drawn between theory and observation, and about the claim to value freedom. As a consequence, there are almost as many differences among contemporary positivist sociologists as there are between positivists as a whole and other sociologists. Hence the coverage given in Part One to four different research traditions. No single research tradition, much less a single individual, is necessarily "purely" positivist in the sense described above. And yet, positivism is a metatheory with distinct ideas about the proper subject matter of sociology and the most appropriate methods for studying it. In what follows, we can anticipate some differences, but they are merely variations on a theme.

POSITIVIST ONTOLOGY: THE NATURE OF SOCIAL REALITY

Social reality consists of events and phenomena in the same sense that the natural world consists of objects and processes. This reality resembles a machine or an organism in that it consists of parts interrelated in some determinate and determinable way. However, human beings are not exactly like parts of a machine. They do not automatically or instinctively respond to social forces because they have "inner states" (e.g. motives, attitudes, beliefs) which intervene between stimulus and response.

These inner states are not directly observable like physical movements. Nevertheless, they can be incorporated into a scientific account in the form of intervening variables which help to explain the connection between observed stimulus and observed response. To help explain why blacks in the United States vote in such large numbers for candidates of the Democratic Party, it might be inferred that they have attitudes of political liberalism. This attitude links being black and voting Democrat. It can be measured by using a liberalism scale. Variations in behavior can also be explained by positing the existence of different values acquired during socialization. The higher birth rate of Catholics might be explained by inferring and trying to measure different values attached to birth control and family life.

The existence of inner states does not contradict the positivists' determinism. Social conduct is only apparently free. In reality, it is determined by the combined effect of numerous circumstances, including past experiences, situational influences, and personality dispositions. Present difficulties in accurately specifying these circumstances and predicting behavior are the result of cognitive limitations. They do not indicate that the properties of the social world are different from those of the natural world.

EPISTEMOLOGY—KNOWING THE SOCIAL WORLD

Social life is assumed to have properties (e.g. the degree of social inequality) which vary over time. The goal of theory is to formulate propositions which predict the quantity of this variation from one setting to another, using other variations to explain it. The assumption is that social action is concrete, quantifiable, and susceptible to scientific analysis.

Empiricism

Positivism is a variant of empiricism. The principal tenet of empiricism is that our "beliefs about the external world are worthy of the description 'knowledge' only if they can be put to the test of experience" (Benton, 1977:21). Experience means sensory observation. Entities that are totally inaccessible to observation are dismissed as "metaphysical," outside the bounds of the subject matter of science.

Taken at face value, empiricism poses severe problems for sociologists. They cannot ignore the role played by attitudes and beliefs in human conduct. Attitudes and beliefs are not directly observable and, according to a strict interpretation of empiricism, would not be acknowledged as part of the domain of science. One solution to this problem is to admit the existence of such phenomena but point out that the same admission has to be made by the natural scientist. The engineer must recognize stress as a condition attributable to certain metals under certain conditions; but it is no more possible to directly observe this than the feeling of stress experienced by an individual. In both cases the condition has to be inferred from physical manifestations.

Another solution to the problem of empiricism is to treat beliefs and attitudes as if they *were* observable. For example, feelings of hostility and distrust toward a minority group can be observed by constructing a racial prejudice scale and asking respondents to mark their position on it. The responses become our empirical data.

The problem of empiricism can also be surmounted by treating inferences about motives and attitudes as only preliminary information to guide sociological research. While this information is not reliable in itself, it can lead to data that are. Positivists thus acknowledge that making sense of what people do often requires that we use empathy. We have to be able to see the world as others see it. However, empathic insight is not scientific knowledge because it is not empirically grounded. Empathy must be used as a preliminary source of hypotheses which may then be validated against behavior we can directly observe (Abel, 1970:71). The probability of a connection between the action we observe and the inner state we impute through empathy can only be judged by an objective test. Empathy might therefore suggest an explanation but it does not constitute an explanation in its own right. Accordingly, empathic understanding should not be regarded as part of scientific knowledge, however useful it might be in leading to that knowledge (Cohen, 1980:10).

A final strategy for dealing with inner states empirically is to assume that inner states are very simple and highly predictable. We might assume that people always act rationally. Inner states are thereby reduced to an assessment of the most efficient way of performing a task given certain built-in preferences. Having made this assumption, we are able to take inner states for granted, devoting our attention to the environmental conditions which govern rational choice and the behavior which results from it. Unlike inner states, both of these can be empirically ascertained.

Explanation

Positivists believe that sociology should be concerned with making statements about social events or phenomena (such as petitions for divorce or acts of burglary) and explaining these events or phenomena by searching for their determining causes. The rise in the divorce rate is caused by a rise in income levels of women; acts of burglary are caused by poverty. Such statements do not simply mean that the effect always follows from the cause. They mean that the effect *had* to follow from the cause. In other words, an explanation of a relationship is given by indicating *why* the effect followed the cause. And to do this, we make reference to a broader generalization. For example, a regular association is found between being Catholic and voting Democrat. This association is explained if we subsume it under some more general statement that members of minority groups (e.g. Catholics) are more likely to vote for parties of the left (e.g. Democrat) than for parties of the right. This more general statement is lawlike because it makes no reference to specific religious groups or parties. Not only does such a law-like statement enable us to make predictions about the behavior of other minority groups (e.g. Jews), but it also enables us to predict that, were Catholics to become a majority group within the same kind of political system, *they* would support the party of the right. Lawlike statements are thus not only universal, but they must also support "counterfactuals" — statements contrary to known or presumed facts. They allow us to antici- pate what would happen given a set of hypothesized but not presently existing circumstances. In this example, the law states that if the Catholics were to become the majority group, their voting practices would change.

Laws are abstract in the sense that they refer to classes of objects rather than specific and unique objects. But even the most general law is not universal in the sense of applying to all times and places. The law stated above would apply only to societies where there are left- and right-wing parties. Positivists do not claim that laws must be universal in scope. They simply claim that, whenever the scope conditions are met (i.e. in all societies with left- and right-wing parties) the law will apply.

Laws are accepted as explanations only because they are grounded in theory. It is theory that helps account for the empirical uniformities described by laws. For example, the laws which describe the relation of supply and demand for certain kinds of labor are accounted for by theories having to do with how individuals make decisions on the basis of calculations as to the rewards and costs of various choices. The theory makes sense of the law and helps connect one statement (e.g. the price of labor) with another statement (e.g. the price of consumer goods).

Theories are not simply summaries of existing knowledge. They are ways of generating new knowledge. They can perform this function because they consist of *sets* of interrelated propositions which can be arranged and rearranged in various combinations by the use of formal logic. For example, assume that an embryonic theory of divorce exists. Two statements in the theory describe existing findings. The first says that marital instability is more common among members of the lower classes while the second says that members of the upper classes have less freedom in choosing marriage partners than members of the lower classes. A sociologist might want to take these two propositions and combine them in a theory to suggest new facts and throw more light on divorce. Logically, it is valid to argue:

> *If* freedom of mate choice is inversely related to social class
> *And* marital instability is inversely related to social class
> *Then* marital instability is positively related to freedom of mate choice.

The three propositions in combination comprise a theory of divorce which is falsifiable once appropriate measures are devised (Winton, 1974:11).

The use of logic to create new propositions also helps us work from an empirical generalization we are interested in explaining to theoretical statements we think combine to form an explanation. For example, if we find that more highly urbanized societies tend to have higher degrees of the division of labor, we can formulate this as a proposition, "population density increases with the division of labor." The explanation for this association can be found in two other statements. The first says that the more opportunities people have to interact with each other the greater will be the division of labor between them (Blau, 1977:195). The second says that the probability of association between people increases with the size and population density of a community. These two propositions, in combination, help account for the empirical generalization that cities have more division of labor than rural areas.

Validation

The manner of theory testing in positivism reflects its empiricist underpinning, the purpose of theory being to explain what goes on in the realm of "basic, uninterpreted, hard facts" (Bernstein, 1978:111). The most appropriate test of a theory is its capacity to withstand falsification when set against those facts. This position (known as "falsificationism") assumes that there are "a finite number of possible conjectures or theories about nature, such that by progressively refuting them we get nearer and nearer the 'truth'" (Giddens, 1977:61). Accordingly, observations are made and experiments conducted in order to see if theory predictions can be falsified. If they are, the theory should be abandoned or modified. If they are confirmed, the theory is provisionally retained.

In actual practice, positivists acknowledge that "a single failure of a prediction derived from a knowledge claim, even when scope conditions are met, is not sufficient grounds for rejecting the knowledge claim" (Cohen, 1980:127). Theories are rarely abandoned upon a single disproof. It takes repeated predictive failure to bring a theory seriously into question, and even then it will be abandoned only if a clearly superior replacement has been developed (Lakatos, 1970). Accordingly, direct competition between positivist theories is rare. None of the competing theories has sufficient empirical grounding to provide what might be considered a crucial test. This condition of "underdetermination" can be attributed to technical difficulties (such as the failure to control experiments properly), the difficulty of replicating studies on human beings, or the intractability of social reality to precise measurement.

Concepts

A concept is an idea of a class of objects. The term "bureaucracy" signifies a certain idea of the formal structure of a real organization. To define bureaucracy is to spell out the idea for which the term is a label. The precise term used is less important than the definition given of the idea.

Positivists believe that sociology must develop a set of concepts in which the social world is described as it exists. The concepts should approximate as closely as possible a pane of clear glass (Gusfield, 1981:84). As this metaphor suggests, the external world is believed to exist independently of whatever is believed of it by human beings: the knower is distinguishable from the known.

Positivists do not pretend that concepts describe the world in all its detail. Concepts indicate the manner in which each theorist has chosen to abstract from experience. In sharpening their perception of some aspect of reality, the positivists are aware that their vision becomes blurred with regard to others. Concepts are both a way of seeing and a way of not seeing.

Positivists evaluate concepts mainly in terms of their utility. A concept is useful if there exists a shared understanding of the idea to which it refers. Concepts are provisional terms, always open to further refinement to enhance their utility. They can be refined by incorporating them into hypotheses. The more useful concepts will be those which "can be embedded in a variety of different types of statement rather than being so narrowly conceived that they can be fitted into only one law-like statement" (Cohen, 1980:138).

The statements defining sociological concepts are not, therefore, true or false. There can be no absolutely correct way to abstract from experience. Concepts vary only in their degree of significance. A significant concept is one that occurs repeatedly in statements of a law-like nature that we believe to be true.

Much effort is expended by positivists in trying to ensure that their concepts have precise and consistent meaning. For example, efforts are made to define and derive empirical measurements of "racial prejudice," such that the concept refers to the same thing, whether used in the ghettos of Harlem, the barrios of Los Angeles, or the affluent, white suburbs of Chicago. A concept like racial prejudice and its measurement by a "racial attitude scale" is thus accorded the same epistemological status as a concept like energy transfer and its measurement by a mercury thermometer.

TESTING THEORY

Positivists, as their name implies, attack the negative, critical commentary of those who claim to know what society ought to be like and who focus on the hidden or negative side of social life. They argue, instead, that they have no preconceived model of society and are purely objective in their search for general laws. Indeed, to truly discover the social world, it is necessary for sociologists to exclude their own opinions from their work as sociologists. Furthermore, what they discover as sociologists is a description of what is. By itself, it says nothing about what ought to be.

Positivist sociology thus stresses the objective, rational side of social investigation. Insight, guesswork, luck, even political biases might well play a role in the *origin* of theories, but adherence of the scientific community to the scientific method is expressly intended to eliminate these sources of bias in the development and testing of theories.

Values do enter into positivist sociology, but only in certain ways which leave the basic procedures of science unscathed. Values enter into the choice of problem to study and method to be used in the study. However, the collecting and analyzing of data must be value-free. Values enter into the interpretation of findings, into the allocation of "significance" to different results. But the community of disinterested scholars will act as jury on this interpretation. Values enter into the work of the individual sociologist by virtue of his biography and work-setting. But science comprises a community of scholars with an explicit normative system which weeds out obvious political biases. Finally, values are present in the canons of the scientific method itself. Objectivity itself is a value. However, these values are not considered by positivists to entail metaphysical commitments.

Positivists are anxious that their sociology be used in policy making but they distinguish between "basic" and "applied" sociology. While applied sociology might well be shaped by political needs and social values, the problems of basic sociology are always purely intellectual problems. Basic sociology is indifferent to social problems and evaluates itself according to its own internal standards rather than by lay appreciation of its accomplishments (Cohen, 1980:51). Applied sociology is concerned with the discovery of the uses of knowledge, in applying the knowledge produced by the "pure" sociologist. More specifically, some sociologists concern themselves with how given problems can be solved by whatever sociological knowledge exists: these are "social engineers." Sociological theory thus has only an indirect relationship to social practice; thought and action are separated. Science itself is not thought to be competent to make value decisions as to the use of knowledge, and the findings of sociology are not thought themselves to be good or bad, but correct or false.

In the chapters which comprise Part One, several research traditions will be described. If positivism means slightly different things to each of these research traditions, it is because the introduction of philosophical assumptions into a research enterprise always creates a series of quite specific difficulties and calls forth a variety of solutions. One way or another, however, these research traditions share a number of ideas about sociology: that a natural science of society is possible; that law-like generalizations about social reality are conceivable; that sociology has a technical character, neutral in respect of values. In the commentary on each of these research traditions we shall have occasion to question this commitment to a positivist sociology—its ability to deal with subjectivity and meaning, its ability to explain and predict social behavior on the basis of laws, and the validity of its claim to be free of value commitments.

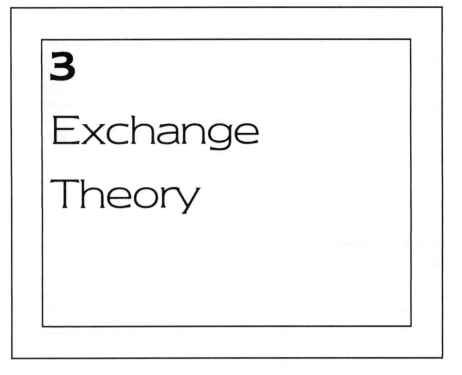

3

Exchange

Theory

At the core of exchange theory lies the very simple assumption that human beings will form and sustain relationships if they believe that the rewards they derive from such relationships will exceed the costs. This idea has a familiar ring to most of us because it is part of a very influential movement in social thought called "utilitarianism." Utilitarians teach that it is human nature for people to want to avoid pain and maximize pleasure. Because people's capabilities are limited, their search for pleasure often leads them to form relationships in which they exchange what they can produce and have a surfeit of for what they cannot produce and yet desire.

Utilitarianism gained favor as a way of comprehending social life at the time when the new capitalist or bourgeois class was supplanting the old aristocracy. The bourgeoisie maintained that social rewards should be allocated on the basis of talent and energy rather than birth or inherited social identity. This class naturally believed that the measure of a person's worth should be the usefulness of that person for satisfying social needs. This standard of utility was gradually adopted as an ethical position by the new order of industrial capitalism and came to dominate political and economic thinking as well as the young social sciences.

The impact of utilitarian thinking on social thought is evident in the following widely held beliefs. First, the basic unit of social life and the unit of analysis in social thought is the individual actor. Second, the individual actor is a utility maximizer: "for each person each state of the world has a particular *utility* level, where utility is that which the person seeks to maximize through his actions" (Coleman, 1975:81). Third, social order is possible because individuals find that, by pursuing their own interest, the interest of all is maximized. Social relations endure because "actors are beneficial to one another—by 'accident' if you will—because each is interested only in his own welfare; yet each, in using the other as a means to his own end, must aid the other's welfare in order to benefit his own" (Coleman, 1975:82).

HOMANS'S ELEMENTARY FORMS OF SOCIAL BEHAVIOR

Constructing theories on the assumption that "all contacts among men rest on the schema of giving and retaining equivalents" (Simmel, 1950:387) is therefore hardly new. However, exchange theory as such, the idea that the principles underlying social life can be stated in terms of exchange processes, is of fairly recent vintage. The basic propositions of modern exchange theory were formally stated by George Homans in 1961.

Homans's propositions bear the mark of two nonsociological research traditions. The first is behavioral psychology. In behavioral psychology the individual is portrayed as unwittingly reflecting the impact of reward-and-punishment conditioning. This idea of "operant conditioning" is clearly evident in three of Homans's propositions. The first states that "for all actions taken by persons, the more often a particular action of a person is rewarded, the more likely the person is to perform that action" (Homans, 1974:16). The second states that "if in the past the occurrence of a particular stimulus, or set of stimuli, has been the occasion on which a person's action has been rewarded, and the more similar the present stimuli are to the past ones, the more likely the person is to perform the action, or some similar action now" (Homans, 1974:22). The third proposition states that "when a person's action does not receive the reward he expected, or receives punishment he did not expect, he will be angry; he becomes more likely to perform aggressive behavior" (Homans, 1974:43).

Homans's thinking was also influenced by microeconomics. There the assumption is made that an individual's wants are central to his behavior. Man is assumed to be a profit maximizer. The influence of microeconomics is evident in the remainder of Homans's propositions. The first states that "the greater the profit a person receives as a result of his action, the more likely he is to perform the action" (Homans, 1974:31). In microeconomics, profit always means reward minus cost. The cost of something is "the foregone reward of an alternative action not performed." The second proposition drawn from microeconomics states that "the more often in the recent past a person has received a particular reward the less valuable any further unit of that reward becomes for him" (Homans, 1974:29). This is the familiar idea of "marginal utility"—the value of a good decreases the more we have of it relative to other goods.

Homans contends that these five propositions in combination describe the most elementary processes of all human conduct. They can be summed up in a "rationality principle": "In choosing between alternative actions, a person will choose that one for which, as perceived by him at the time, the value (V) of the result multiplied by the probability (P) of getting the result, is the greater" (Homans, 1974:29). The idea of rational choice and rational action thus plays a central role in exchange theory.

The fact that Homans's formulation of exchange theory bears the stamp of two rather different social science theories is neither coincidental nor inconsequential. We shall see that modern exchange theory combines these founding theories with only partial success. We will find that some exchange theorists adhere scrupulously to the principles of behavioralism, in which conditioning is thought to be most important and choice insignificant. Others stress the microeconomic aspects of exchange theory, devoting their energies to studying how people make decisions based on profit and loss considerations.

Exchange theorists are united, however, in subscribing to positivism. They believe that sociology should construct comprehensive, predictive, and testable theories about a subject matter which, to all intents and purposes, is no different from the subject matter of the natural sciences. Although each social actor is an extremely complex bundle of wants, his or her behavior can be explained by reference to laws of society. Exchange theorists begin their search for these laws by drastically simplifying their model of man in order to reveal the elementary processes which govern his behavior. They then proceed to work out deductively how the actor will behave in a situation which presents options, assuming all the while that goals are pursued rationally.

The research tradition I describe in this chapter is closer to the rational-choice version of exchange theory than the behavioral version because it seems to be a more authentically sociological research tradition, taking into account much better than the behavioral version the problem of consciousness.

THE MEANING OF RATIONAL CHOICE

Exchange theorists characterize human beings as rational, decision-making people, seeking to maximize their rewards and minimize their costs. They are assumed to exhibit certain tendencies of action: they are goal-seeking;

they prefer some goals over others; they are capable of anticipating the outcomes of their actions; and they are assumed to direct their actions toward preferred anticipated outcomes.

This model does not assume that people *always* know what they want, or that they expect their actions to automatically produce desired outcomes, or that they are always aware of all the options available to them. "Whatever a man's information, perceptions, and designs might conceivably be, if he does not in fact possess the best possible ones but acts in accordance with those he does possess, though they may be wrong or inadequate, he is acting rationally" (Homans, 1974:48).

The rational choice model thus begins with the fact that at all times, human behavior rests on some previous choice. At the very least, a person will have chosen whether to continue what he is doing or switch to something else. The model predicts that the alternative chosen will be more rewarding or have higher "utility," provided the actor estimates that the alternative will indeed bring him the outcome he desires.

Knowing what a person values is not in itself a sufficient basis for predicting his behavior. We also must know the individual's "subjective probability estimates." We need to know what estimation he has made as to the likelihood of a desired outcome resulting from the action he is considering. Where the expectation is low, even though the outcome is greatly desired, the actor will not select that option. These probability estimates are made on the basis of past experiences, by observing the behavior of others, and by generalizing from one decision to others similar in nature (Blalock and Wilken, 1979:83). The accuracy of the estimates will vary according to the recency of previous decisions of a similar kind, the success of such decisions, the degree of support from other people for the estimate, and so on. On the assumption that people normally act rationally, exchange theorists conceptualize variations in estimates as deviations from objective probability. In other words, complete accuracy in estimation is considered the modal case and any departures from such accuracy become something to be explained by auxiliary statements in the theory.

The utility of the outcome of an action or course of action depends upon the degree of goal fulfillment it provides and the importance of the goal it fulfills. Actually, utilities refer not only to the outcome of what we do but to the absence of the outcome of what we do *not* do. We weigh the utility of one outcome against the utility of the other outcome, choosing the outcome with the highest estimated utility. Therefore, rewards should be thought of as including outcomes that increase goal fulfillment *or* preclude a loss in goal fulfillment, and costs should include outcomes that decrease goal fulfillment *or* do not provide an increase in goal fulfillment.

Generally speaking, the greater the degree of goal fulfillment provided by an outcome the greater will be its utility to the actor. But experimental research has shown, and no small amount of observation of everyday life confirms, that people become satiated with an outcome with varying degrees of rapidity. The first "units" of goal fulfillment may therefore yield greater utility than subsequent units. This is the familiar economists' principle of "marginal utility." Knowing that outcomes have relative rather than absolute utility is important. When people choose they are comparing the utility of various outcome options available to them. The more they have of one thing, the less valuable any further units of it become and the more valuable further units of another thing will be. People's choices thus reflect preferences among combinations of commodities (Heath, 1976:11). When a man decides whether or not to work overtime he is deciding which *combination* of units of work and leisure will be most satisfying to him.

SELECTING ACTION ALTERNATIVES

Initiating the Selection Process

Actors begin to consider changing a course of action when they judge that greater utility can be obtained through enactment of an alternative. The decision to switch from action A to action B will be made if (i) the gap between outcome and goal fulfillment in action A is narrower than the gap between outcome and goal fulfillment in action B, (ii) the goal to which action A is oriented is less important than the goal toward which action B is oriented, or (iii) the outcomes of action A do not meet the actor's expectations.

Selecting the Alternative

At minimum actors will choose between continuing the alternative they are currently enacting and switching to a different alternative. They may also consider enacting the same alternative at a different level of intensity, and they may be trying to fulfill either the goal they are currently fulfilling or a goal that is substantially underfulfilled.... choices among alternatives will be made on the basis of their subjective expected utilities. Generally we expect them to switch to a different alternative if that alternative has greater subjective expected utility than continuation of their current alternative has. This means that actors may continue enacting a given alternative even though they are experiencing severe deprivation on other goals simply because they perceive no alternatives with greater subjective expected utility available to fulfill those goals (Blalock and Wilken, 1979:147).

Early rational choice models simply assumed that people scanned all available alternatives until they located that which would yield the greatest excess of reward over cost. Later models incorporated the more realistic idea that people do not always seek to maximize profits but rest content instead with an option that is simply "good enough." "That is, rather than strictly maximizing their benefits, men may continue to search for better alternative outcomes only until minimally satisfying ones are found" (Homans, 1974:122). This is "satisficing" behavior. Satisficing is most likely to occur where information about choices is scarce and costly to obtain.

Exchange theorists are conscious of the fact that their model of human behavior is very simple and that real life is much more complex. However, for a number of reasons, they see this as no impediment to building valid theory from its premises. They point out, first, that real life is not as complicated as we might suppose. In real life people deliberately simplify their world in order to make it manageable. They settle for relative rather than absolute judgements about alternatives—a better choice rather than the best choice; they treat as equivalents the rewards of various outcomes so that they can lump them together; they refrain from precise calculation of probabilities, setting the odds at zero or at one-to-one; they also satisfice rather than maximize.

Second, exchange theorists acknowledge that their model is a simplification of the "subjective component" (the way we think and feel about choices), adding that all theories must simplify some aspects of reality in order to make others comprehendable. The complexity in rational choice theory lies in "the structural configuration within which this simple man acts" (Coleman, 75b:81). By assuming that people act rationally we "suspend" certain problems in order to devote our attention to other matters.

Third, exchange theorists acknowledge that making choices is determined in large part by a complex and subtle process whereby we must put ourselves in other people's shoes and imagine what their wants are. They deal with this by trying to formalize this process of "taking the role of the other." For example, they postulate that an actor will be able to accurately anticipate the reaction of the other if he has often performed the act in the past, if the other is familiar to him, if the other gives off plentiful cues, where there are no third parties influencing the interpretation, and so on (Blalock and Wilken, 1979:188). Social interaction is thus not a process incapable of simplification and formalization—especially if the interaction is sustained and orderly.

SIMPLE SOCIAL EXCHANGE

Once we turn our attention to social exchange we confront what most sociologists would consider the truly social world in which the behavior of actors is influenced by their anticipation of how others will react to what they do. Social relationships demand that we estimate, not only our own utilities, but the utilities of others. They require not only that we make choices but that we anticipate what choices others would make.

The introduction of the concept of social exchange thus enormously complicates exchange theory. The actor can no longer be treated as an isolated being. Fortunately, real life rarely exhausts all the logical possibilities of exchange processes. Some exchange relations are much more important than others because they concern "primary goals" such as getting enough to eat and obtaining shelter for the night. Some exchange relations become so routine that the other's reaction to what we do can be predicted with confidence. Many of our exchange relations follow predictable sequences—an exchange of greetings would be an example. Finally, social exchange relations are similar to, but not completely identical with, economic transactions. Social exchanges involve "unspecified obligations" (Blau, 1964:93). The rewards or sanctions exchanged are not specified precisely. The actors trust each other to reciprocate in some fashion at a later time. Unspecified obligations relieve actors of the burden of precisely calculating the nature and timing of appropriate responses. In this kind of "generalized exchange," people help each other "not in response to any specific benefit received, but rather in honor of the social exchange relation itself, that relation being a *series* of reciprocating benefits extending into the experienced past and the anticipated future" (Emerson, 1981:33). Actors trust each other to reciprocate in social exchange, whereas purely economic exchange is likely to be hedged about with stipulations and requirements. The importance of trust for alleviating the burden of calculation is indicated by the fact that, where trust breaks down, social relations become less certain, people tend to become more calculative toward each other and demand immediate payment for their services (Chadwick-Jones, 1976:343). The existence of unspecified obligations makes the sociologist's problem of analysis much simpler.

Rational choice in the context of complex social exchange processes is also simplified by norms. Social norms prescribe who can enter an exchange relationship, what are the legitimate alternatives for the actors in the relationship, and the appropriate level of profit each party can realize. Without norms proscribing force and fraud the trust which makes unspecified obligations possible would break down (Blau, 1964:255). Norms also facilitate indirect exchange: wealthy businessmen who make philanthropic contributions "do so to conform with normative expectations that prevail in their social class and to earn the social approval of their peers, not necessarily in order to earn the gratitude of the individuals who benefit from their charity, who they may never meet" (Blau, 1964:260). Exchange theorists do not have to argue, then, that exchange brings about social integration by a process in which all individuals exchange with all other individuals. We "exchange" with society—or at least with those groups we think stand for society. Thus, when a person rescues another from drowning, the gratitude of the person rescued is supplemented by the respect and admiration forthcoming from witnesses, and it is the anticipation of their reward (or sanction in the case of a failure to act) which is the primary motive for the act (Goode, 1978:19).

NORMS   As this example suggests, conformity to norms can itself become a reward. People conform to norms because it brings them social approval and they find social approval rewarding. Norms thus account for many actions which would otherwise appear unaccountable in the strictly rational model. People who refuse to cheat, even though cheating would help them achieve a desired goal, do act rationally and do act in their self-interest "if the peace of mind and social approval they obtain from their honesty is more rewarding to them than the gains they could make by cheating" (Blau, 1964:258).

COMPLEX SOCIAL EXCHANGE

Simple exchange consists of transactions in which the action of one party constitutes a direct outcome for the other party. More complex forms of exchange occur whenever more than two people enter the relationship. Indirect exchange involves two parties each giving something to a third party, who then allocates outcomes among the original two parties. Any kind of "gatekeeping" role will involve indirect exchange: the basketball scout, the professor recommending students for jobs, the talent agent placing clients, and the social hostess seating guests are all allocating outcomes on the basis of assumed inputs. Mediated exchange involves an intermediary, as in the case of a wholesaler facilitating the exchange between producer and retailer.

Complex forms of exchange alter the meaning of utility. Goods and services are created in complex exchange which cannot be created in simple exchange, where A rewards B with x and B rewards A with y. In complex exchange a third good or service is produced which both A and B can enjoy. In a game of tennis, what A gives to B and what B gives to A interact to produce a rewarding outcome for both players (Emerson, 1969:395). In a game of tennis played for a prize derived from fee-paying spectators even more complex utilities are yielded. In this case, the game of tennis A and B jointly produce is exchanged for what each of them desires. This is but one example of the division of labor in exchange relations in which a good that could only be jointly produced by each party performing a specialized function is exchanged for a reward which neither of them could have produced on his own. "Value is produced in the social process from behavioral contributions that have little or no value taken by themselves" (Emerson, 1981:34).

EXCHANGE NETWORKS

The sum of exchange opportunities confronting an actor is called an exchange network. The exchange network connects the actor with other actors through a series of exchange relations. Each actor will have the opportunity to transact business with at least one other participant in the network, although not all actors have equal opportunities to initiate or respond to transactions (Tallman and Ihinger-Tallman, 1979:218). Most people are members of a number of exchange networks and they must learn to balance the payoffs in one exchange network relation with the payoffs in another. A husband has to balance what he owes his wife and friends against what he owes his employer and workmates.

Networks add to the possibility for indirect exchange. Individual A can give to B in the expectation that C will eventually reciprocate. The individual assumes that *some* member of the network will reward him. Thus, in extending a dinner party invitation, we do not necessarily anticipate a direct return from those we entertain, but merely that, from somewhere in our social circle, a return invitation will be issued (Kadushin, 1981:239).

EQUITY

People will enter relations of exchange voluntarily only if they anticipate an acceptable rate of exchange. Enduring relations settle at a rate of exchange more or less satisfactory to all parties. The exchange rate is determined mainly by supply and demand. In his study of the interaction between employees of a federal agency, Blau (1955) discovered that a relationship of exchange had formed between expert workers and less experienced colleagues in which advice and assistance were exchanged for respect and compliance and that the rate at which this exchange took place had been established over a long period of time. Blau found that the value of any one of many consultations became deflated for nonexperts and the value of any one of many solicitations for advice became deflated for the experts in accordance with the principle of marginal utility. The exchange relation thus settled at that point where the last unit of advice was worth more to the nonexpert than the self-abasement it cost him and the last unit of flattery was worth more to the expert than the time he spent giving the advice. The marginal utilities of the respective parties in the consulting relationship established the going rate of exchange. This rate could be altered at any time by a change in demand or supply. The cost of advice would diminish if the proportion of experts increased and advice became plentiful. The cost of advice might also fall if the nonexperts formed a coalition to make flattery scarce.

The rate at which rewards are exchanged in a relationship is not determined exclusively by supply and demand, however. Ideas about what is fair or just also influence the exchange rate. Such ideas derive from a comparison the individual makes with other people and the judgement she makes whether she is receiving as much as she ought to receive when compared with the effort they expend (Homans, 1974:252). In other words, the individual wishes to feel he is being treated equitably.

Equity exists when the ratio of inputs to outcomes for participants in an exchange relation is equal to the ratio for other people involved. It is less important that outcomes be equal than that the ratio of inputs to outcomes be equal. Whether or not a worker is satisfied with her pay depends less on her being paid the same as her fellow workers and more on her getting paid in relation to her expenditure of effort and time (and her qualifications) at a ratio that is the same as that of her fellow workers.

If a person receives less than her due, she suffers from negative inequity. A person receiving more than her due is enjoying positive inequity. Satisfying relationships require that both partners believe they enjoy equity, but they need not share equity judgements. One person might see the exchange as equitable, the other inequitable; one person might see positive inequity, the other negative inequity; both might believe they benefit—and both might believe they lose (Blalock and Wilken, 1979:249). The judgement of equity is obviously an uncertain business. However, it is worth noting that people tend to make equity judgements by comparing their lot with people who are already like them in many ways, which makes the judgement easier (Blalock and Wilken, 1979:234). People also tend to form equity judgements by comparing themselves, not to particular people, which would make the judgements difficult, but with a "generalized other." A student might compare the ratio of her work and grade not with a particular student but with the ratio thought to pertain among students in general.

People who feel unjustly treated will be dissatisfied and become angry, especially if the degree of inequity is great and it is believed to be deliberate. Such people can try to increase their outcomes, lower the outcomes of others, reduce their inputs, increase the inputs of others, or leave the relationship. People are not always able to find more equitable relationships and must learn to live with what they have. In this case they might seek to restore "psychological equity" by altering their perception of respective inputs and outcomes (Walster, Berscheid and Walster, 1976:6–7). Those who enjoy positive inequity are likely to feel guilt, especially if the inequitable exchange was initiated by them. Where such feelings are strong (or where retaliation is feared), beneficiaries will either increase the rewards of their victims or seek to excuse their part in the exchange by denying intentionality or responsibility.

Equity analysis can deal not only with interpersonal relations (such as those between parents and children) but also with macro-level relations (such as those between labor and management, between a majority group and a minority group, or between one nation and another). Labor-management relations are clearly shaped by judgements of parity among workers of similar occupations, and racial discrimination exists where inequitable outcomes result from equivalent social inputs by members of different racial groups. Exchange theory thus shows its ability to link the microprocesses of interpersonal relations to the broader social issues of intergroup and international relations.

POWER

I have already alluded to the fact that actors might have to tolerate an inequitable relationship if no better is available. This is likely to be a situation where one actor (A) has greater need for what another actor (B) can provide him than B has need for what A can provide him. In a relationship characterized by the extreme dependency of one partner on another an imbalance of power prevails. B's power over A is approximately the same as A's dependency on B (Emerson, 1976). "The greater the difference between the benefits an individual supplies to others and those they can obtain elsewhere, the greater his power over them is likely to be" (Blau, 1964:120). The "principle of least interest" will therefore determine who has the most power in a relationship (Cook and Emerson, 1978:724).

The power of one individual over another will be greater if what she offers is highly valued by the other, if the other is willing and able to meet her needs, and if the other cannot resign himself to living without the service she provides. The more powerful individual is in a position to offer rewards for compliance and punishment for noncompliance (Blalock and Wilken, 1979:177).

Relations of extreme dependency border on servitude, and this raises the question of the place of physical force or coercion in a theory which stresses above all the role of rational decision making in social action. Many exchange theorists deliberately exclude coercion from their model, although they have no wish to understate the role it plays in social life. Goode (1973:174), on the other hand, argues for the inclusion of physical coercion or "force threat" in exchange theories on the grounds that people can and do "buy" protection from force. Goode is right in a sense: robbery or kidnapping is an exchange relationship in which life is exchanged for money. However, "bargains" such as these are almost involuntary, the freedom to excercise choice being so limited that they must be regarded as marking the outer limits of the scope of exchange theory. Its failure to deal with these situations facilely is no criticism of the theory.

MACRO-LEVEL PROCESSES

When exchange theorists move beyond the simple world of isolated individuals and try to explain complex social institutions and social processes, how do they proceed? One strategy is to treat the social world as if it were composed, not of unique individuals, but of categories of people. Since people simplify their social world by "lumping together various other actors and by assuming a high degree of homogeneity or similarity between them," the sociologist is warranted in treating social behavior as the interaction between categories of actors who exhibit tendencies to act in certain ways (Blalock and Wilken, 1979:288).

A second means of dealing with the complexity of social institutions and structures is to argue that people treat much of their social world as given, not subject to modification by anything they might do as individuals. The actor's choices are thus constrained by what he takes to be "natural" and "objective." An actor's behavior toward members of a minority group might be influenced by what he believes are the attitudes of people like him. These attitudes are part of the actor's context, and the sociologist can treat them as a "contextual effect." The average rate of racial prejudice in a population is thus used to help explain the individual's behavior toward a member of a minority group. This strategy of mixing micro- and macro-levels of analysis is described by Blalock and Wilken (1979:290).

> First, ... we may use macro-level variables in micro-level equations. For instance, in studying the behavior of a person we may use explanatory variables such as average level of prejudice in his or her environment ... or the behavior levels of peers or other significant persons. Second, we may use aggregated individual scores in a macro model. Thus, in comparing communities or nations we may introduce such variables as median income levels, literacy rates, frequency of violent acts, or percentages of persons having specified traits (Blalock and Wilken, 1979:290).

In addition to permitting macro-level phenomena to enter as contextual effects, exchange theorists also move beyond a discussion of individuals when they discuss intergroup processes. Groups, like individuals, can be thought of as having goals, selecting alternatives, having utilities, and possessing resources (Goode, 1978:101). The only difference between individuals and groups is the accuracy with which most of these variables can be measured. Groups thus function as "corporate actors," and their actions can be explained using variables identical to those used in the explanation of individual behavior, "provided that we also introduce additional variables to take care of problems of coordination, dissensus, conflicting interests and rivalries, defections and social control, and the like" (Blalock and Wilken, 1979:335).

Blalock and Wilken also deal with macro-level phenomena when they describe "allocation processes." Here, the distribution of reward among actors is not the unintended consequence of myriad individuals pursuing their self-interests, but the result of indirect exchange in which third parties determine outcomes: for example, a businessman might allocate jobs to applicants, an editor allocates space in his journal to writers, or the legal system "allocates" punishments to the accused. These allocation processes are a major determinant of the distribution of power and prestige in society.

The manner in which exchange theory is applied to a social pattern like race relations is illustrated by a model of interracial contact formulated by Blalock and Wilken (1979:558). The model focuses on the rewards and costs of interracial contact for the individual. Macro-level variables enter the picture as factors affecting the shapes and levels of the reward and cost functions. The dependent variable is defined behavioristically and consists of two dimensions:

> Frequency: "the total number of times (in some specified time period) in which a given pair or set of actors is engaged in interaction."
> Duration: "the length of time that elapses between the onset and completion of each particular interaction."

The frequency and duration of voluntary interracial contact is taken to be a direct consequence of the rewards and costs expected from such contact. Rewards include not only concrete goods and services but also less tangible outcomes such as exposure to persons with different life styles, beliefs, and experiences. Costs include not only "expenses" such as time consumed, travel costs, and so on, but the possibility of embarrassment and humiliation. The calculation of rewards and costs is in turn affected by a large number of other factors, the elaboration of which forms the body of the theory. Many of these factors have to do with the character of the contact itself. Thus, the rewards and costs of interracial contact will be influenced by the degree to which the contact involves intimacy, conflict, is visible, implies equal status, is considered legitimate, and so on. Some of these factors concern the actor's biography, such as the actor's previous contact with similar partners, his vulnerability to group sanctions, and his degree of dependence on making the contact.

As these examples demonstrate, exchange theory claims to be able to deal with macro-level processes as easily as it deals with face-to-face interaction. Exchange theorists are quick to point out that social institutions will endure only because "people want to carry out the specific, concrete acts or tasks that make up those larger social patterns" (Goode, 1978:14). They believe that there must always be traceable a link between individual actors and the larger needs of society, these larger needs reflecting in some way or another a process in which individuals are forced to do what others want, in return for which they get cooperation and help from others. Thus, even if analysis does begin at the macro-level, it will eventually have to concern itself with "relations among persons" (Coleman, 1975b:86).

COMMENTS

Few sociologists deny that many social relations are based on exchange. But not so many are willing to accept the argument that the principles which govern exchange relations are the most elementary and fundamental forms of social behavior to which all others are reducible. Criticisms of exchange theory take a number of forms. Some sociologists refuse to believe that exchange theory really explains social behavior at all, charging that the model is either merely a description of what happens or a prescription about what ought to happen if human beings are to be rational. Other critics believe that exchange theory is too strongly committed to empiricism to cope with the subjective component in social action. There are still others who believe that rational choice theory is not empiricist enough. A fourth group of sociologists believe that exchange theory is incapable of explaining macro-level processes.

DOES EXCHANGE THEORY EXPLAIN SOCIAL BEHAVIOR?

There is an attractive simplicity to the idea that people do things because they find them rewarding. All we need do to explain a person's actions is to find out what he finds rewarding and what he is prepared to do in order to obtain it. The problem is that such explanations can easily become circular. We might say that an act is performed because it is rewarding—and cite as proof that it is rewarding the fact that it was performed. Or we might claim that a pattern of behavior persists because it has paid off for a society (whatever has not been rewarding has not been permitted to remain), but the only way we know what patterns of behavior are rewarding is if they persist. Neither argument escapes circularity unless independent evidence of what is found rewarding is provided.

Even when it is possible to ascertain in advance what a person values, it is also necessary to know in advance how much that person is willing to pay for it. Thus we might account for a politician's advocacy of a certain policy in the course of an election campaign by arguing that she is exchanging her advocacy for campaign contributions. But this theory explains her advocacy only if we can say what amount of advocacy she is willing to exchange for the amount of campaign contributions she desires.

What is more, we ought to be able to make this determination in advance of testing the theory. If all our theory says is that X amount of advocacy will be exchanged for Y amount of contributions and if the *only* means we have of measuring the value the politician places on Y amount of contributions is the amount of advocacy we see her exchange for it, it is a circular argument.

Exchange theorists are aware of these logical difficulties. Homans (1974:36) acknowledges that his basic propositions are susceptible to circular argumentation. He claims, however, that these propositions can be rendered invulnerable to this criticism once they are properly specified. The basic proposition "the more valuable to a person is the result of his action, the more likely is he to perform that action" can be protected against circularity by adding the assumption "a man inexperienced in his job is likely to find some amount of advice about how to do the job more valuable than the result of just doing the job without advice." This assumption makes possible the hypothesis that "an inexperienced man is more likely to try to get some advice than an experienced man." Presumably, whether or not a man is experienced and whether or not he finds advice rewarding can be ascertained in advance of the testing of the theory. Carefully used, then, the exchange theory can avoid circularity.

Exchange theorists regard such problems as technical difficulties which will be resolved once independent measures of outcomes and rewards are found. Many experimental studies have been conducted which show how people decide on the utility of various outcomes and arrive at estimates of the likelihood of particular outcomes yielding particular rewards. While the applicability of these experimental studies to real life must be open to question, they do protect exchange theory from the criticism that it is inherently circular and would never be falsifiable.

The charge that exchange theory is not falsifiable comes from another quarter. Here the charge concerns the practice of adding "auxiliary statements" to exchange theory—statements added to the theory after the fact to protect it against disconfirmation. Some critics claim that exchange theorists are prone to use these statements to save their theory. An illustrative example is provided by rational choice theories of voter turnout in elections.

What explains the behavior of people at election time? Exchange theory would encourage us to believe that people vote in elections because they calculate that they will be better off if they go to the polls than if they remain at home. The problem with this theory is that people would never vote at all if they were really rational. The usual rewards of voting are "collective" or "public" goods, such as economic stability, clean air, and national defense. Such goods are available to the whole population regardless of whether they voted. As voting always entails some cost, and as each voter, if rational, will calculate that an individual vote will make no difference to the overall election outcome, the most rational choice would be to leave the voting to others. And yet people do vote in elections. Does this invalidate exchange theory?

Given our understanding of the requirement that a theory remain in use only as long as the facts fail to falsify it, it would seem that the voting example should throw serious doubt on the validity of exchange theory. But the reaction to this kind of disconfirmation usually takes the form of introducing auxiliary statements which explain away the apparent anomaly. It might be argued that the voter actually goes to the poll because he feels he has a long-term investment in the survival of the electoral system. Or it might be argued that he goes to the poll because he will gain short-term rewards from meeting his friends. By adding auxiliary statements, the theorist is able to declare irrelevant the outcomes formerly treated as rewards and postulate new rewards in order to make the observed pattern of behavior appear rational. These kinds of *ad hoc* adjustments to the theory provide no test of the theory itself because the idea that people do things because they find them rewarding is protected from disconfirmation.

It is possible to modify exchange theory so that it can explain going to the polls and still be testable, however. We could invoke the idea of satisficing. We could propose that potential voters do not seek to maximize gains so much as minimize losses. This is quite plausible as voting is normally conducted under conditions of uncertainty and risk. The theory would now lead us to expect that people will vote given only the slightest incentive simply to ensure that nothing really bad happens to them. We do not have to suppose that they have precisely calculated the profit to be reaped. This modification is not an auxiliary statement. It reconceptualizes what is meant by rational choice rather than what is meant by a reward. The theory's scope has been enhanced while retaining its essential features (Moon, 1974:196–203).

IS EXCHANGE THEORY EMPIRICAL ENOUGH?

Some critics argue that exchange theory is not truly scientific because it pays too much attention to and relies too heavily on "unobservables" like attitudes and expectations. These critics are behavioralists. Behavioralism is the name given to the set of theories which have in common the idea that social behavior can be explained in terms of observable physical motions and their relation to preceding (or simultaneous) physical events. Behavioralism is strictly empiricist: the focus is upon overt behavior rather than upon what goes on in people's minds.

Behavioralists do not deny the existence of mental states but they are extremely cautious about admitting any reference to them into scientific theory. "Hypotheses which include the internal state as an important variable are difficult to test (and refute) since validated measuring devices are yet to be constructed..." (Kunkel, 1969:333). Behavioralists believe that imputation of inner states should play as small a role as possible in sociological explanations.

The heavy reliance on knowing what a person expects to result from her action is a cause of great discomfort to behavioralists who want to use exchange theory. Expectations are mental states, not amenable to empirical observation. Molm and Wiggins (1979) propose an exchange theory which makes no reference to expectations at all. It is assumed that people enter social relations with little or no information concerning possible outcomes. People initially sample various options and some of these are reinforced or rewarded. This reinforcement forms the basis of stable interaction. Predictions about behavior are based on "actual rather than expected reinforcement" (Molm and Wiggins, 1979:1160). No assumptions need be made about the probable rewards of an action. Nor need we assume that the actions which will be rewarded are known in advance by the actor.

Homans (1974:37) also adheres firmly to empiricism. Although expectations are frequently referred to in his exchange theory, they are defined in strictly empirical terms.

> What a man expects to get by way of reward or punishment under a given set of circumstances (stimuli) is what he has in fact received, observed, or was told others received, under similar circumstances in the past; and none of these things are private events confined within the individual's head.

Expectations are determined by what a person has received in the past, and the judgement of the sociologist in this regard will be as accurate as his subject's.

Behavioralists treat other mental states such as norms and values in the same way as expectations. We value what we have been conditioned to value. Values are "the product of an individual's reinforcement history" (Burgess and Bushnell, 1969:279). Values are learned over the course of previous efforts to maximize utilities. They can therefore be inferred from objective evidence—the individual's past behavior. Value can thus be defined as "the probability of an action's occurrence" (Kunkel, 1969:343). In other words, if an individual behaves in a way defined as honest by the observer, it is assumed that the individual values honesty under those conditions.

Norms are also reinterpreted by behavioralists. They become "rules according to which certain classes of behavior will be reinforced, while, in the same situation, other behaviors will be punished" (Burgess and Bushnell, 1969:279). Norms are strictly conditioning factors which establish the parameters of acceptable behavior. This contrasts with the approach to norms by rational choice theorists who include the idea of expectation in their definition of norms. Normative behavior is not defined as simply the typical way of doing something: it includes a sense of "the way one *should* respond" (Blalock and Wilken, 1979:195).

The behavioralists' discomfiture with the rational choice model is inspired by more than epistemological doubts. They also believe that the image of man presented by the rational choice model is misleading. They find it hard to believe that people routinely calculate probabilities and survey alternatives in the fashion suggested by the model. Behavioralists see human conduct as resulting from operant conditioning where rational choice plays only a limited role. The operant conditioning model needs fewer assumptions about what a person is able to do:

> men *do not* have to spell out all or most of their alternatives, list the various outcomes of each alternative in terms of their respective utilities and probabilities, and choose among these alternatives on the basis of the expected value of each ... [because] action and, if you will, choice depend on past experiences in a specific way. If in the past some activity in some context was rewarded however that activity came to be initially performed, it is more likely to be performed again in that context. This likelihood varies with the degree of reward that followed that activity, the frequency with which the reward occurred, the pattern of that frequency (the reinforcement schedule) and the degree to which the actor is deprived of that reward, which is a function of how recently he received it (Waldman, 1972:213).

In other words, we do not have to deal with the problems the rational choice model creates: people are not completely free to deliberate on alternatives, to imagine new rewards, or to search for more profitable courses of action. Habit and conditioning play a much bigger role in determining social behavior than many exchange theorists seem willing to admit.

Neither side in this debate is necessarily wrong. There is no incompatibility between behavioralists and rational choice theorists. Behavioralism is well suited to explaining how people come to formulate their preference schedules in the first place. Rational choice theorists take these for granted and assume some cognitive weighing of alternative actions in the process of selecting among them. Further developments in exchange theory might specify the manner in which conditioning and decision making "operate together in some situations and are given salience, one over the other, in other situations" (Emerson, 1981:41).

IS EXCHANGE THEORY TOO DETERMINISTIC?

Most exchange theorists reject the behavioralists' rather narrow definition of exchange theory, believing that its emphasis on environmental conditioning slights the decision-making processes which enter into exchange relations. Many sociologists who are not positivists believe that the treatment of the subjective component by all exchange theorists is deficient. They believe that even the rational choice model distorts our image of social action, portraying it as a series of discrete choices between fixed alternatives, rather than as a process.

Where rational choice theorists talk of "acts" and "decisions," other sociologists talk of "acting" and "deciding." The distinction is important because the terms "acting" and "deciding" are chosen to capture the idea that social interaction is a process. Acts have no fixed or clear beginning and end. "Acts" happen, but "actions" flow. "Acts" take place but "actions" take time.

Rational choice theory also impoverishes our understanding of the individual and his relation to society. The "self" is taken for granted, treated as a fixed resource which the individual brings to the exchange relation. As a factor in the exchange it determines the outcome of the exchange but is otherwise unaffected. Other sociologists do not look upon the self as being fixed. They believe that we have a self that is appropriate to each of the settings and each of the relations we enter. Furthermore, this self needs perpetual care and maintenance. Much of what we do is an effort to protect and enhance our sense of self. A son, wishing to borrow money from his parents, may incur (as a cost of obtaining his loan) the time and effort involved in protecting his identity as an obedient and loving child (Weinstein and Tanur, 1978:142).

While the model of the rational decision maker appears to acknowledge the subjective component, then, it actually distorts and reduces it. The self becomes merely a package of "hierarchically arranged interests" (Weinstein and Tanur, 1978:142). This self is not much of an individual at all. Its uniqueness consists only in being a particular combination of preference schedules. Ironically, exchange theory which, as we shall see, is criticized for reducing sociological theory to the study of individual, micro-level phenomena, is here criticized for having a very inadequate view of individual behavior.

CAN EXCHANGE THEORY EXPLAIN SOCIAL STRUCTURE?

The basic constituents of exchange theory are individuals and groups treated as if they were individuals. The individual actor is more real to the exchange theorist than social structure. Macro-level processes, such as the growth of cities, are treated as if they were simply aggregations of a large number of individual decisions.

Other sociologists regard structures as more real than individuals. They believe that the treatment of the individual in exchange theory is a form of blindness concerning the true subject matter of sociology, which should be the relations between individuals. Boudon's (1975:398) explanation of the differences in the amount of schooling Americans receive can serve as an example of this myopia. Boudon assumes that patterns of inequality in educational achievement (like any other social pattern) reflect the aggregation of individual actions, in which everybody attempts to serve his own interest in the best way. Some people are able to obtain more years of schooling because they bring different resources to the choice of whether or not to stay in school. Going to school one more year represents a cost to the student, a cost which will be a function of that student's parental income. The smaller the income the greater the cost. This explains why children from poorer homes obtain fewer years of schooling than children from rich homes.

Critics of exchange theory charge that Boudon's focus upon the individual profit maximizer in this explanation takes for granted precisely that which needs to be explained. Boudon pays virtually no attention to education as an institution, nor does he seem interested in the relation between education and other social institutions like the family. Boudon has no theory to explain why money is the major cost of education, why education is a reward, why that much reward is thought to be worth that much cost or why parental income is so important in determining cost. Boudon is able to explain why choices are made, but he is unable to explain why those are the choices that are available.

Were Boudon's exchange theory of education sufficient, it would follow that developments in education as a social institution would reflect changing demands among the population for education. But this has not been the case. Education in the United States has developed in accordance with changes in the structure of production. "The process of individual choice aggregation, even when it is relevant to educational change, works within economic constraints determined almost entirely outside both the consumer's and the citizen's arena of choice" (Bowles and Gintis, 1975:78).

The exchange theorist asserts that macro-level phenomena (e.g. patterns of inequality in educational achievement) are the outgrowth of individual profit maximization decisions. The critic of the exchange theory replies that those decisions have been shaped and limited by other social structures. This is a debate over logical and causal priority. Exchange theorists begin with the self-interested actor faced with the problem of choice. They assume that the working out of these choices will generate social structures. But the reverse is equally plausible. Social structure—particularly the distribution of power in society—determines not only the terms of exchange in a relationship, but the interests of actors too (Parsons, 1954:62). In particular, what the actor thinks is in her interest, what she considers to be her range of choices, has been determined by the power structure within which she is situated. People do not simply wait to be given power by those who need their services. They actively shape other people's needs so that they are the only ones who can satisfy them. Power is not the effect but the cause of exchange (Marx, 1973:156).

Exchange theorists are not unaware that rewards and interests are to some degree determined by social institutions. "Sometimes," writes Homans (1974:367), "the activities exchanged in elementary social behavior derive their value from the rules of the institution." (Goode (1978:262) acknowledges that it is "partly individuals' knowledge" of social structure which patterns their social behavior. However, they insist that these "rules of the institution" can themselves be explained by exchange theory. They, too, result from previous exchange relations. For example, Homans recognizes that the bureaucratization of formal organizations can impose fresh constraints on the individual's freedom of choice. However, bureaucratization itself can be explained by reference to the fact that executives in expanding organizations find bureaucratic methods more rewarding. Blau (1970:335) criticizes this theory on the grounds that it offers no explanation at all for differences between organizations. He believes that the most appropriate method of explaining bureaucratization is not by reference to the interests and utilities of individuals in the organization but by reference to the structure of the organization. We need to know what distinguishes those organizations which have developed bureaucracies from those that have not. We will answer this question not with data about individuals but with data about organizations. Thus we might find that bureaucracy tends to develop in organizations with a highly advanced division of labor. This structural feature might, in turn, explain why executives in one organization find bureaucratization more rewarding than executives in another.

CONCLUSION

Much of the debate over exchange theory concerns not so much its validity as the scope of the conditions under which it is valid. Many sociologists willing to acknowledge the validity of its analysis of exchange processes are reluctant to rely upon exchange theory exclusively. And exchange theorists themselves acknowledge the weakness of their theory when it comes to explaining the role of ideologies, emotions, and physical force in social life (Blau, 1964:89; Blalock and Wilken, 1979:176).

Exchange theory tends to be more convincing when rewards are extrinsic and plausibly exhaustible. It is less convincing where rewards and costs are low and hard to quantify (Barry, 1978:160). In political sociology, for example, it is most at home "when applied to the bargaining of committees and caucuses, to the adoption of platforms by candidates, to voting, and to readiness to participate in political activity" (Benn, 1976:247). That is, it is plausible wherever social life resembles a market place. Its applicability to other aspects of social life continues to be debated.

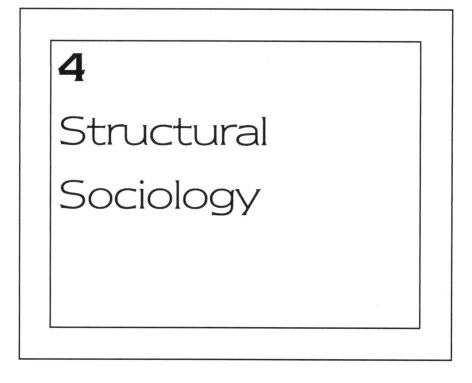

4

Structural Sociology

One of the things that distinguishes the sociological perspective on social life is its preoccupation with the forms or patterns to be found there. Sociologists are more interested in *King* John than King *John,* more interested in the role of king as played by John than in the unique attributes and motives of John who happens to be King. To be King is to occupy a social position, to perform a role, to be part of a structure of authority called monarchy (Coser, 1977:180).

The idea of structure thus plays some role in the work of all sociologists. However, a research tradition has emerged in which structural analysis plays a central, if not the only, role in forming research problems and suggesting solutions. There are variations within this research tradition, as there are in the others. Some structural analysts use structure merely as a descriptive term, to delineate the phenomenon to be explained. Others treat the idea of structure as an explanatory tool to identify the cause of the social relationships observed. Despite these differences, however, they are united in their belief that sociologists must always think structurally. They must always remember that the arrangement of the parts is more important than the parts themselves.

THE MEANING
OF STRUCTURE

A structure is an orderly arrangement of elements. The parts of a structure are less important than the relation between them. Indeed, it is only when we have formed an idea of the relation that we truly know the parts. We recognize this woman as a wife and that man as a husband because we have previously conceptualized the relation, marriage.

Some of the founding fathers of sociology believed that this focus upon structure was the most distinctive feature of their new discipline, firmly establishing its independence of psychology. Thus Durkheim (1960a:13) maintained that if sociology had any legitimacy at all, "societies must be assumed to have a certain nature which results from the nature and arrangement of the elements composing them, and which is the source of social phenomena." There are contemporary scholars who believe that the discovery of the structuredness of social life is the greatest single contribution to the understanding of society sociologists have ever made (Nisbet, 1974:73).

In one sense or another, all sociologists make use of the idea of structure. Exchange theorists, although their unit of analysis is the individual, find the idea of networks useful in describing complex forms of exchange between individuals. In the hands of the structural sociologist, however, the concept of structure becomes the pivot around which all analysis revolves. Structure is no longer treated as the outcome of, or the context for, individual behavior. Structure assumes logical priority over the parts that comprise it.

What does it mean to accord logical priority to the whole over the parts? Consider our understanding of a traffic signal. We do not know what the color amber means until we know it is part of a structure called a traffic signal in which red and green are also constituents. More important, we would not know the precise function of amber if we did not know how amber, red, and green are arranged in the signal. We need to know where all the parts are in relation to the others before we can know the meaning of any one. In the same fashion, the information that a person is black has no sociological significance unless we know the relation of which blackness is a part. In societies other than the United States, blackness might signify being in the majority rather than the minority, or it and other skin colors might play no role in marking relations of dominance and submission. We do not start with the part (blackness) and build upon it our knowledge of the relation (between black and white). We start with the relation and build upon it our knowledge of the part.

Structures are descriptions of the aggregate as a whole, not of its constituent elements. "The aggregate is merely the sum of the elements, but the structure depends on their relationships, in the broadest sense, including under relationships relative positions and indirect influences as well as direct connections" (Blau, 1981:9). Structures are emergent properties because they emerge from the arrangement or interaction between the parts. The division of labor is an emergent property because it refers to the distribution of the labor force among many different occupations. The greater the division of labor in a population, the greater the likelihood that two persons in that population would have different occupations. An individual occupation cannot have the property of the division of labor. However, as this example shows, emergent properties grow out of constituent elements and tell us something about them.

What is confusing to those unfamiliar with structural analysis is that the social world seems to be populated by and observable only through individuals. Although these individuals share certain "obvious" characteristics and attributes (e.g. sex, age, ethnicity) and although they do form patterns (e.g. age grading in school), it would seem that they should be the units with which analysis must begin. And until we learn to think about social structure properly, individuals *are* more apparent than structure.

Social structure is revealed by thinking away the unique attributes of individuals and their relationships and leaving only that which is invariant. What remains is the form or the structure in which those individuals and relationships are "placed" (Nadel, 1957:7). From a varied set of social encounters we might abstract the form or the structure we call "friendship." This form remains constant whether the individuals concerned are young or old, men or women, black or white, and whether the friendship revolves around music, gardening, a job, or some other shared interest. The form transcends particular times, places, and people.

In this preoccupation with form, structural sociology resembles geometry.

> Geometric abstraction investigates only the spatial forms of bodies although empirically these forms are given merely as the form of some material content. Similarly, if society is conceived as interaction among individuals, the description of the forms of this interaction is the task of the science of society in its strictest and most essential sense (Simmel, 1950:21).

Because content is infinitely variable, the pattern or regularity with which the science of society should concern itself must be the form. "Sociology is primarily concerned with social forms, not with the unique content of these forms" (Mayhew and Schollaert, 1980:5).

Abstracting form does not make content totally irrelevant. It simply means that content is explained in terms of form. We know why blackness is important because we know the pattern of majority-minority relations in which it plays a part. We can predict that, were whites in the minority position, they would behave in much the same way as blacks do now. The ultimate goal of structural theory might thus be to explain both form and content, with the former having priority. A theory which states that interpersonal conflict depends on opportunity for social contact predicts that any social condition that increases social contact (e.g. the growth of cities) will also increase interpersonal conflict. The theory is valid whether the contact takes place between different classes, ethnic groups, religious bodies, or sports fans. Of course, the manner in which the form is experienced by social actors will be modified by the content of the interaction. Friendships formed in the workplace are probably different from those formed in the leisure sphere.

THE "MENTAL IMAGE" OF SOCIAL STRUCTURE

Structural sociology is a distinct research tradition but it is not homogeneous. Some structural sociologists merely invoke the idea of structure to suggest a context or background against which individual actions can be understood. Others use structure to describe how actors relate to each other in conscious ways, using their sense of how things are or should be arranged to determine their choices. Some mean by structure an organized quality of social life of which actors are probably unaware. Finally, there are those who think of structure in very abstract terms, as nothing but "a communication network mapped on some population" (Mayhew, 1980:338).

These might be considered differences between "weak" and "strong" versions of structural analysis. They differ in their strength of commitment to the position that *all* the theorist needs to know is the arrangement of the parts. When examining a particular example of structural analysis, the strength of this commitment can be measured by asking certain questions. Does the analysis emphasize the parts (as seen in the context of the whole) or is the emphasis upon the whole itself? Is the emphasis on the content (as modified by the form) or upon the form (as manifested in the content)? Is structure immediately observable in social relations or does it underly those relations in a manner of which the actors are unaware? Is structure open to modification and change by self-conscious actors, or is it intransitive, like a force of nature? Is structure a description of what is observed which we must explain by some other theory, or is structure an explanation of what we observe?

In this chapter I will keep these questions in mind as I progress to successively stronger versions of structural analysis. I will begin with those versions in which the mental image of social structure is rather vague and shadowy. In these versions, structure means little more than "category" or "place." As I move through the chapter, the idea of structure will come more sharply into focus, subordinating content to form, part to whole, description to explanation.

STRUCTURE AS LOCATION

In some usages, social structure describes an individual's social location. In a study of newspaper readership, Wright (1975) used structural analysis to explain variations in exposure to the mass media. He used the concept "social structure" to divide the observed population into those earning high incomes and those earning low incomes. Newspaper readership was more common in one location (the high income category) than in any other. In this example, the concept of social structure simply refers to categorical differences within aggregates of individuals. This is a relatively weak sense of structure. It "merely assumes the existence of structure in order to study its impact on individuals" (Mayhew, 1980:339). The individual, not the structure, is the unit of analysis. Social structure simply means the social categories into which the population has been divided. It enables us to place or locate each member of the population. But the resulting categories do not really describe structure at all. They tell us nothing about how the individuals are arranged in relation to each other nor the effect this has on their behavior. Wright's categories not only tell us nothing about the distribution of income in the population (i.e. the structure of income inequality), but they tell us nothing about the effect of variation in income levels on the organization of social relations. There is little sense of the whole, and little sense of any arrangement or organization of parts.

This is not to say that a structural sociologist must dismiss as irrelevant all individual data. Data on the incomes of individuals are relevant because they can tell us how income earners are distributed or arranged in the population (e.g. the degree of income inequality), just as data on the age of individuals can be used to describe the age structure (e.g. whether or not the population as a whole is "old" or "young" in relation to another population), and data on individuals' jobs can describe the occupational structure. All that is required of such data is that they describe the population as a whole rather than a sample of it.

STRUCTURE AS ROLE

A more abstract definition of social structure refers to patterned social relations in which the parts which comprise the pattern are not categories of individuals but role players. Accounting for a person's behavior by pointing to the role being performed is inherently relational because roles are, by definition, part of a relationship. An individual identified as playing the husband role is part of the marriage relationship. A husband logically implies a wife, just as a teacher logically implies a student and friends imply strangers. Performing a role means that certain things are expected of us, and certain constraints are placed on our behavior. Some roles allow intimacy, others prescribe distance; some roles are formal, others informal. Notice how this treatment of the role concept rules out the use of this term to apply to those behavioral clusters where no relation, no structure, is implied, as in the "role" of the scapegoat (Biddle, 1979:66).

Roles can be thought of as "packages of expected behavior." The expectations specify the "limitations within which behavior must fall" (Katz, 1976:16). The individual is left with room for choice within these limitations. Social structure is therefore an expression of tolerable limits of variation. In the doctor-patient relationship, the doctor is expected to enjoy considerable freedom and discretion in his treatment of the patient. But there are limits on the extent of that discretion. The patient should not be kept totally "in the dark," and has some rights as a patient to know what kind of treatment he is receiving. In return, the patient is expected to be submissive, but he is not expected to abandon all self-determination.

The structure of roles accounts for the choices an individual makes. To explain a person's conduct, the sociologist would want to know (given that the available choice is between option A and option B) what the rate of choice is of either option for people in role X as opposed to people in role Y (Stinchcombe, 1975:12). What happens to people's choices about voluntary association membership when they cease being childless and become parents? This kind of inquiry assumes that roles impose constraints on the individual to the extent that no single individual can alter the role in any significant fashion, although he can refuse to perform it.

Each individual actor performs many roles. Each role is part of a set of roles. This "role-set" is the total complex of roles with which a particular role is characteristically connected. For example, the role of medical student entails relations with an instructor, nurse, physician, orderly, medical technician, and patient. Each of these relations will make different demands on the student. Becoming a medical student means learning how to balance and integrate these demands.

The role-set determines how the individual role player will perform her role. The medical student will designate some relations more important than others; she will find that some role players have more power over her than others; she will find that other role players vary in their visibility. The role-set encourages certain kinds of behavior (e.g. the student might turn down a social invitation from fellow students, begging the priority of an instructor's homework demands) and discourage others (the student learns to give low priority to nurse's demands). The individual student does not have to make these decisions on an *ad hoc* basis. They have been made for her by the role-set of which she is a part (Merton, 1968:423–424).

Organizations, as well as individual roles, constitute "sets," and their conduct can be explained in much the same way. An organization set consists of all those organizations with which a focal organization is typically linked. The set is held together by the role expectations of the organizations involved (Aldrich, 1979:219).

When an individual's role-set changes, his attitudes and behavior will also change. When the children of the family leave home permanently, they leave behind them an "empty nest." The parents' role-set has changed its shape. As a result, each spouse's attitude toward the family as a unit and toward each other is likely to change.

As this example suggests, structural sociologists believe that people's consciousness—their attitudes and beliefs—tends to follow from the roles they play rather than vice versa. They deny that people first adopt attitudes and then step into the roles which seem consonant with those attitudes. A person's work role, for example, affects his perceptions and values because it confronts him with demands he must try to meet. "These demands, in turn, are to a great extent determined by the job's location in the larger structure of the economy and society" (Kohn and Schooler, 1973:117). Research has shown that workers promoted to foreman (workers whose role-set has changed) come to see the company as a better place in which to work. They also develop more positive attitudes toward management. Those who later returned to the ranks as a result of a recession reverted to prounion and antimanagement views. In both instances, the workers' attitudes "seem to be molded by the roles which they occupy at a given time" (Lieberman, 1956:400).

Studies such as this, in which one of the variables describes the characteristics of the individual (e.g. her attitudes), are not wholly structural. A more satisfactorily structural approach to role-sets is to consider the role-set as a whole in relation to some other arrangement of roles. Thus we might ask: What is the degree of role-differentiation in this organization as opposed to that one? To what degree are roles better integrated in this role-set as opposed to another role-set? What is the relation between the family as a structure of roles and the workplace as a structure of roles? Do certain kinds of work place structure encourage or facilitate certain kinds of family structure (Smelser, 1959)? In this kind of analysis, there is a clearer image of structure comprising a whole. Structure is conceived as an arrangement within a totality. An even clearer image of the whole is conveyed by the type of structural sociology described in the next section.

STRUCTURE AS ORGANIZATION

To indicate the difference between structural sociology as the study of roles and structural sociology as the study of social organization it might be *(margin handwritten note: SOCIAL RELATIONSHIPS. (ROLES))*

helpful to distinguish between social relationships on the one hand and structural relations on the other. Social relationships are visible associations between concrete actors about which empirical generalizations can be made. The doctor-patient relationship would be an example. We infer motives, invoke norms, or postulate values in order to explain these generalizations.

Structural relations are not obvious on the surface. They are not immediately detectable in social interaction. For example, if we wish to explain why one factory has higher productivity than another, we might find out if the level of satisfaction that workers have with the performance of their fellow workers varies from one factory to another. In this case we would be studying social relations within each factory. But there is a structure beneath these social relationships. The structure is the way work is organized in the factory. The factory has a structure that is independent of the social relationships within it. It might turn out that variations in productivity are closely associated with how decentralized decision making is in the factory. We need to study the structure before we can make sense of the social relations within it.

This distinction between social relationships between actors and structural relations between dimensions of an organization makes sense of Mayhew's (1980:339) argument that structural sociologists do not study human behavior at all. "The behavior they do study is that of the variables which define various aspects of social organization." Social relationships are defined in terms of social organization. For example, an individual's social relationships (e.g. the degree of intimacy or conflict within them) are determined by the position of the individual in the life cycle. Structural relations serve to limit the range of social relationships. "People are constantly choosing which of several possible relations to pursue and how to behave in them, but they are choosing from among a small set of socially structured alternatives" (Fischer, 1977:viii).

The problem of explaining why there are inequalities of income in society will serve to illustrate the technique of using structure to mean social organization. Why do some groups in society (e.g. blacks, women) consistently earn less than the average? One answer to this question is provided by exchange theorists. Differences in earnings are said to reflect differences in "investments" or "human capital" that individual workers bring to the labor market. This market is just like the market for goods. Each worker tries to sell his or her labor for the highest price: the employer tries to get the most skill and effort for the least wages. It is assumed that wages will reflect the worker's marginal productivity and will respond to changes in the supply and demand in different parts of the market.

According to this "human capital" theory, income inequalities result from individual differences in skills and abilities as these are augmented by training and experience. The labor market is not completely open, but in the long run wages are assumed to settle at a rate which is the competitively determined return on individual capital. The idea of the market (which is a structural idea because it represents an arrangement of opportunities) is rather shadowy in human capital theory. It is little more than an arena where the hiring and firing occur. Any imperfections in the market (such as those restrictions on worker mobility imposed by unions operating closed shops) are treated as the effect of individual competitiveness rather than the effect of other structural forces. "The structural context ... is such that when it is assumed to be working according to theoretical specification, it need not be included in analyses" (Beck et al., 1978:705).

Structural sociologists account for patterns of income inequality much less by pointing to differences in individual skills and attributes, assigning more importance to the constraining influence of the labor market itself and the larger economic forces this market reflects. The labor market is not merely an arena but an extremely complicated social structure. It includes "the means by which workers are distributed among jobs and the rules that govern employment, mobility, and the acquisition of skills and training, and the distribution of wages and other rewards obtained contingent upon participation in the system" (Kalleberg and Sorenson, 1979:351). The market is not simply the place where employer and employee meet. It defines and limits the options available to them. Indeed, it determines who shall and who shall not be employers and employees.

The characteristics of the labor market in the United States have been closely scrutinized by structural sociologists in recent years. Several "segmented" labor market theories have been formulated. One argues that there are at least two markets. In the "primary" job market, a few large corporations dominate. Price fixing among these corporations is common, trade unions are fairly strong, and increases in costs can be passed on to the consumer. Rewards, negotiated on a national or industrial basis by the union, are not directly related to individual skill or effort. In the primary market, wages depend less on aggregate levels of supply and demand for particular kinds of labor and more on the historical influences of technological change and customs in hiring and firing. "Everything else equal, workers' wages will tend to increase with age as the simple effect of institutional seniority privileges, fixed through bargaining and custom" (Gordon, 1972:50).

In the "secondary" labor market, firms are more competitive, profit margins are narrower, and labor costs proportionately higher. Unions are weak and piece-rate work common. Dismissals frequently occur when product demand falls. In this sector,

> variations in total individual incomes are likely to depend more heavily on variations in hours than in wages.... Employers act as if all present and potential employees have more or less equal productivities.... As a result, wages will generally not reflect variations in individual characteristics but will be largely determined by the aggregate balance of

supply and demand in the secondary market ... individual income will
depend primarily on the number of hours worked (Gordon, 1972:51).

The two labor markets determine the opportunities available to individuals.
The opportunity to earn high income and have a steady job is much greater
for the individual who enters the primary sector than for the individual
who enters the secondary sector. Income differences are explained not by
differences in individual skills and ambition but by the structure of the
labor market.

Human capital theory would predict that wage differences between
people with similar training and abilities will narrow over time because
employers want to offer no more than necessary for workers in a given skill
category and workers will move to another employer if he pays higher
wages. One problem for the human capital theorist is that this kind of wage
equalization does not seem to occur. Wage inequalities show no signs of
diminishing in the United States, and worker mobility in search of higher
pay for the same qualifications is rare (Bibb and Form, 1977:975). Instead,
workers tend to get "locked in" to the industrial sector they initially enter.

Structural sociologists are able to explain this lack of equalization by
pointing out that the primary market shields workers from competition
from workers in the secondary market while binding them to their
employer by seniority rights and pension benefits. Furthermore, workers
who are forced to take jobs in the secondary market tend to develop
attitudes and behavior patterns congruent with secondary market job
characteristics—weak commitment, anticipation of failure, little inclination
to learn new skills, and so on. Income inequalities are explained, not by the
characteristics of the workers themselves, but by the characteristics of the
jobs they hold and the market in which those jobs are found.

This analysis of the social organization of job opportunities helps
explain the lower average income of minority groups like blacks and
women. These groups tend to be overrepresented in the secondary labor
market. The primary market has traditionally been dominated by white
males. As blacks and women have entered the labor force they have either
(a) been blocked from the primary sector and channeled into the secondary
sector or (b) segregated within a few occupations within the primary sector.
As this structure has crystallized, blacks and women have learned that their
chances of landing and keeping a job in the primary sector are low and have
adopted work orientations congruent with the secondary labor market.

Two features of this explanation of income inequalities are noteworthy. First, differences in qualifications are treated as the effect of the
structure of opportunities rather than as the cause of differential performance in it. Human capital theorists argue that blacks and women receive
inferior rewards because they have less "capital" to invest and are less
productive. A structural sociologist would argue that the labor market is

organized in such a way that some jobs receive higher rewards than others and that income inequalities reflect entry into different labor markets rather than differences in human capital. To support this argument they would cite evidence that sex differences in income are much more closely related to labor market position than to individual differences in investments like schooling (Bibb and Form, 1977). What is also noteworthy about the structural theory is that it does not rely on evidence of overt discrimination by employers for an explanation of income inequalities by race or sex. Employers have no need to discriminate overtly against women, for example, who are structurally tied to kinship roles which make entry into the primary market difficult and who, in any case, typically do not offer themselves for primary sector jobs.

The market for labor constitutes a vast opportunity structure. Within each employing organization there is an internal market for labor governing placement and mobility within the organization. This opportunity structure, indicated by promotional criteria, the frequency of promotion reviews for different positions, and the number of rungs on the career ladder, determines an individual's level of reward and rate of mobility.

As is the case on a national scale, organizations exhibit inequalities in income and mobility. The typical organization is arranged in such a way that certain departments (e.g. accounting) have ladders of upward mobility that extend further than those in other departments (e.g. personnel work). Members of the organization located on the bottom rungs of tall ladders have more opportunity for being mobile than those situated on the bottom rungs of short ladders. The opportunity structure thus prohibits certain options. One reason why women are less mobile in large corporations is that they are located in shorter chains of opportunity. This, rather than lack of "human capital" explains why they do not advance as far as men.

Opportunity structures do not work in a blind and mechanical fashion. Structures shape behavior and attitudes in such ways as to fit the prevailing options. The results can be self-confirming.

> Those people set on high mobility tracks tend to develop attitudes and values that impel them further along the track: work commitment, high aspirations, and upward orientations. Those set on low mobility tracks tend to become indifferent, to give up, and thus to "prove" that their initial placement was correct (Kanter, 1977:158).

Each position in an organization carries its own inducements and constraints which reflect where that position is located in the underlying social organization of the firm. These inducements and constraints encourage the individual to behave in ways appropriate to the position, thus creating the impression that the incumbent does indeed "fit" the position, and rendering her even less capable of transcending its limitations.

The social-psychological consequences of social organization are even more in evidence in the case of those few individuals who find themselves "out of place," individuals like the "token woman" in an organization dominated by males. The token stands out, attracts more attention and gossip, is more distinctly remembered by nontokens, and suffers from this visibility when mistakes are made. The presence of a token minority in its midst makes the majority draw closer together, to close ranks, and to reemphasize their distinctiveness (Kanter, 1980).

The social-psychological consequences of tokenism probably explain the relatively poor performance of minority group members in all organizations. For example, women in law school tend to get poorer grades than men. But the level of their inferiority is much greater where their proportion in the law school is very low. The more women there are in the law school, the better they perform relative to men (Spangler, et al., 1978). This finding is unlikely to be significantly different no matter which minority group is involved. The chances are that were men in the minority, their performance would follow a similar pattern.

STRUCTURE AS DISTRIBUTION

When we think of social structure as social organization we have in mind rules and procedures people follow. A more abstract understanding of social structure is to think of it in terms of arrangement or distribution. In this case structure means how various kinds of social positions are arranged and how people are distributed among those positions. Attention focuses on the social associations (e.g. cooperation, domination) and social processes (e.g. social mobility) which are a consequence of the arrangement of positions and of the distribution of people across those positions.

One of the most important concepts in this kind of structural theory is "heterogeneity." It refers to the number of distinctions made within a population. The sociological problem is to predict the effects of variations in heterogeneity on the social life of a population. For example, in a population with just one distinction (i.e. two groups distinguished by some features such as sex, age, or race), the members of the smaller of the two groups will find it easier to mix with people not in their group than will members of the larger group. This is explained not by the values or interests of group members but simply by how the population is distributed. This kind of theory explains why liberal whites have so few black friends although they are convinced they are not racially prejudiced: there are simply not enough blacks for all of them to have one as a friend (Blau, 1977:21).

As this example shows, structure conceived as distribution is more abstract than structure conceived as social organization because less concrete detail is required before the idea can be used to explain social behavior. The division of the population into categories and the precise distribution of people across these divisions is enough to account for social behavior. Thus, religious intermarriage is more simply explained by the relative size of different groups than by factors such as religious sanctions. Religious beliefs and ethics might modify the impact of structural conditions but these conditions remain the most important determining factors. Furthermore, these beliefs and ethics might change in response to changing structural conditions (Blau, 1977:25).

When we think of structure as distribution our attention is no longer directed to the roles people perform but to the positions of which they are incumbents. Their behavior can be explained by finding out how their position is arranged in relation to other positions. Consider the impact of social class position on dating behavior.

> It has been observed that marriages to persons outside one's own socioeconomic stratum are more prevalent in higher than in lower socioeconomic strata. Boys and girls from higher social classes have also been found to be more likely than those from lower classes to have dates with partners whose class differs from their own (Blau, 1977:49).

In other words, patterns of dating and marriage can be explained without assuming that class differences have less psychological significance for persons in the middle class than in the working class. Structural conditions are sufficient to explain marriage and dating patterns. To the skeptic who points out that this all depends on what an individual makes of class differences, the structural sociologist replies that what an individual makes of class differences has itself been caused by structural factors.

> Class lines may appear to be less rigid to persons in upper than those in lower strata, because the social reality experienced by the latter actually restricts interpersonal relations more by class lines than that experienced by the former. But such differences in views and attitudes that may make class distinctions less significant in the thinking of the upper strata are the consequence of the more prevalent associations across class lines among the upper than the lower, not their cause, which is accounted for by the structural variation in stratum size (Blau, 1977:50).

Causal priority is given to structure rather than to beliefs and attitudes of persons.

Distributional theories do not exclude reference to attitudes and beliefs altogether, but such matters of individual psychology are treated as "minor premises." The major premise of the theory is always structural. The minor premise will usually be some tendency of individuals assumed to be invariant for the purposes of the theory. By virtue of this minor premise individuals are treated as "standard, interchangeable elements" so that the distinct impact of structure can be isolated (Mayhew and Schollaert, 1980:5).

Many of the minor premises in Blau's work are drawn from psychology. In seeking to explain the rate of social contact between racial groups, Blau treats as a minor premise the fact that people prefer to mix with their own kind. The major premise of the theory is that the more group memberships cross-cut each other, the greater the proportion of intergroup contacts made. This part of the theory says nothing about people's attitudes. It simply states that, in a population where group memberships overlap (so that, for example, religious-group membership cross-cuts racial-group membership in such a way that blacks and whites might belong to the same church), the proportion of contacts which are interracial must be higher than in a population where the amount of cross-cutting is less.

Other structural theorists reject this reliance on psychological premises but their method of theory building is much the same. Typical is Aldrich's use of a "population ecology" model to explain the behavior of organizations. Variations in organizational structure are accounted for by a theory of social selection. Organizations not adapted to their social environments fail. Changes in the environment impel structural changes through either the elimination or the modification of the existing structure.

The population ecology model contains no reference to psychological factors and makes no assumptions about individual choices or motives. At the level of organization, we need only assume that organizations adopting the innovations of relatively successful predecessors will have at least a short-term advantage over others that do not. The environment selects the form, not the individuals in the organization, who may only dimly understand the reason for the success of their particular activities. Individuals may have a wide variety of motives for their actions, but structural and historical conditions make possible the fulfillment of some and not others. Aldrich (1979:54) concedes that "some non-adaptive partial structures or activities survive because they are tightly linked to an adaptive characteristic, because they are insulated from direct environmental pressures, or simply by chance alone," but motives do not explain these exceptions any more than motives explain the survival of "non-adapted" natural species.

STRUCTURE AS NETWORK

The proper focus of structural sociology should be the whole rather than any position or relation within it. The idea of the whole is implicit in "role-set," but attention is nevertheless directed primarily at the impact of the role-set on the individual. The idea of the whole is more explicit where structure is conceived as social organization, and even more explicit where structure means distribution. However, for some sociologists, these efforts at structural analysis, with their preoccupation with aggregates and categories, can only provide a proxy measure of structural relations (Wellman, 1980:12).

Where structure is conceptualized as a network, the sense of the whole is unequivocal. Here the network of relations is the unit of analysis, not the individual. Network analysis goes beyond the treatment of individuals as role players or as incumbents of positions. Whereas in role analysis the individual is the sum of the roles he plays, in network analysis the individual is the sum of his network ties.

The idea that social behavior can be described and explained in terms of social networks has a long history in anthropology (Nadel, 1957) and was introduced into sociology by researchers investigating visiting and helping relations among family members (Bott, 1957; Mitchell, 1969). The idea of network was found to be a useful way of thinking about family relations and helped account for different forms of the division of labor within the family.

A social network is a collection of individuals among whom there are a number of direct social connections. A person's place in the network is the principal determinant of that person's conduct.

> Society affects us largely through tugs on the strands of our networks—shaping our attitudes, providing opportunities, making demands on us, and so forth. And it is by tugging at those same strands that we make our individual impact on society—influencing other people's opinions, obtaining favors from "insiders," forming action groups (Fischer, 1977:vii).

An individual's freedom to marry for love is greater where the family network is small. Where spouses are both members of large nonfamily networks, the division of labor within the family is greater (Lee, 1979). Networks influence migration patterns, as when immigrants are drawn to particular cities and jobs by the kin and countrymen who have preceded them (Fischer, 1977:23).

The idea of networks also entered sociology from the social-psychological experiments of Jacob Moreno, whose "sociograms" mapped or diagrammed the web of relations to be found in small groups. A sociogram was especially effective in locating friendship choices, leadership patterns, cliques, and isolated individuals.

The social-psychological approach to network analysis popularized by Moreno focuses upon the individual social agent and emphasizes individual decisions, interdependence, mutual reliance, and exchange transactions between directly and indirectly linked individuals. Networks are conceived as "sets of direct and indirect social relations, centered around given persons" (Andersen and Carlos, 1976:28). The network is "ego-centered," in that the network radiates from a central individual. The researcher's interest is in the impact of the network on the individual. The links in the network consist of social relationships.

More abstract and formal network analysis abandons this social-psychological position, focusing not on the individual and his relationships but on the whole and the links that comprise it. The links are represented in matrix rather than sociometric form, with the matrix representing all possible links in a system. The possibility of thus demonstrating the presence *or absence* of a tie between two persons enhances the visibility of the overall connectedness of individuals in the network. After all, ties which an individual could have but does not are as important as the ties he has (Burt, 1980:91). This focus also makes it possible to theorize about the characteristics of networks as wholes and to analyze the relation of one network to another. It distinguishes network structure theory from exchange theory, which looks at structural patterns primarily as they condition dyadic ties (Wellman, 1981:18).

More abstract and formal network theories also differ from social-psychological versions in their focus on underlying structures rather than social relationships. The ties do not consist of social relationships between individuals. A tie might simply mean that two positions in a network are "structurally equivalent" and have the same pattern of relations with other positions. Occupants of equivalent positions need never meet or know of one another's existence.

Network structure analysis requires data on relations as they are conceived as structuring the whole:

> ...they are data on what relations obtain between pairs of entities. The entities may be people or organizations of any other defined social entity. The relations may be any kind of socially meaningful tie. What is of interest to the social scientist is how the relations are arranged, how the behavior of individuals depends on their location in this arrangement, and how the qualities of individuals influence the arrangement (Leinhardt, 1977:xiii).

The "whole" can be anything the sociologist wants it to be in the light of his research interests (Fischer, 1977:34). It might be all actors in a given geographical area, all actors sharing a common goal, all potential partners in an exchange relation, and so on. The entities can be individuals or organizations. "An interorganizational network consists of all organizations linked by a specific type of relation, and is constructed by finding the ties between all organizations in a population" (Aldrich, 1979:281).

Thinking about social life in terms of networks forces us to acknowledge the constraints on individual behavior inherent in the way social relations are organized. There is a limit on the amount and intensity of ties any individual or organization can maintain. Relations will not be evenly distributed across the matrix of all possible relations. Cliques, factions, and elites tend to form in all networks (Laumann, et al., 1978:458).

The network is thus a kind of social topology. People occupy positions which are either "close" or "distant." Positions are close if they have identical relations with other positions in the whole—if they are structurally equivalent. The analytical technique of "blockmodeling" is a method of ascertaining the degree of structural equivalence among individuals in a whole. Instead of dealing with social relations between people, it deals with relations between blocks of people: that is, people who are structurally equivalent in the sense that they have approximately the same patterns of relations among themselves and with people in other blocks (Light and Mullins, 1979:87).

Network structures consist of ties between positions or between activities. An example of an interposition network is the group of individuals who occupy seats on all the boards of a given group of corporations (e.g. banks). The whole is comprised of the relations between positions. An interactivity network is measured by the number of activities in which two actors are simultaneously involved. In this case the network would consist of those activities in which a given group of individuals participate. The greater the number of activities shared, the denser the network. Density is usually measured by comparing the number of actual relations among a set of people or positions to the number of possible relations.

Network structure analysis clearly accords priority to the whole over the parts. In the study of interlocking directorates, the focus is not who becomes a director but what is the pattern of interlocks between corporations.

> Are the connections denser in some parts of the network than others? If so, what are the components of the dense modes? Do some firms or types of firms occupy more central positions? (Sonquist and Koenig, 1976:62).

Where the focus upon the whole is so sharp, data must always pertain to the whole population under observation: a saturation sample rather than a representative sample would be most appropriate. And techniques of data analysis should be chosen which deal in patterns and wholes rather than in frequency distributions and covariation. Graph theory is especially suitable for dealing with networks because it is a configuration of points and lines. In the study of interlocking directorates, a person who holds a membership on two boards is treated as a line and the two corporations are points. A graph enables the investigator to assess the density and extensiveness of the ties between the various nodes in the network.

Network analysts have sought answers to three questions. What is the effect on the actor of his location in the network? What is the effect of network structure as a whole on the actor's behavior? What is the effect of one network on another?

People's ability to achieve their aims is determined by their position in social networks. A network shapes the flow of resources between actors. To the extent that social power rests on the resources an actor commands, the distribution of power in a population will reflect how positions are arranged within it. Social power is thus measured by the number of open lines of action available to the actor (Abramson, et al., 1958:22). Although command over resources might *appear* to be the basis of social power, the actor has acquired these resources by virtue of her location within a network and is only able to use those resources to the extent that her position in the network allows (Galaskcewicz, 1979:24). Community power studies show that actors in the center of a network are more powerful than those on the periphery because they have more ties to occupants of other positions.

This method of accounting for the distribution of power is different from the kind of structural analysis described at the beginning of this chapter. Network structure analysts dismiss role theories as "psychological" because they rely on the attribution of expectations to actors. Network structure analysts believe that behavior can be explained adequately by describing the social distribution of possibilities. Norms and roles are variously seen as irrelevant for explaining social behavior (White, 1970), as being determined by an underlying network structure (Burt, 1980), or as being secondary in importance to structure (Wellman, 1981).

The effect of the network structure as a whole on a person's behavior can be observed in studies of "open" and "closed" networks. In a closed network all or most actors know each other and share information. By the same token, they have few contacts with people outside the network. This means that the amount of information available to each person in a closed network is less than the amount available to people in an open network. Consequently, people in open networks find it easier to learn about new opportunities, such as new jobs.

> There is a structural tendency for those to whom one is only weakly tied to have better access to job information one does not already have. Acquaintances, as compared to close friends, are more prone to move in different circles than one's self. Those to whom one is closest are likely to have the greatest overlap in contact with those one already knows, so that information to which they are privy is likely to be much the same as that which one already has...(Granovetter, 1974:53).

It is not the characteristics of the individual job seeker nor the nature of the employing organization that determines access to job information but the connections between the particular job seeker and the hiring organization.

How closed a network is has also been found to have an effect on how easily people obtain psychiatric care, prenatal service, and abortions (Horwitz, 1977). It accounts for the fact that some people are more readily mobilized than others to join social movements (Useem, 1980). And it explains why some firms are more innovative than others—information is more likely to disseminate in an open network where ties are weak (Aldrich, 1979:99).

The third issue addressed in network analysis is the relation between one network and another. What is the impact of network A on network B? Do networks which share members tend to converge in structural properties like density and degree of connectedness? Erickson (1981) has demonstrated that the structure of secret societies varies in part by structural context. She defines a secret society as "a persisting form of relationships which, directly or indirectly, links the participants in related secret activities," that is, as a social network. Secret societies can be classified by their degree of approximation to a hierarchy. The principal determinant of the degree of hierarchy is the preexisting network from which members are recruited. Particularly when control over recruitment is centralized, prior networks which are hierarchical will generate a hierarchical structure within the society. This particular approach to secret societies focuses on linkages between structures, a pattern of ties, and relatively abstract features such as their strength, rather than on the content of those ties or the motivations of the people involved.

In analyses such as these, nothing is said about people's motives, attitudes, or values. The impact of network position can be ascertained without referring to rational choices, or inferring values. Structure is not a system of roles but simply a system of concrete ties. Network analysis is thus the most abstract form of structural analysis. Despite these variations, however, this research tradition is united in a commitment to positivist principles of scientific method. In no other research tradition do we find this combination of an objectivist ontology (ignoring subjective states), an emphasis on form over content, and an argument that differences in social position are the major influence on social relationships.

COMMENTS

During the course of its development, structural sociology has become increasingly abstract and deterministic. Reference to willing, choosing actors has been expunged from analysis. Social structure is defined without reference to expectations. It is simply "regularities in the patterns of relations among concrete entities" (White, et al., 1976:77). The reasons for this are both epistemological and ontological. Structural sociologists all "share the empiricist notion of scientific explanation" (Rossi, 1981:46) and define social structure as empirically observable patterns of interaction (Blau, 1981:2). Ontologically, social order is assumed to rest not on shared values or reciprocal expectations but on the coordination of activities through network processes. It is patterns of relations that bind people to society, not values (Burt, 1980:892). Questions of "social sentiments" are believed to occupy a "secondary position" in the analysis of social structure (Wellman, 1979:1202). Structural sociologists therefore reject the argument that sociologists are impelled by their subject matter to interpret social behavior, to understand the subjective meaning of people's actions. "It would be easier to identify with a spider than a human, because the range of behavior options for the spider is more restricted" (Mayhew, 1981:645).

Stinchcombe (1975:27), himself a structural sociologist, acknowledges "the crude picture of individuals that structural explanations tend to give." Having stripped away the "subjective component" for onotological and epistemological reasons, structural sociology is left with a model of individual behavior which is deterministic and crudely mechanical. Social action *is* structured, but this does not entail the limitations on outcomes implied by structural analysis. The structuredness of social interaction can only mean that some outcomes are more probable than others (Coser, 1975a:211).

Structural sociologists deal much better with the fact that social life is reproduced—reaffirmed, repeated—than with the fact that it is produced by human beings. Social structures constitute the work of willing, thinking subjects. "Every act which contributes to the reproduction of a structure is also an act of production, a novel enterprise, and as such may initiate change by altering that structure at the same time as it reproduces it—as the meanings of words change—in and through their use" (Giddens, 1976:128).

Structural sociology is not only deterministic, it is also crudely objectivist in its approach to social action, relegating the symbolic component of social interaction to a secondary position. Meaning flows from structure rather than vice versa. But an adequate study of social patterns *must* refer to meaning. At the very least, people recognize some aspects of their lives as structure: they take for granted certain things and not others.

> Even a biologically based structure, like the communication network of a viral disease in a human group, creates a meaning structure in the group. History reveals that people expecting the plague relate differently than do those who expect death from old age (Gannon and Freidheim, 1982:880).

What a structure is and how the structure operates is comprehensible only by understanding how people interpret their situation.

Structural analysts acknowledge that people have intentions and motives, but they have those motives only because the structure "allows" it. What is more important, the discovery of laws of structural variation is not seen as depending on knowledge of what is going on in people's heads. But is this really true? Are the laws of structural sociology truly explanatory without help from an understanding of motives? Take the "law" which states that there is a positive relation between the size of an organization and the size of its administrative component. This statement reads like a natural law. But the relationship it describes holds only if people follow certain practices that are consistent with the pattern. The law depends upon people's motives. The members of the organization can change their goals, adopt different motives, change their practices, and thereby violate the law. They might decide to put a cap on the size of the administrative component in their organization while allowing the organization to continue its growth (Turner, 1977:28). The reference to laws implies that this relation is as unalterable as a law of nature. But the causal laws of sociology cannot be identical to the causal laws of the natural sciences because the relations they describe are in principle mutable in the light of human knowledge. Structural sociologists have lost sight of the duality of structure—it is both "the medium and the outcome of social acts" (Giddens, 1981:8).

Structural sociologists write as if reference to motives were necessary only in order to make the general principles of structural covariation comprehensible and convincing to the lay reader. They imply that interpretation is merely the "scaffolding that can be removed once an edifice of generally accepted laws is erected" (Turner, 1977:25). But as we can see in the example of the "law" that describes the relation between size of administrative component and organization size, reference to motives is always necessary. The link is neither mechanical nor inexorable, beyond alteration or debate. For one thing, this treatment of the relationship as "mechanical" disguises the extent to which dominant organizational groups impose their sectional interests or goals, "their conception of 'the organizational goal' and attempts to achieve it through their notion of proper, necessary or suitable procedures" (Salaman, 1979:85). On close inspection, then, many of the "laws" of structural sociology turn out to be little more than correlations. Their explanatory power rests entirely on the attribution of motives, interests, and projects to the actors concerned. Structural effects admittedly operate independently of the will of particular individuals, but they do not operate independently of subjectivity altogether.

The foregoing criticisms of structural sociology emanate from sociologists who draw their inspiration from idealism. They share a concern with the loss of voluntarism implied by a sociology which seems to define individual spontaneity as outside the boundaries of social science. The other source of criticism of structural sociology is the realist research tradition called historical materialism. From the standpoint of historical materialism, the treatment given structure by structural sociologists is ahistorical and static. I can illustrate what this means by referring to the earlier discussion of labor markets.

Structural sociologists reject the human capital model of income determination which emphasizes individual-level variables such as amount of schooling, work experiences, and family background. They substitute a "dual economy" model in which the existence of two economic sectors is postulated. In the "primary" sector firms tend to be large, highly productive, very profitable, heavily capitalized, monopolistic, and unionized; in the "secondary" sector firms tend to be small, labor intensive, highly competitive, paying low wages, and making small profits. The existence of these sectors has important consequences for the distribution of earnings in the American population (Beck, et al., 1978). Differences in individual earnings can be explained better by finding out in which sector the individual's job is located than by finding out how much human capital she has.

How adequate is this structural theory of income differentials? In the opinion of historical materialists this "theory" offers no explanation at all. It is merely a description. The important question is not how the economy is organized but *why* it is organized into sectors. Structural sociologists by and large have been willing to use technological factors to explain the growth of a monopolistic sector (Averitt, 1968). Their critics reject this introduction of nonsociological factors. Instead, they put forward a theory which explains the emergence and operation of the dual economy in terms of the struggle for control over the labor process, a struggle inherent in the capitalist mode of production (Edwards, 1979). While structural sociologists assume that job design and recruitment patterns reflect technological requisites and employee needs (e.g. for job security), Marxists argue that they are determined by employers, who have both productivity and class considerations in mind: "they will design certain jobs, for instance, in order most efficiently to forestall the development of class consciousness among certain workers" (Gordon, 1972:128).

Marxists maintain that their theory of income determination is both structural and exclusively sociological, having no need to rely on assumptions of technological imperatives or individual motivation to explain why sectors and markets arise. The segmentation of the economy reflects the efforts on the part of an increasingly consolidated capitalist class to undermine the increasing power of the proletariat.

Different research traditions lead to different conclusions. Structural sociologists picture the two economies as being different: one sector simply has more of something than the other sector. The Marxist model is more authentically structural because each sector is conceived as a necessary condition for the existence of the other. There is an underlying dynamic within capitalism which creates an interdependence between the two sectors and yet sets up an opposition between them. This dynamic constantly shifts the boundaries and respective strengths of the two sectors. A model which does not capture this movement is ahistorical because it portrays as permanent and natural a structure which is actually only a stage or moment in a long process of transformation.

CONCLUSION

In structural analysis, human actions are assumed to be patterned without reference to the will or design of any particular person or group. Patterns of behavior are accounted for by citing the inhibitions of some of the possible alternatives in a situation. The structure "de-randomises persons impersonally" in terms of attributes like sex, age, and ethnicity (Gouldner, 1980:95).

The persuasiveness of structural analysis stems in large part from the fact that structures are often unrecognized, partially hidden from the layperson. They must be uncovered by techniques of analysis which focus on social relationships conceived as an organized whole. The impact of structural analysis is also due in part to the fact that it demonstrates that actions are not only shaped by intentions: there are unintended consequences to action, effects of the actions of many individuals of which they are usually unaware. Structural analysis serves to reveal these unintended consequences. This idea plays a much more central role, however, in the research tradition to be described in the following chapter, functionalism.

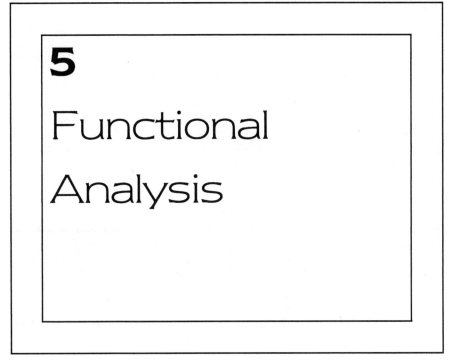

5

Functional Analysis

The term "function" means the contribution which an activity makes to the total set of activities of which it is a part. The activity persists because it is necessary for the survival of the whole. Thus we speak of the heart functioning to pump blood and thus ensure the survival of the organism. And we can also speak of an institution like marriage functioning to ensure orderly procreation and child nurturance and thus ensure the survival of society from one generation to another.

Functional analysis shares with structural sociology the assumption that society is not merely an aggregate of discrete individuals. Rather, it has a structure of its own, just as an organism has a structure. The difference lies in the priority functionalists give to the needs of society when explaining structures. For structural sociologists, "function" is what structures do. For functionalists, "function" is the cause and structure is the effect. Structures exist because they have functions. Structural sociologists would argue that because we have legs we walk; functionalists would argue that, in order to walk, we must develop legs.

Functional analysis is distinguishable from structural sociology in being a form of teleological inquiry. Social practices are explained by reference to the ends or purposes they serve. Function is always judged "in relation to some social end" (Durkheim, 1938:III). Thus, in seeking to account for the existence of a taboo on incest, functionalists are not simply concerned with how it is related to other social norms but with its relation to the needs of society as a whole. Assuming that societies must transmit cultural values from one generation to another in order to survive, the argument could be made that the taboo on incest prevents the undermining of parental authority by its ban on sexual unions between parents and children, and thus ensures the generational transmission of values.

It might seem odd that the causes of a pattern of behavior are to be found in its effects. But for a number of reasons the investigation of social institutions frequently calls for functional analysis. People's actions often have consequences which they did not intend and of which they are not fully aware. These consequences are not without social significance, because they either encourage or discourage the repetition of the actions. The reason most people would give for attending church is that they wish to worship God. But church attendance often enhances the sense of social cohesiveness worshippers feel. If they find this comforting they are likely to repeat the action without being fully aware that this is one of the reasons for their regular attendance.

Functional analysis also makes sense because the consequences of a pattern of behavior do not necessarily change as the motives of those engaging in that behavior change. "It might, in truth, still play the same role as before, but without being perceived" (Durkheim, 1960b:87). People might alter their reasons for attending church but the effect of church attendance on society remains the same.

Finally, functional analysis makes sense whenever the sociologist feels that it is pointless to assign causal status to one particular structural element and designate another element as the effect. Social structures are so complex, their parts so interdependent, that a change in one part will have ramifications for the other parts, and when *they* change, the original part will also be affected. There is no "first cause" where the analysis must begin. We could break into this complex process at almost any point and begin analysis.

A PARADIGM FOR FUNCTIONAL ANALYSIS

The procedures for conducting functional analysis were formally stated by Robert Merton in 1949. His "paradigm" provides a convenient way of explicating functionalism. The analysis takes place in a series of steps.

Functional analysis begins with the identification of an "item" which the sociologist wishes to explain. This will typically be some aspect of social structure—a role, an institutional pattern, a social process, a particular norm, and so on (Merton, 1968:104). The second step is to make sense of this item. What meaning does it have for those involved? What meaning

function

does it have in the society at large? For example, what is the meaning of dating? Apart from a means of finding a marriage partner, is it a form of recreation, is it a means of claiming status in peer groups, is it a form of social experimentation?

The third step in the analysis is to identify the objective consequences of the item. If these consequences are judged to help the system adapt to its environment they are called "functions." If they lessen the adjustment of the system they are called "dysfunctions." If they are recognized by members of society they are called "manifest." If they are unrecognized they are called "latent."

Part of the fascination of functional analysis is the way in which it frequently helps us discern the unanticipated and unrecognized consequences of people's behavior. If we set out to explain a religious ritual, like the Rain Dance among the Hopi Indians, we have selected for study a standardized and recurrent social action. The "meaning" or stated purpose of the dance is to appease the rain gods and ensure rain.

> But with the concept of latent function, we continue our inquiry, examining the consequences of the ceremony not for the rain gods or for meteorological phenomena, but for the groups which conduct the ceremony. And here it may be found, as many observers indicate, that the ceremonial does indeed have functions—but functions which are non-purposed or latent.
>
> Ceremonials may fulfill the latent function of reinforcing the group identity by providing a periodic occasion on which the scattered members of a group assemble to engage in a common activity ... such ceremonials are a means by which collective expression is afforded the sentiments which, in further analysis, are found to be a basic source of group unity (Merton, 1968:118).

Identifying objective consequences is thus no easy task. It demands that we look beyond the obvious and straightforward effects which people intend and consider some of the hidden and long-term results of their actions.

The functionalist's fourth step, logically implied in the third, is to specify the larger whole for which the structure in question is thought to have consequences. Usually this is simply "society," but any whole qualifies as long as we can think of it as seeking to maintain itself. Small groups, organizations, or cities could qualify. Functionalism is distinctive in this teleological form of argument: social phenomena are accounted for by pointing to the end or purpose they serve.

The fifth step in analysis is to decide what the survival requirements of the whole are. An explanation of a pattern of behavior by reference to the *effect* it has makes no sense unless we can claim that the effect is needed by the whole of which the item is a part. The fifth step thus postulates the existence of a need. The item is said to meet this need. The sixth step closes the circle by identifying the mechanism whereby the satisfaction of the need acts back upon the original item. This is called a "feedback circuit." A complete functional explanation requires the demonstration not merely of the consequences of item A for some larger whole B. It also requires that the satisfaction of some need of the larger whole in turn maintains item A.

It makes little sense to explain a pattern of behavior by its effect if this effect cannot be shown in some way to feed back to the original pattern of behavior. Functionalists assume that patterns of behavior persist because people find them rewarding. A pattern of behavior which is functional for society will command more resources with which to reward those engaging in it. Highly rewarded activities will both reproduce the social system and reward the individual member (Winch, 1977).

The impact of a social structure (that is, its ability to control and motivate social behavior) is related to the function it serves. A structure performing a minor function exercises less influence than a structure performing an important function. Take the case of rules of inheritance. All societies in which there is something substantial to pass from one generation to another have rules of inheritance. These rules determine more or less uniquely who is to inherit each good. It is noticeable, however, that these inheritance rules are "usually firmer, clearer, and better enforced, and better obeyed in the landed upper class than in the poor rural lower classes" (Stinchcombe, 1968:83). The function that inheritance rules perform is more important where the need for them is greater. And consequently, as the theory would predict, the structure has more impact where its function is more important. In this fashion, functionalists explain both the survival of the system as a whole and the motivation of the individuals to reproduce its structures. Inheritance rules function to facilitate the orderly transmission of property at the same time as they furnish motivation for individual members of society.

Merton demonstrated the power of functional analysis by explaining the persistence of "machine" politics in cities like New York, Chicago, Boston, and Philadelphia. The "machine" was loosely based upon a considerable modification of the formal democratic system of municipal government. Political "bosses" controlled the administration of urban services in return for votes, money, and loyalty from citizens in their precinct. Many people regarded the machine as corrupt, a perversion of the democractic ideal. But the machine had survived repeated attempts to destroy it. Merton was thus alerted to the possibility that the machine performed functions not carried out by the official political structure.

How did the citizenry view the machine? What was the meaning of this "item"? The machine was not considered corrupt by those who benefited from it. For many recent immigrants, more interested in earning a living than in legal and political issues, the machine provided immediate and effective help in a manner which spoke directly to their capacities and needs. Both the machine and the official structure offered help in exchange for support, but the machine provided this help in a manner more finely tuned to the needs of recent immigrants.

How did the machine serve each city's needs? The machine helped overcome a chronic weakness of municipal government in the United States—the constitutional separation of powers. In most large cities political power was widely dispersed, rendering decision making extremely difficult. Not only this, but tenure of office was limited and rotation of office the norm. These operating deficiencies generated an alternative and unofficial structure to fulfill the need for effective decision making. The machine was able to pull together the various decision-making agencies. With the loyalty of satisfied voters assured, it managed to operate as a strong city government. The machine was a different structural arrangement for performing the same purpose as the official structure.

If the machine added stability and continuity to the city, how did this consequence "feed back" and sustain the machine? The machine provided votes for politicians and favors for voters. But the official structure was also set up to do this. Politicians would promise policies in return for votes at election time. The machine was distinctive in the *way* in which this exchange was managed. Votes were provided on the basis of patronage rather than policies. They were tied to the needs of the boss rather than to changing party platforms. The favors, too, were provided in a distinctive, personal way. Newly arrived immigrants preferred to see their precinct captain for assistance than go to the official social welfare agency. The machine humanized and personalized "all manner of assistance." The machine therefore operated as a functional equivalent, eventually supplanting the official structure and withstanding numerous attempts to abolish it by well-meaning reformers who did not recognize its real functions.

These direct kinds of feedback were supplemented by a complex network of interdependencies between actors who also relied on the machine in one way or another. The machine provided alternative ways for businessmen to serve illegal but profitable markets. It also provided alternative careers for lawyers. All these groups fought against the abolition of the machine. It died only when the needs of urban dwellers began to change. When they began to assign lower priority to obtaining help and attributing more importance to having a just political system, and when they began to receive more federal aid, the power and prestige of local machine politicians waned and reform efforts were successful.

Merton has thus explained the growth and decline of the most remarkable of urban America's social institutions. He has done so by pointing out the link between the structure and operation of the machine and the particular needs of cities. The function is the link between the part (the machine) and the whole (the city). The machine was structurally different from but functionally equivalent to the legitimate political structure it supplanted. This idea of "functional equivalence" is a very powerful tool in functional analysis. A more detailed consideration of its use will demonstrate its importance.

FUNCTIONAL EQUIVALENCE

Functional analysis gives priority to function and treats structure as secondary. Structures exist because they perform functions. This idea is made clear in the concept of functional equivalence. Society is assumed to have certain chronic needs. If one structure does not satisfy them, another will. The structures are functionally equivalent. In the case of religion:

> If belief 'deteriorates' markedly, this implies that at least for a considerable segment—if not for all members—of a society the religious function can no longer be adequately fulfilled by the traditional religious structure—the church. At this point, we invoke the concept of functional equivalence. That is, we look about to discover what other relationships and institutional structures take over some part of the religious function (Winch, 1963:145).

Functional equivalence means that responsibility for important functions passes from one structure to another, with important consequences for the rest of society. For example, as more sophisticated scientific and technological knowledge becomes necessary for participation in the labor force, the transmission of occupational skills from one generation to another becomes impossible for the traditional family to carry out. A new and functionally equivalent structure (formal schooling) emerges to meet this need. The function of the family also changes "from that of providing education to one of providing the opportunity to be educated" (Winch, 1963:122). The function of channeling people into different positions within society thus falls to the school rather than the family—today's employer is much more interested in what school you attended than in your family background.

A Functional Analysis of Social Inequality

One of the better known functional analyses is Davis and Moore's (1945) explanation for inequalities of reward. Why do different social positions carry different amounts of prestige and pay? As functionalists, Davis and Moore were interested in the objective consequences of this social pattern. They argued that unequal rewards serve as an inducement to attract people to specific social positions. The richer the rewards, the more attractive the position. But what accounts for the particular ranking of positions? Why is it that certain occupations are more highly rewarded than others?

Functional analysis would direct our attention to the requirements of the society in which the pattern of social inequality exists. Some social positions are more important to a society's purposes than others. If the society is to fulfill those purposes, the most important social positions must be filled by the most qualified people. The number of qualified people being in short supply, it is necessary to offer high rewards to ensure that they are motivated to fill the most important jobs. The rewards must be sufficient both to attract adequate numbers of individuals to those positions and to motivate them to work hard. Positions of great functional importance for which qualified personnel are scarce will presumably be the most highly rewarded. A Supreme Court Justice is highly rewarded because the position is functionally important and the skills required to fill it are scarce. If either functional importance or supply of qualified personnel changes, rewards are also likely to change.

The Davis-Moore theory has generated considerable debate and several empirical studies. Cullen and Novick's study (1979) is typical in finding only indirect support for the theory. Higher rewards (measured by income and prestige) do go to jobs judged to be socially important and for which elaborate training and scarce talents are required. However, training contributes more to the explanation of rewards than did perceived importance, as does required talent. It is clear from this and other studies that supply factors (required talent and training) are more important than the demand factors (what society needs) that the functional theory emphasizes.

Abrahamson (1979) applied the functional theory of stratification to income inequalities within organizations. The organizations he examined were baseball franchises. He defined organizational survival as winning. He assumed that functional importance to the goal of winning could be calculated on the basis of past contribution of a position to victory. Scarcity was measured by rate of turnover in a position, on the assumption that the greater the number of separate individuals appearing in a position, the more abundant the talents needed to fill it. Abrahamson found that salaries of positions do vary according to functional importance. However, they vary even more according to the scarcity of talents. Once again, supply factors are more important than demand.

Direct and explicit tests such as these are not the only contemporary examples of functional approaches to stratification. Recent efforts to ascertain the determinants of an individual's income and occupational attainment are functionalist at base even though their unit of analysis is the individual. They uniformly conceptualize inequality as if it were "a continuum of presumably consensual, popular evaluations in which differences can only be a matter of degree" (Horan, 1978:535). In other words, they think of inequality in terms of occupational prestige—where prestige is believed to indicate the moral evaluation placed upon a position, its importance for the society as a whole (Parsons, 1954:74).

Many studies of social mobility are also functionalist at base. Studies of "structural mobility" (in which the movement of individuals is accounted for by changes in the occupational structure) are functionalist. The model of structural mobility assumes that jobs in certain sectors become more abundant and more highly rewarded as that sector becomes more socially valuable. Jobs in other sectors become fewer and not as well rewarded as they lose functional importance. An increasingly service-oriented society needs more white-collar workers and professionals. A highly mechanized society needs fewer farm laborers (Collins, 1975:432).

Functional Analysis of Deviance

Merton's analysis of politics and functional analyses of social inequality describe patterns of behavior as socially useful which many might regard as harmful for society. Each institution has unintended and largely latent consequences which are functional for society and which help explain why it persists. In this respect, functionalists display a keen sense of irony. A sense of irony alerts us to results which are the opposite of what was expected or considered appropriate. A sense of irony is also evident in functional analyses of deviance.

Crime and its punishment is universal: no society has been discovered without it. Nor does deviance show any sign of declining with the advance of civilization. Could it be that crime and punishment are somehow needed by society? After all, if a strong commitment to values is necessary for the survival of society, any practice which defends and reaffirms this commitment would be functional. Emile Durkheim (1960b:118) clearly believed that the punishment of crime could be explained in functional terms.

> Although [the punishment of crime is] ... a quite mechanical reaction, from movements which are passionate and in great part non-reflective, it does play a useful role. Only this role is not where we ordinarily look for it. It does not serve, or else only serves quite secondarily, in correcting the culpable or in intimidating possible followers. From this point of view, its efficacy is justly doubtful and, in any case, mediocre. Its true function is to maintain social cohesion intact, while maintaining its vitality in the common conscience.

Punishment is meant not for the criminal but for the honest. Crime and its punishment perform a service for society by drawing people together in a common posture of anger and indignation. In identifying an act as deviant and in seeking to punish the act, the society "is declaring how much variability and diversity can be tolerated within the group before it begins to lose its distinctive shape, its unique identity" (Erikson, 1966:11). In searching out and apprehending deviants, the community, with the intended and manifest purpose of punishment and retribution, produces in a latent and unintended manner tighter bonds of solidarity among those who are "normal."

> By only a slight extension, one could argue from this to the social utility of misbehavior. That is, by adding only the assumption of a probable atrophy of moral sentiments if they remain unchallenged, with seeming slight deviation increasingly tolerated, gradual demoralization might ensue if conspicuous deviance did not occur and provoke the emotional reaction of the community (Moore, 1978:329).

The detection and punishment of the abnormal is necessary to sustain an awareness of what is normal.

The functional approach to deviance generates a number of intriguing insights. It suggests that no act or actor is intrinsically deviant: "we must not say that an action shocks the common conscience because it is criminal but rather that it is criminal because it shocks the common conscience" (Durkheim, 1960a:81). What kind of behavior is defined as deviant varies from time to time according to society's needs. Accordingly, the sociologist should ask what kinds of needs produce what kinds of deviance and how the "deviance" is produced. It is also important to examine the consequences for society of the creation and maintenance of deviance. Functionalism suggests that society "creates" deviance by the very act of organizing agencies (e.g. police forces, mental hospitals) to control it. Agencies whose manifest function it is to eliminate deviance have the latent function of maintaining it.

Functional analysis also suggests that a rise in the rate of deviance is probably related to growing concerns about community boundaries. When a community becomes uncertain about its identity and about the nature and limits of socially acceptable behavior, a deviance "scare" is likely to occur. Erikson's (1966) study of the Salem witchcraft trials serves to illustrate this point. The trials were sparked by growing concern among the inhabitants of the Bay Colony about the practice of witchcraft in the community. The scare was occasioned by political and religious disturbances in the community, chief among which was the revocation of the Bay's charter by the English. The trials and executions provided a dramatic way of reaffirming Puritan values and ideals and of reasserting the limits of permissible behavior. Erikson suggested that witchhunts such as these serve not only the manifest purpose of punishing criminals but also the latent function of redefining moral boundaries which have grown indistinct. He thereby alerts us to the possibility that a social group will more severely reject and stigmatize odd people when it is threatened with dissolution. Perhaps the frequent "crime waves" that have swept over American society reflect not an increase in the actual commission of crime but an increase in the level of anxiety among the population.

The premise of all these functional analyses is simple: the explanation of any belief, rule, structure, or practice is to be found, not in people's motives and not in some distant point of social origin, but in its linkages with other parts of society or in its contribution to the survival of the system and its members. Functionalists direct our attention to the objective consequences of social action. What do structures actually do? Functionalism is most compelling when pointing out the positive consequences of normally disapproved patterns of behavior. Thus, in a piece remarkable for its wealth of insight, Gans (1972) speculated in functional terms about the "causes" of poverty, pointing out that poor people perform many functions for society—they do "dirty work," they create jobs for those who cater to the poor (e.g. policemen, social workers, pawnbrokers), they buy goods others will not consume (e.g. day-old bread), they absorb most of the costs of economic and political change (e.g. urban renewal), and so on. Gans's sense of irony borders on comedy, but his purpose is serious. He is concerned to show that many groups in society are motivated to maintain poverty rather than eliminate it, that the poor are always likely to be with us. Moore (1978:340) is probably right when he argues that this orientation to tracing the true consequences of structures constitutes the major claim for functionalism in society. But as a research tradition is it sufficient for all sociological purposes? A review of some of the more commonly found criticisms of functionalism will answer this question.

COMMENTS

FUNCTIONALISM AND MOTIVES

Functionalism sees the social world as a concrete reality governed by observable functional relations amenable to scientific investigation. The purpose of analysis is to uncover the law-like relations which exist between social structures. Functionalism does not rely in any significant way on data concerning motives or intentions. Although functionalists frequently use words like "purpose" which seem to refer to what actors intend by their actions, their statements do not refer to human agency or design or assume its presence. The emphasis is less upon the actor and more upon the structure in which the actor is located. In the opinion of many sociologists social structure and its functioning should not be divorced from social action in this way. Sociologists should not simply assume a social structure and examine its interrelation with other structures but should analyze the mechanisms whereby the reality of that structure is continually constructed anew by conscious participants. In this respect, functionalism is subject to the same brand of criticism leveled at structural sociology. More of this line of criticism will be elucidated in Part Two of this book.

FUNCTIONALISM AND STRUCTURE

Functionalism captures more successfully than structural sociology the dynamic, fluid character of social life. Functional processes take time to unfold. Rather than simply taking snapshots of structural covariation, functionalists examine the workings of feedback loops to ascertain the contribution of structures to the maintenance of the system and the reasons for the reproduction of structures. And yet, this separation of structure and function carries with it a distinct danger of reifying social structure. It is common in biology to refer to structure as the part and to function as the working of that part. A biologist might say "this is the heart and here is how it works to pump blood around the body!" This easy separation of structure and function cannot be made when we turn our attention to social life. Social reality is not divisible into parts and their functioning. Social patterns exist only "in so far as they are constantly produced and reproduced in human action" (Giddens, 1977:114). It is inconceivable that we could first know a part of society and subsequently determine its function. We know structures only in their functioning, in their operation. Functionalists, attempting to conceptualize the dynamics and flow of social interaction thus reaffirm the false distinction between structure which they originally sought to overcome and leave us with the impression that structures are like things.

FUNCTIONALISM AND EXPLANATION

Research traditions like functionalism are not theories but ways of building theories. Functionalism does not consist of a set of propositions about what the world is like but a set of guidelines to study that world. Admittedly, these guidelines are based upon some initial assumptions about what the world is probably like and these assumptions have shaped the guidelines. But it is true nevertheless that functionalism is a way of arriving at and judging theories rather than a theory itself. A paradigm of functional analysis is therefore an heuristic tool. It is to be judged by its utility, not by its validity. Does the paradigm suggest law-like relationships between structures? Does it imply plausible motives for action? Does it point to fruitful avenues of research? Does it enrich our appreciation of the interconnections of social phenomena?

If the utility of functional analysis is to be judged by how well it leads to theory, two important criteria have to be met. The theories must stipulate law-like relations between phenomena such that a causal explanation is given. And the theory must be falsifiable by empirical data. As we shall see, functional analysis has been unable to meet either of these criteria satisfactorily.

Although functional analysis seems to differ from causal analysis in its preoccupation with the effect rather than the cause of structures, the ultimate goal of functional analysis is to give a causal explanation. Providing a causal explanation by means of the attribution of function can only be achieved in the following way. In simple cause and effect relationships, A is an event that causes B. In functional relationships, A, causing B, continues to be operative and will be reproduced by B. This is implied by the principle of feedback on which functional analysis rests. In functional models phenomena are conceived in dynamic terms—as interrelated processes. The "item" with which functional analysis begins is always "standardized" (i.e. patterned and repetitive). Visualized as an ongoing series of events or social practices, social structures can be interpreted as partly products of their own functioning.

It is logically conceivable, then, that a structure can be "self-maintaining." Its effects can be traced through a feedback loop back to their origin. But why should the effects necessarily help reproduce the structure rather than destroy it? Here functionalists seem to rely on a kind of natural selection argument. The structure to which function is attributed continues to exist because it has survival value for the system of which it is a part. Systems without that structure have failed to survive. The analogy here with biological sciences is obvious. But how well can this analogy work in the social sciences? In order for us to be able to think about social systems in terms of natural selection the following requirements must be satisfied:

(1)   Some criterion of "normal functioning" or system survival must be identified. Some means must be found for deciding when a system has "died"—or at least is not functioning normally—so that the process of selection can be observed.

(2)   The needs of the social system must be identified. Merton's paradigm acknowledges this. The "functional requirements" of the system under observation must be ascertained. Merton added, however, that the notion of functional requirements was "one of the cloudiest and empirically most debatable concepts in functional theory." In the next chapter we shall see one solution to this problem in the work of Talcott Parsons, who believed that he had identified the functional prerequisites of all social systems. Functionalists who have not followed Parsons remained wedded to the idea of functional requisites without, however, making clear what these requisites are.

(3)   Law-like statements have to be formulated to link the pattern of behavior to be explained with the society as a whole. To "explain" religious ritual in terms of its integrative consequences, for example, is tantamount to the statement of a law to the effect that whenever the ritual fails to occur system disintegration follows. Performance of the ritual is a necessary condition for the existence of the required level of integration. Without such law-like statements, we cannot explain why one pattern of behavior rather than another exists. Functionalists have been reluctant to argue that any structure is indispensable to social life and have been obliged to admit the possibility of functional alternatives, as we have seen. For example, if religion declines, an alternative structure (e.g.

baseball) arises to perform the function in its stead. However, the idea of functional alternatives removes all the deductive rigor from the functional analysis, leaving only the rather weak argument that, if a given level of social integration is necessary for social survival, something *like* a religious ritual will have to be present.

(4) The exact meaning of natural selection has to be specified. In the biological sciences, natural selection rests firmly on a theory of genetically transmitted traits. Although the idea of "social selection" can assume that one generation learns from the previous generation, this is actually no explanation at all of *how* or *why* patterns of behavior persist. It does not describe the means by which this pattern of behavior or that pattern is "selected" to survive.

In the opinion of many critics, these requirements for converting functional analysis into causal explanation are so daunting that further work in this research tradition should be abandoned. They believe that the clear specification of the logic of functional analysis, with its base in the idea of functional requisites and system survival, only reveals the unfalsifiability of theories derived from it.

FUNCTION AND SOCIAL INTEGRATION

Functionalists have been criticized for being preoccupied with the contributions structures make to social order and for failing to pay enough attention to the causes of instability and disintegration. Functionalism is not inherently "biased" toward stability and integration. The research tradition is based on the unobjectionable assumption that society can be conceived of as an organic whole in which the parts are interdependent. However, functionalists frequently tend to shift from this assumption about *system* integration to the much more questionable assumption of *social* integration. They assume, in other words, that societies would not survive unless there was consensus at the level of values and norms.

A common value system is assumed in the argument that social inequalities reflect a society's evaluation of the functional importance of social positions. It is also assumed in functionalist theories of deviance. But is there a *common* value system or simply a *dominant* value system? The answer is more likely to be the latter. We know that the criteria on which popular rankings of occupations rest tend to correspond to dominant group attributes (Crompton and Gubbay, 1978:155). The definition of which occupations are most important (and the specified ways of filling those occupations) is based as much on the threat of force as on common, agreed ideas about what society needs. We also know that definitions of deviance are likely to reflect dominant values.

The assumption that social order rests on a common value system also exaggerates the extent to which people have similar needs. Merton was aware of this bias and instructs us in his paradigm to ask for whom a given structure is functional. What is functional for one group might be dysfunctional for another. Gans (1972:276) actually restricts the meaning he gives to function to "those observed consequences which are positive as judged by the group under analysis." He thereby acknowledges that it is impossible to speak of "society's needs" because there are likely to be deep conflicts of interest in any society.

Assuming that we agree to carry out a functional analysis of a structure like the political machine without assuming a common value system, we must still acknowledge that the consequences of social structures vary in scope. Not all consequences are of equal significance. Some flow directly back to city officials, some flow more generally back to the majority of citizens, and some consequences are very general and impact upon the political system as a whole. The last kind of consequence is the focus of attention of functionalists, but it is more likely that the machine itself is sustained by the most immediate of consequences—the payoff to city officials.

As they modify their analysis to accommodate conflicting interests, Merton and Gans move further away from the idea that structures can be explained in terms of societal needs and closer to the position that specific interests and power groups sustain social institutions. Merton's analysis of the political machine shows that *any* particular social structure can be shown to have contributed to the maintenance of society. It is inconceivable to Merton that one and only one method of satisfying a social need has been identified. Once the idea of structural alternatives has been introduced, the possibility has also been admitted that the present structure was deliberately chosen by those with the power to do so. The interests of those in power explain the presence of a pattern of behavior rather than "functional necessity." Social life is indeed organized, but it is organized in such a way as to benefit some more than others.

FUNCTION AND DYSFUNCTION

Functionalism logically permits the idea that a pattern of behavior might be disintegrative or dysfunctional. Merton was aware that the same structure could have both functional and dysfunctional consequences. However, functionalists usually assume that a pattern of behavior would not survive unless its functions outweighed its dysfunctions. Thus, in the analysis of the political machine, Merton assumed that the machine's survival was a sign that the net balance of functions must have been positive. He acknowledges the theoretical possibility of dysfunctions but he does not discuss them. Instead he stresses the gains to be reaped from the machine, omitting to mention at whose expense these gains were obtained. The machine did provide gains and mobility for some people but it also exploited the "vast majority of the ethnic poor along with the more fortunate good citizens" (Matza, 1969:62).

Even when dysfunctions are analyzed they are treated as pathologies of the system. Patterns of behavior are categorized as dysfunctional if they work against the maintenance of the system. However, systems have short-term and long-term maintenance needs. Changes might threaten short-term needs but meet long-term goals. Functionalists are somewhat too ready to define change as dysfunctional. They tend to ignore the possibility that what is presently dysfunctional (e.g. a social movement creating disturbances) might be functional in the long run.

FUNCTION AND CHANGE

Finally, functionalism has been criticized for being unable to deal with social change. The burden of functional analysis has been placed upon the study of the contribution or functioning of parts to some whole. The original functionalists were really interested in "how societies survive and cohere in the face of external pressures and internal strain, not how they change" (Smith, 1973:4). By emphasizing the conditions that make for stability, social change is treated as abnormal and threatening. And by emphasizing the way in which the parts of a system are interdependent, the possibilities of endogenously induced change are minimized (Friedrichs, 1970:26).

Critics acknowledge that later functionalism has not prohibited the analysis of social change. After all, any model which allows room for imbalanced exchange, conflict, dysfunction, disequilibrium, and so on must be able to talk about change. "The static bias must not be considered as a principal and insurmountable deficiency of systemic-functional models as such, but, at most, as the factual defect of some particular implementations of these models" (Sztompka, 1974:160). Be this as it may, the functionalist model of change lacks precision. It needs "a specification of what types of malintegration, anomie, breakdown in mechanisms or failure to meet needs will cause, under what conditions, what types of change in varying types of social systems" (Turner and Maryanski, 1979:117).

If change is, as many functionalists claim (Smelser 1968:258), a continuous round of adjustment between the different parts of society, the question of why any part should become unadjusted in the first place remains unanswered. Unless functionalists can explain why dissatisfactions arise, why incompatibilities occur, their treatment of change remains merely a description of what happens once a disturbance has happened. This difficulty of dealing with change reflects a problem faced by all sociologists working within this research tradition. The research tradition has failed to develop theories which satisfactorily explain why social structures persist. It is hardly surprising, then, that it has been unable to explain why social structures change (Cohen, 1968:57).

CONCLUSION

Under the weight of these and other criticisms, functionalists' claim to provide a sufficient research tradition for sociology has been rejected. This is not to say that the functionalist approach is not useful in directing the sociologist's attention to the possibilities of a particular type of cause and effect relation which may help explain puzzling patterns of behavior. But all the efforts to modify functionalism so that it will fit the positivist canons of scientific explanation have only resulted in destroying any promise of uniqueness it might have had.

In this chapter we have dealt with sociologists who, in using functional analysis, focus on a particular structure, using its contributions to the system as a source of information about the structure itself. Attention is directed principally at the part, using the whole as "a kind of backboard off of which to bounce effects and consequences" (Demerath, 1967:506). In the next chapter we will look at a research tradition in which the focus is upon the system itself. In this case, knowledge of structures is a means to the end of knowledge about the system as a whole.

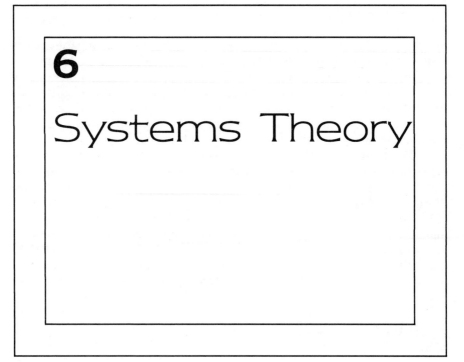

6

Systems Theory

Sociologists agree that the various forms of human activity are intercon-nected. Societies are comprised of many different parts which are related to each other in complex ways such that a change in one of the parts will have widespread but barely discernible consequences for the other parts. A change in the method of manufacturing and marketing of a good induced by technological innovation might place pressure on family and educational institutions to produce a different and perhaps more skilled worker; it might change the flow of migration between regions of the country; it might create new markets for labor; it might form new classes, mobilize new kinds of political association, and even encourage new expressions of religion (Smelser, 1971:8). These changes, in turn, will in all probability react upon the processes of manufacturing and marketing with which the cycle began. And the resulting society is different from the society that existed when the whole process started.

Many sociologists believe that dealing with this kind of organized complexity demands the use of a systems model. Such a model makes a number of assumptions about social life. First, social life comprises an interrelated whole such that a change in one part will affect the other parts—the internal arrangement of the system is less variable than its external environment. Second, the whole is more than the sum of its parts—it has an organization which imparts characteristics to the whole that

79

are not found in the components alone. Third, a boundary separates each system from its environment and each system tends to be boundary-maintaining. Fourth, the operation of a system consists of processes of input, throughput, and output as the system engages in interchange with its environment; this environment includes other systems. Finally, the operations of the system must be interpreted as oriented to the achievement of system goals—these goals are equilibrium and system survival.

These assumptions provide the foundation for a wide variety of systems theories. They apply to systems varying widely in their size, time scale, and content. Typically, a systems theory will contain concepts that distinguish different kinds of systems (e.g. open or closed), describe hierarchical levels in each system (e.g. subsystems and sub-subsystems), delineate aspects of the internal organization of a system (e.g. its degree of differentiation), identify the mode of interaction of a system with its environment (e.g. inputs and outputs), describe system tendencies (e.g. equilibrium), and identify sources of system crisis (e.g. system strain).

SYSTEMS THEORY AND SOCIOLOGY

Systems theory is intended to apply to many different fields, including not only physics and biology but political science and sociology as well. Within sociology, there are "literally dozens" of systems theories (Ball, 1978:115). Some of these theories employ "mechanical models." Elements are said to be mutually interrelated, tending toward a state of equilibrium "such that any moderate change in the elements or their interrelations away from the equilibrium position are counterbalanced by changes tending to restore it" (Buckley, 1967:9). Others use "organic models," in which the concept of equilibrium is replaced by that of homeostasis, on the grounds that organisms (or societies) do not have fixed states of balance but a fixed *relation* with their environment. Furthermore, the system is thought to be capable of elaborating and changing structure in order to maintain homeostasis. In the "process model," structure "is an abstract construct, not something distinct from the ongoing interactive process but rather a temporary, accommodative representation of it at any one time" (Buckley, 1967:18). The model is called a process model because it focuses on the action and interaction of the components of the system on the assumption that structures are continually arising, dissolving, and changing.

In the mechanical system model the parts are simple, their relations narrowly restricted and unchanging; the system is closed and little allowance is made for internally generated tension or strain. In the organic model, the parts are complex (they have their own organization), relations are fluid; the system is open, and internally generated strain is allowed for, although only as an occasional disturbance. In the process model, the parts are conceived of as events, the relations consist of flows of information; the system is open, and the possibility of internally generated strain is chronic.

I cannot hope to cover adequately the entire range of systems theories in sociology in one chapter. Instead, I will focus on "action theory," not only because it has attracted the most attention within the sociological community, but also because it occupies the middle ground in systems thinking between the largely discredited mechanical models of functionalism and the largely unproven processual models of Buckley (1967), Etzioni (1968), and Emery and Trist (1972).

Although the name Talcott Parsons is closely associated with action theory, the latter has been modified to such an extent by others working within the systems-theory framework that it should not be regarded as the product of one man (Loubser, 1976:1). Nor should Parsons be classified exclusively as a systems theorist (Alexander, 1978; Munch, 1981; 1982). However, the fact that Parsons entitled his intellectual autobiography "On Building Systems Theory" is not without significance. He became increasingly convinced during the course of his career, and successfully persuaded others, that sociology should adopt the same kind of systems models as used by biologists. Society is no longer thought of as resembling a system; it is a system. Parsons' incorporation of the action theory into systems theory is not therefore a radical departure from his early work "but a filling out of the systems analysis with which he began" (DiTomaso, 1982:17).

ACTION THEORY AND FUNCTIONALISM

Action theory has its roots in Parsons' first major work, *The Structure of Social Action*. In a "voluntaristic theory of action" Parsons proposed that the basic unit of sociological analysis be the social act, conceived as "a process in which the concrete human being plays an active, not merely an adaptive role." He dismissed as crudely deterministic rational choice theories because they recognized "no criterion for the selection of human actions other than the rationality which weighs actions as means to ends" (Munch, 1981:722). He also rejected those theories which interpreted social action as the direct expression of values. Sociology could become a science only if it treated "the ultimate common value element *in its relations* to the other elements of action" (Parsons, 1937:440).

In its original formulation, then, the theory of action was systemic, seeking to conceptualize the "interpenetration of means-ends rationality and a normative limitation on the free play of such rationality" (Munch, 1981:722). The effort to elaborate this idea of system initially led Parsons in the direction of functionalism (Munch, 1982:780). But this functionalist phase ended soon after the publication in 1951 of *The Social System* (Adriaansen, 1980:88). Parsons became increasingly disillusioned with functionalism. He believed that functionalism would "become intolerably confusing" unless the nature of the "larger whole" was specified more carefully (Parsons, 1975:73). His functionalist writings proved to be merely a sketch of the action theory he was to develop in the 1950s and 1960s when he began to borrow heavily from general systems theory and cybernetics (Rocher, 1975:10). Eventually, he would formulate a theory of all "action systems," assuming that all living systems share certain fundamental properties.

In certain respects Parsons adhered more scrupulously to classic functionalism than did functionalists themselves.

> In the days of Comte, Spencer and their organicist followers, the notion of structure was ancillary to the concept of function because of the following assumptions (a) every organism taken as a self-sufficient totality has its own functional needs for survival; (b) these needs are satisfied by organs which are parts dependent on the whole represented by the social body taken as an organism; (c) the 'organ-parts' exist in order to satisfy functional needs of the whole and for this purpose only; they are therefore dependent and irreplaceable; (d) the whole influences the existence and the structure of the parts, i.e. the overall structure conditions the single institutional structures (Barbano, 1968:46).

Nineteenth-century functionalists studied the function of patterns of behavior in the total system of which they were a part. Function was determined with respect to the integration of the total system. Items for analysis were thus defined with respect to the total system and its requirements: "the possibility of an *autonomous* definition of the items ... was not even foreseen or considered" (Barbano, 1968:53).

As we have seen, Merton's paradigm makes no reference to abstract system properties or to universal functional requirements. Merton was more concerned with structural connections and with the fact that such connections limit the choice of alternatives open to an institution for it to fulfill its purposes. Merton abandoned the holism that had been the hallmark of the original functionalists. In doing so he reversed the principle of functional analysis, transforming it from the study of the consequences of the system for certain structures into the study of the consequences of certain structures for the system (Barbano, 1968:52). The result was to make functionalism logically untenable (Slabbert, 1976:48–51).

Action theorists believe that it is impossible to use functionalist concepts or theories without committing oneself to the idea of a self-maintaining system. Functionalists use system as a metaphor: society can be studied most efficiently if we suppose it to be a system. In action theory systems are real, not metaphors. When functionalists refer to needs, they have in mind the needs of concrete societies as they have been suggested to them by the organism metaphor. When the action theorists refer to needs, they have in mind the needs which any system must fulfill in order to remain a system. These are not social needs but system needs.

Action theory also differs from functionalism in attempting to formalize references to system needs. Rather than simply saying that a structure has consequences, the action theorist wants to be able to say that the structure exists because it has those consequences. Instead of drawing up a list of needs in an *ad hoc* manner, the action theorist seeks to ground a complete and comprehensive classification of needs in general theoretical principles so that they can be used to predict structures.

A further difference between functionalism and action theory follows from Parsons' stronger commitment to the idea of system. Parsons, more than the functionalists, wanted to develop a complete set of structural categories so as to provide an adequate description of the empirical social system. He was strongly committed to the idea that social phenomena must be treated as dynamically interdependent processes. The essential problem of dynamic analysis is how to treat a system of variables simultaneously. Parsons used structural categories to make this possible. To simplify the problem of dealing with a complex of interrelated variables, groups of them are removed from study and treated as structural categories, i.e. not as variables but as constants. These categories become the setting for dynamic analysis. Merton, being less committed to viewing the social system as a whole, felt no need to "map" the social structure in this way.

THE ACTION FRAME
OF REFERENCE

A frame of reference is the most general framework of categories in terms of which scientific work in a field makes sense. It furnishes a language in which to speak about reality. In classical mechanics the language would include categories like space, time, mass, and location. Parsons believed that the construction of such a frame of reference was a prerequisite for building sociological theory. The frame of reference would say what is meant by social action, what its dimensions are, and how it should be explained.

The action frame of reference is based on the belief that social structure always involves a *normative order.* Parsons did not accept the utilitarian theory that social order was based on principles of rational choice and equitable exchange. Parsons believed that social order must rest on shared understandings and shared norms. Thus, a relationship forms only when I take into account not only my expectations about myself but my ideas about what *you* expect of me.

When I engage in interaction with others my actions are shaped by the goals I have in mind. But I must also take into account what other people want me to do in light of their goals. They, in turn, must do the same. Orderly interaction will not take place unless this "double contingency" bond is formed. I must want to do what you want me to do, and you must want to do what I want you to do. The building block of social order is not the individual but this bond of double contingency. In this sense, even the smallest social relationship comprises a social system. The behavior of one "part" or actor directly shapes— and is shaped by—the behavior of the other part, and the two together form a "whole" which is more than the sum of its parts.

Systems theory is a way of thinking about connections and interdependencies. Thinking of social relations systemically means abstracting their qualities of interdependence and boundedness. System properties are not immediately visible. They must be brought out and accentuated in the course of analysis. Social groups, collectivities, and organizations are not systems. As concrete groups, they will probably lack certain features of systems while other features will be disproportionately dominant (Munch, 1982:787). This distinction between abstract and concrete systems is important for a proper understanding of the theory of action, which often makes unconventional distinctions and suggests surprising connections between apparently dissimilar spheres of social life.

SYSTEMS AND FUNCTIONS

Thinking about human action in terms of systems raises theoretical issues of a distinctive kind.

> The analyst will consider *system problems,* for example, problems of boundary maintenance, problems of resource procurement and allocation, and problems of pattern maintenance .... He will be drawn toward attempting: (1) to define problems, and (2) to identify mechanisms that, however adequately or inadequately, 'resolve' the problems and (3) to state the conditions and consequences of adequate or inadequate resolution (Ackerman and Parsons, 1966:28–9).

These issues suggest a new way of ordering sociology's subject matter. The known range of patterns of social behavior is only a fraction of those which are logically possible. Why should this be so? What causes social structure? Parsons (1977:180) believed that *function* was the "only basis" for theoretically ordering social structure. Function or system problem analysis must be used to identify and explain structure. Structures are to be classified and explained as mechanisms of this or that kind helping solve system problems.

THE A-G-I-L SCHEME

The idea that social systems confront certain endemic problems and that structures form to confront these problems was first suggested to Parsons during his collaboration in a study of role-differentiation in small groups. These mini-systems faced problems of two kinds: they had to balance problems of relations with the environment (external) with problems of coordination (internal), and they had to balance short-term, expressive needs (consummatory) with actions directed toward the achievement of long-term goals (instrumental). Parsons had the idea of applying this systems analysis to complex systems like societies. By conceiving of these system problems as aligned along two axes (external/internal and instrumental/consummatory), four system problems were revealed, as the following figure illustrates.

Figure 1.

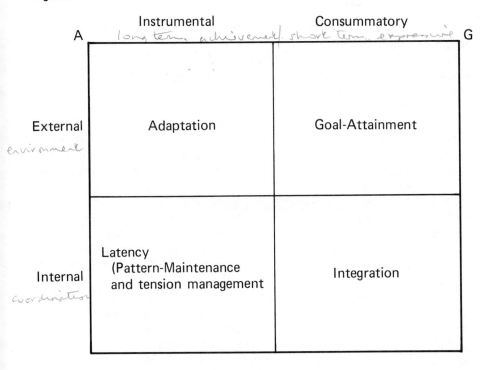

	Instrumental	Consummatory
External	Adaptation	Goal-Attainment
Internal	Latency (Pattern-Maintenance and tension management	Integration

A ... G

Pattern-maintenance, or latency, is the problem of maintaining the distinctive pattern of the system despite internal processes of change and new inputs to the system. Integration is the problem of securing the mutual adjustment of the parts of the system. Goal-attainment has to do with setting and achieving long-range goals. Adaptation is the problem of securing sufficient resources from the environment for goal achievement. A functional subsystem consists of those system activities oriented toward the resolution of a particular system problem.

SYSTEMS OF ACTION

The ordering of systems and subsystems according to their function carries through the entire theory of action. At the most general level, four action systems are distinguished. These coincide approximately with what are usually considered quite distinct fields of study. The "behavioral system" is the biological constitution of the actor; the "personality system" refers to his psychological makeup; the "social system" is the pattern of interaction; and the "cultural system" refers to complexes of meaning expressed in beliefs and values. Each system performs a distinct function: cultural systems maintain patterns, social systems integrate, personality systems shape goals, and behavioral systems are adaptive.

The cultural system consists of patterns of meaning and the symbolic codes in which they are expressed. Whereas social systems are organized around the interaction of people and groups, cultural systems are organized around meaningful patterns of relations between symbols. To see culture as a system is to suppose that it has its own needs and its own laws of development. A culture can develop independently of social systems. "Thus classical Greek culture persists many centuries after classical Greek society has ceased to exist" (Parsons and Platt, 1973:8–9). Culture is therefore autonomous, analytically separable from what people do in the same sense that the language of a people is analytically separable from what they happen to say.

Cultural and social systems interpenetrate. Culture is transmitted, learned, and shared, penetrating society by providing the framework of meaning upon which a society's institutions rest. Conversely, the social system provides inputs to the cultural system. If culture were not daily confirmed in people's experiences it would die and be mummified in museums.

The personality system makes its own inputs to the social system. It provides a level of motivation adequate for participation in socially valued and authorized patterns of behavior. In turn, the personality system is shaped by the social system (receiving social rewards for proper role performance) and by the behavioral systems (in the form of genetic endowments).

The behavioral system contributes to the personality system motivational energy, response capacity, and the ability to integrate and learn. "In return the personality generates outputs with respect to the organic system in the form of 'motive force'" (Devereux, 1961:30).

Any concrete social pattern will be shaped by all four action systems. Sickness not only has obvious biological aspects, but it is also a psychological condition, in the sense that it requires motivation to accept help—we must admit we are ill and need treatment. Sickness is also a social condition, in the sense that there is a "sick role" to complement that of the healer. And it is a cultural condition insofar as modern medical practice is organized around the application of scientific knowledge, which teaches that sickness is a natural rather than a supernatural phenomenon.

The four action subsystems are cybernetically related. A cybernetic relation exists when systems consisting of high information but low energy direct the action of systems consisting of low information but high energy. For example, the room thermostat uses very little energy but much information to control the tremendous heat-producing capacity of a furnace. The cultural system is the "control center" which gives ultimate direction to action. The behavioral organism provides the energy for action to move toward its goal.

To use the example of sickness once more, in modern societies sickness is defined and treated on the basis of strongly felt cultural commitments to the idea that illness is impersonally caused by microorganisms and the like rather than supernatural agencies. This implies normatively expected ways of thinking about illness such that someone who refuses to perform the sick role is considered deviant. Psychological attributes, in turn, are molded by these cultural and social conditions such that a disposition to be healed is generated, shaping the reaction of the behavioral system.

The Social System

Each of the four action systems can be decomposed into its own subsystems. The model of the social system, the subject of special concern to sociologists, contains an adaptive subsystem ("the economy") which produces and allocates disposable resources, a goal-attainment subsystem ("the polity") which organizes the system for the purposes of reaching its goals, an integrative subsystem ("the societal community") which promotes social solidarity, and a pattern-maintenance subsystem ("the fiduciary") which conserves and perpetuates meaning.

Social structures and processes can be understood and accounted for by placing them in one or another of these subsystems. The integrative subsystem includes legal institutions because they determine under what conditions norms of interaction apply. But it also includes systems of social stratification because they are means of allocating people to positions and

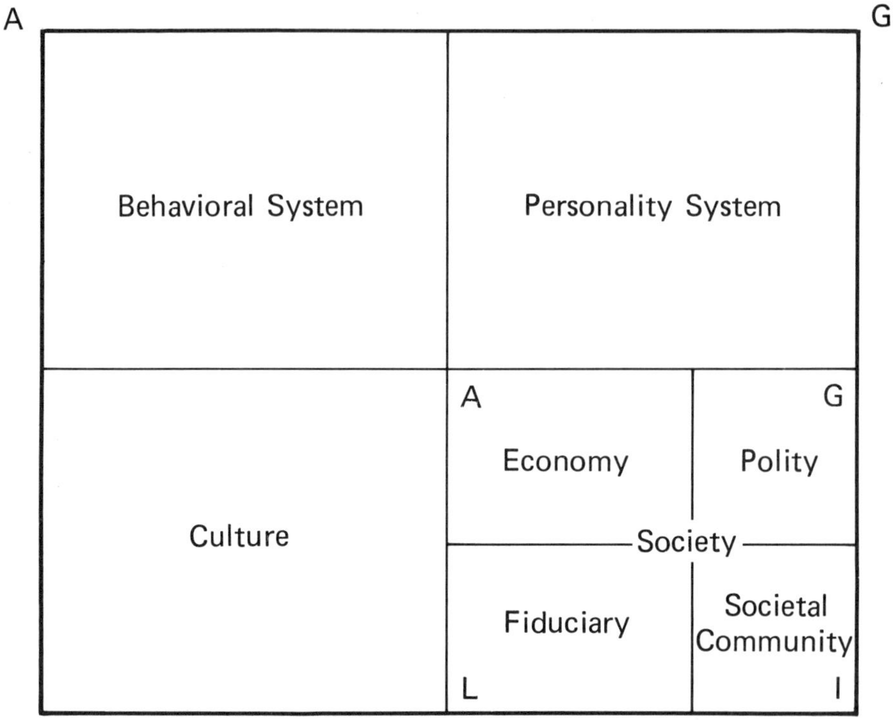

Figure 2

assessing their social contributions according to the system's scheme of values. Medical care would also be part of the integrative system to the extent that it preserves and enhances the capacity of the individual to perform social roles when that capacity is threatened by illness or death.

Functional systems are thus abstractions from institutions. The latter tend to focus on social concerns. Functional systems concern only selected aspects of human behavior. Any given functional system, on the other hand, will span a number of social institutions. The polity

> includes not only the primary function of government and its relation to the societal community, but also corresponding aspects of any collectivity.... The business firm, universities, and churches have political aspects (Parsons, 1971:16).

Conversely, social institutions can be multifunctional. Political institutions perform several functions. And religious institutions are not only integrative but they also have political and economic aspects (Smelser, 1963:28). The family, too, is multifunctional, contributing to the integrative, adaptive, pattern-maintenance, and goal-attainment functions of the social system (Parsons, 1971:11).

The four subsystems of the social system must solve their own problems if they are to survive. Although the economy performs adaptive functions for the social system as a whole, considered as a system in its own right, it must meet its *own* adaptive, goal-attainment, integrative, and latency needs. It is possible in this way to conceive of the economy as an autonomous system, with its own survival needs often in conflict with the function it must perform for the social system as a whole. .

Subsystem Exchange

Each subsystem of the social system specializes in the production of some kind of output which it contributes to the other subsystems. The output of the economy is goods; the output of the societal community is social solidarity; the polity produces effective decision making; and the output of the fiduciary subsystem is value commitments.

The subsystems of the social system are thus engaged in a complex process of exchange as each contributes to the others what they need and receives in turn what it needs in order to generate its output. Actors within the polity (e.g. Congressmen) rely on outputs from actors in the societal community (citizens) in the form of support for their decisions and legitimacy for their office. In return, they provide for role-players in the societal community effective decision making at the societal level. Expressed more bluntly, votes are exchanged for political decisions.

Generalized Media of Exchange

Exchange between subsystems would not be possible unless there existed some generalized medium through which the exchange could take place. Were the exchange to remain at the level of barter, only very simple transactions could occur, for barter is the exchange of something specific for something else also specific. A medium of exchange is generalized to the extent that it can be exchanged for a wide variety of goods and services. It has no intrinsic value: "although it has no utility itself, *it stands for utility,* since it can be exchanged for things that do" (Johnson, 1973:209). In the action frame of reference, the media of exchange are institutionalized means of exchanging inputs and outputs between subsystems.

The concept of medium of exchange is intended to make possible the abstract analysis of subsystem interdependencies. It is a means of conceptualizing the dynamic interchange occurring between the different parts of society. The media of exchange link the differentiated subsystems, regulating and integrating the transactions between them. Parsons

(1977:209) hoped by this device to avoid the "static bias" which often plagues structural-functional analysis.

There is a generalized medium of exchange "anchored" in each of the four subsystems. Transactions with the economy take place via the medium of money. This medium is the vehicle for exchanging economically valued commodities. For example, the fiduciary system produces "labor commitments" (i.e. the motivation to work) and allocates them to the economy, which utilizes them in the production of goods and services. The economy produces goods and services and allocates them to the fiduciary system. The exchange takes the form of wages for labor and prices paid for goods and services—and the medium is money.

The second medium of exchange is power. It is the medium through which exchanges with the polity are conducted. Power, like money, is important for what it symbolizes. Power is the "binding obligations" political actors receive in return for making decisions. It rests on a mandate given to those in positions of authority to make decisions on the system's behalf. Politicians are given "credits" by their followers (i.e. the freedom to make certain decisions) in the expectation that the "investment" will pay off for all concerned. In modern societies, the medium of power has become highly generalized: that is, political agents are given periodic authorization to exercise political power but they are not asked to provide specific decisions in return for specific kinds of support.

The third medium of exchange is influence. It is "anchored" in the societal community. Influence is a medium in the sense that it "flows" from one actor to another. Influence is "carried" in the symbolism of offices, titles, insignia, and so on. These symbols are valuable not in themselves but in what they stand for. They are the "currency" of persuasion.

The fourth medium of exchange is called "value commitments." It is anchored in the fiduciary system. Value commitments, like money, power, and influence, are important for what they represent, namely, obligations and duty. The actual "currency" in which they are transmitted takes the form of potent symbols, like "motherhood" or more concretely, national monuments. Such symbols express the willingness of a system's members to commit themselves to the values of the system as a whole.

By introducing the idea of media of exchange, action theorists are able to move closer to processual models of systems in which the operation of the system is conceived in terms of information flows (rather than mechanical movements or chemical reactions). This facilitates the analysis of the functioning of social structures in fluid, dynamic terms. The clearest example of this is the conceptualization of power, which is described not as a resource of which people have more or less but as a medium through which exchange takes place. Power is not divisible in action theory. It flows from one part of the system to another to meet overall system needs. Action theorists thus attribute more importance to process than to structure, for process shows the system in motion while structure arrests that motion. The special treatment given to the relation between process and structure in action theory is worthy of extended comment.

SOCIAL STRUCTURE

Role
Collectivity
Norm
Values

Social structure is any set of relationships between components or elements which can be treated as constant over time and constant over the occurrence of processes. A system will develop mechanisms or specific structures to deal with its functional problems. If function describes what gets done, structure describes how it gets done.

In action theory, social structure is defined as sets of expectations. A relationship is structured to the extent that people know how to act in a situation, when they know what to expect of others and what others expect of them. Some of these expectations have to do with broad categories of action while others are specific. Social structure therefore exists at several different "levels" of generality.

The components of social structure are hierarchically arranged.

> (1) Individuals in roles are organized to form what we call (2) collectivities. Both roles and collectivities, however, are subject to ordering and control by (3) norms that are differentiated according to the functions of these units and to their situations, and by (4) values that define the desirable type of system of relationships (Parsons, 1967:141).

Any concrete social relationship will contain all components or levels.

The most specific component of social structure is the *role*. A role is the normatively regulated participation of a person in a concrete process of social interaction with a specified, concrete role partner. Each individual occupies a number of different roles. To analyze structure at the level of role we would have to ask, What roles are identified? How are they differentiated? How formal are the expectations attached to them? How are people allocated to roles? How are role performances regulated and integrated? *Role*

At the next level of generality, social structure means the *collectivity*. This is a concrete system of interacting persons-in-roles (Parsons, 1960:172). Collectivities are recognized by signs of membership and by differentiation among members in relation to their statuses and functions according to some common purpose (Parsons, 1971:7). Collectivities (such as universities), consist of clusters of roles. The collectivity helps arrange and give meaning to the roles. *Collectivity*

At the next level of generality stand *norms*. Norms are social rules which define expectations of performance for "differentiated units within the system" (Parsons, 1961:44). These "units" might be sex or age categories *Norms* or ethnic groups. Norms range from the formality of legal systems to the informality of neighborhood mores. A complex of norms is a social institution. Marriage is a social institution to the extent that there exists a body of widely known and supported expectations governing the relation between husband and wife.

Structure at the most general level means *values*. Values comprise a "pattern of desirable orientation for the system as a whole" (Parsons, 1961:44). This pattern is a set of judgements and expectations held by members of a society which defines what for them is the good life. Being the most general component of social structure, values determine the components of social structure beneath it. Values should therefore be "the main point of reference for analyzing the structure of any social system" (Parsons, 1960:20). The direction of action is determined by social norms and the values which legitimate them. People feel a need to conform to shared expectations about right and wrong behavior, both as a result of socialization, and in anticipation of the discipline which would result if they did not conform.

Action theory thus explains the conduct of social actors principally by the fact that they have learned and "internalized" the norms which society has developed. The acquisitiveness of the businessman and the pecuniary disinterestedness of the priest are not due to the greater greed of the businessman but to the different values each has endorsed. Persons who forego the higher incomes of the business world and espouse ideals of altruism are more likely to emphasize "professional" ethics while those who have chosen business as a career must conform to norms which demand the rational pursuit of profit (Marsh and Stafford, 1967:740).

During the course of socialization the individual actor learns the norms of society and even internalizes them so that they become *his* wants. The individual does not thereby become merely a puppet of society, however. In the course of socialization

> the individual has continually opened up for him new worlds within the world of a normative culture, and his attachment to the normative culture is generalized and freed from the tyranny of concrete specifications.... The whole process of socialization, therefore, is a process in which the individual, through the internalization of the normative culture, attains to increasing autonomy of action, but it is also a process in which the bond between the individual and the normative culture is strengthened, because this bond comes to depend less and less on any particular relations of the individual (Munch, 1982:779).

Actors are free to choose in action theory, but their choices are structured by dominant values and norms.

The patterning of choices by structure was conceptualized by Parsons in terms of a "pattern-variable scheme." The idea of this scheme came to Parsons during the course of a study of the relationship between doctor and patient. He observed that physicians and patients relate to each other in certain patterned ways. The physician clearly feels that the patient ought to be treated impersonally. The patient feels obliged to judge the physician by universalistic standards. The doctor would not be expected to "get personal" with the patient. And the patient would not expect to judge the doctor by criteria other than those applicable to the whole profession.

Some of these choices seem to relate to the person and some seem to relate to the nature of the relationship to that person. Furthermore, the choices seem to "hang together" in clusters. One relation might be "communal" in the sense of combining personal attention, intimacy, and affectivity; another relation might be "associational" in being impersonal, distant, and unemotional. Parsons eventually settled upon four such choices.

Diffuseness-Specificity. The occupant of a role might have diffuse and numerous obligations, or those obligations might be specific and strictly limited.

> ...if a doctor asks a patient a question the relevant reaction is to ask why he should answer it, and the legitimizing reply is that the answer is necessary for the specific function the doctor has been called upon to perform, diagnosing an illness for instance. Questions which cannot be legitimized in this way would normally be resented by the patient as 'prying' into his private affairs. The patient's wife, on the other hand, would, according to our predominant sentiments, be entitled to an explanation as to why a question should *not* be answered. The area of the marriage relationship is not functionally specific but diffuse (Parsons, 1954:39).

Affectivity-Affective Neutrality. The actor might feel free to express feelings (affect) in a relationship, or he might feel he must keep his emotions in check. Thus the physician, in his professional capacity, is expected to avoid emotional involvements with his patient, either affection or hatred, moral approval or disapproval. "He should be 'objective' and 'impersonal', treat the patient's condition as a problem, a 'case'" (Parsons, 1954:160).

Ascription - Achievement

Quality-Performance. The actor reacts either to some objective characteristic or quality of the person (e.g. age) or to his accomplishments or performance. The physician expects to be judged on the basis of his accomplishments and abilities rather than his sex or age.

Universalism-Particularism. The actor treats the other person either on the basis of generally accepted standards or on the basis of his particular relationship to that person.

> A heart specialist, for instance, may have to decide whether a given person who comes to his office is eligible for a relatively permanent relation to him as a patient. So far as the decision is taken on technical professional grounds the relevant questions do not relate to *who* the patient is but to *what* is the matter with him. The basis for the decision will be 'universalistic', the consideration of whether he has symptoms which indicate a pathological condition of the heart (Parsons, 1954:41).

On the other hand, the physician might make the decision on the basis of the patient's particular relation to him. In this case, the doctor would be more likely to find time for a kinsman than a stranger.

The pattern variables describe regularities in the way actors orient themselves toward and evaluate other people. They are social-structural guides for decision making. It should be possible to predict from known states of pattern variables (i.e. the normative culture) to less well-known concrete behavior. A concrete pattern of behavior in which two racial groups intermix is predictable where choices have become structured toward that end of the spectrum characterized by universalism, performance, specificity, and affective neutrality.

SOCIAL PROCESS

Action theory is divided into "statics" and "dynamics." Parsons (1961:31) maintained that "stable structural reference points are necessary for determining generalizations about processes." Processes are changes of variables within a given social structure. For example, social mobility is the movement of persons through a status hierarchy. The election process involves the redistribution of political power and turnover of political personnel without, however, a change in political structure.

Social processes are the means by which a system maintains its equilibrium. A system is in equilibrium when its inputs and outputs are in balance. A thermostat, serving to balance heat loss and heat gain, is an equilibrating mechanism governing the process of energy transfer. A social system will contain as many equilibrating processes as there are separate input-output exchanges.

Asserting the need for systems to maintain equilibrium is not the same as claiming that all systems are in equilibrium. Whether equilibrium is actually achieved "is entirely an empirical question" (Parsons, 1961:37). The internalization of norms by members of society could be thought of as a preferred state of the system. If so, any tendency to deviate from these norms could be expected to provoke some sort of reaction in the direction of returning the system to its previous condition. But the reaction may be inadequate and the system may remain disequilibrated. "Perfect equilibrium" is a condition in which the processes of complementary interaction are fully developed and the functional needs of the system are maximally satisfied: it is a theoretically limiting case, never achieved empirically.

The analogy of the temperature-constant room helps us understand the concept of equilibrium, but there are two reasons why it should not be applied too literally to social systems. First, it is rare that the preferred state of a social system can be specified as precisely as the desired temperature of a room, nor is it usual for the values of the inputs and outputs necessary to achieve this goal state to be known with precision or achievable with accuracy. In this sense, the analogy is misleadingly precise. Second, the goal states of social systems are not constant: they change continually in the light of environmental conditions. The analogy is, in this respect, misleadingly static.

SOCIAL CHANGE

Equilibrium analysis deals with short-term "adjustive processes" in society (Parsons, 1977:280). They leave the structure unchanged. Action theory distinguishes between equilibrating processes and changes which represent the emergence of a new structure entirely. These latter changes are set within an evolutionary framework. Societies, like natural species, change by evolving improved methods of meeting environmental problems.

Conceiving of social change as evolution has a number of consequences for sociological theory, the most important of which is the introduction of "a criterion of evolutionary direction" (Parsons, 1966:26). Evolution means improved capability to adapt to environmental exigencies, "an enhancement of adaptive capacity" (Parsons, 1966:21). The achievement of a new equilibrium state means the movement from an initial, unstable point to a new structural arrangement which enables the system to absorb the original disturbance.

In both biological and sociological systems, adaptive upgrading is achieved by structural differentiation: "a unit ... having a single, relatively well-defined place in the society divides into units ... which differ in *both* structure and functional significance for the wider system" (Parsons, 1966:22). Each newly differentiated unit is more efficient at performing its primary function.

The A-G-I-L system can be used to describe differentiation in human action systems. Differentiation "involves the development of sub-systems specialized about more specific functions in the operation of the system as a whole, and of integrative mechanisms which interrelate the functionally differentiated sub-systems" (Parsons, 1966:24). At the most general level, evolution means the differentiation of the cultural, social, personality, and behavioral systems from each other. The cultural system becomes unfastened from the society in which it arose, so that beliefs and values become increasingly self-contained and self-developing. The emergence of distinct religious cosmologies and secular ideologies (e.g. communism) which span social systems would be appropriate examples (Bellah, 1964). The autonomy of cultural systems is also demonstrated when there are unintended consequences of ideas and beliefs. For example, science-based technology might acquire a life of its own, causing people to worry about "runaway" technology.

Within social systems, evolution means the differentiation of social structures around each of the four functional subsystems. Differentiation of goal-attainment functions creates agencies specializing in the definition of societal goals, the emergence of a huge state apparatus being one sign. The differentiation of the integrative function is exemplified by the evolution of autonomous legal systems. Differentiation of adaptive functions produces a market system. And the growing specialization of families, schools, and scientific institutes is one sign of the differentiation of pattern maintenance functions. The changing role of the family is especially noticeable. It has ceased to be an economic unit of production as more and more members enter the labor market to sustain themselves. "The family's activities become more concentrated on emotional gratification and socialization" (Smelser, 1963:108).

If this process of differentiation into increasingly specialized units were to continue without other structural modifications, the system would disintegrate. However, the tendencies toward disintegration are counteracted by the evolution of more sophisticated integrative mechanisms. One prominent modern example is the development of bureaucratic forms of organization. The function of bureaucracy is to coordinate the operation of functionally specialized units. Another example of an integrative mechanism is the voluntary association, which serves to link the family and the state in modern societies.

Differentiation and the more complex exchange and integration processes it brings increase the need for exchangeable resources that are not tied to specific subsystems. More generalized resources are therefore another sign of evolution. The decline of ascriptive criteria to measure performance and the rise of more universalistic criteria (e.g. intelligence tests) would be an example.

Finally, evolution involves value generalization. The more differentiated the social system, the higher the level of generality at which the values must be couched if they are to legitimate the more specific norms of the differentiated parts. An injunction not to exploit others in economic transactions is more general than a specific prohibition against lending money at interest.

Like natural species, societies pass through stages of evolutionary development. The transition from "primitive" to "intermediate" societies took place when a written language developed. The shift to "modern" society was marked by the development of a rational legal system. No single line of evolution exists, however, for there is "considerable variability and branching among lines of evolution" (Parsons, 1966:111). This idea distinguishes this contemporary version of evolutionism from its nineteenth-century forebear.

The transition from one evolutionary stage to another involves a complex process of "variation, selection and adaptation" (Parsons, 1977:180). However, priority is assigned to cultural factors in the evolutionary scheme. The classification itself is cultural: societies are fitted into scheme according to cultural characteristics associated with them (e.g. written language). More important, the principal determinant of change is cultural—the development of more complex and general normative cultures and hence the maximization of cybernetic controls. Parsons (1966:113) described himself as "a cultural determinist" and argued that normative elements were more important in social change than "material interests." He did not deny the empirical effectiveness of power and interests in shaping change but he believed that the interplay of power and interest must always take place within the general system of values in that society (Munch, 1982:795).

In the later developments of action theory, this idea that culture sets the broad direction of societal development was asserted even more firmly. Patterns of culture were treated as equivalent to the "gene pool" which determines biological development. Genes and values alike are inherited and change only slowly. Thus the culture of the United States comprises a single "relatively well-integrated value-system" which had changed little since the nation's founding. This culture has determined the outer limits of change in American society in the same manner as the gene pool has shaped our biological development (Parsons and Platt, 1973:40).

Action theory has steadily developed in the direction of a more sophisticated analysis of subsystems and the analysis of the relation of interpenetration between them (Munch, 1981:735). The major landmarks have been the differentiation of the four "action systems," the formulation of the A-G-I-L scheme, the introduction of cybernetics, the introduction of the concept of the media of exchange, and the formulation of theories of process and change along evolutionary lines. The theory of evolution crowns the theory of action because it brings it closer to empirical data and to the comparative analysis of social systems. There can be no doubt that action theory has done most to generalize and emphasize the relevance of the concept of system to sociologists (Szacki, 1979:514). Whether or not its version of systems theory is the best and whether or not systems theory of any kind is of use to sociologists is the topic of the concluding section.

COMMENTS

It is unlikely that an overall judgement as to the utility of a research tradition as complex and multifaceted as systems theory in general or action theory in particular is possible. In this concluding section, I will discuss only those criticisms of action theory most commonly encountered. Some of these concern the substantive claims implicit in the research tradition (e.g. the bases of social order) while others focus upon the epistemology of action theory (e.g. the status of the "action frame of reference").

THE EMPHASIS
ON INTEGRATION

The concept of "integration" is at the core of action theory. Without integration, social systems would break down. The requisite level of integration rests on "a unitary system of institutionalized values" and "a relatively consistent system of norms that receive unitary formulation and interpretation" (Parsons, 1961:44). Individual actors are integrated into society insofar as "they act so as collectively to avoid disrupting the system and making it impossible to maintain its stability, and ... to 'co-operate' to promote its functioning as a unity" (Parsons, 1954:71).

Parsons recognized that empirical societies vary quite widely in the degree to which they were integrated in this way. He simply used the assumption of integration as an "analytical starting point" (Parsons, 1954:66) in the same way that exchange theorists use the assumption of perfect rationality. The result is, however, that action theory is shaped and weighted by assumptions which accentuate the role of normative elements in social action, especially by the assumption that consensus at the level of values is necessary for social order.

This assumption that social order rests on value consensus causes a number of problems. It describes a condition of complete institutionalization characteristic of only the most permissive and tolerant of communities, in which people communicate fully, where power is legitimated, and where there are no fundamental conflicts of interest (Rex, 1974:75). Even as a provisional assumption with which to begin analysis, the idea tends to be unhelpful. It encourages us to ignore "social unions enforced by naked power or its equivalents," we find it more difficult to explain how new social forms could ever be accepted, and we are blind to the kinds of structural effects which give us different labor markets, intermarriage rates, and so on, which do not necessarily reflect the impact of values at all but which nevertheless sustain the patterns of social life (Swanson, 1971:186).

Action theorists frequently write as if no distinction exists between system integration and social integration. System integration is the degree of fit between system parts. Social integration refers to social relations between concrete groups or individuals. Social integration might depend on value consensus, but system integration need not. It is possible to conceive of system integration without also assuming consensus. The union organizer and the employer sustain an orderly relationship, each having his or her needs met by the arrangement, but they need not share either values or long-term goals. The union organizer is able to show that the goods can be delivered and the employer can show the shareholders a profit even though they disagree fundamentally over goals.

Moral considerations are not necessarily paramount in social relations. Values should not automatically be placed at the top of the hierarchy of control over human behavior. People conform to norms not only (and perhaps not principally) because they have "internalized" them but because of ulterior considerations—such as those found in economic self-interest. Patterns of behavior are therefore as likely to reflect the clash and compromise of economic interests as shared, internalized norms (Lockwood, 1967:284). And even if norms are recognized to be influential, it has also to be acknowledged that what is moral or normative is often uncertain, and that those groups with the most power will exert the most influence in determining what a norm means and how it should be applied (Burger, 1977:323).

The second consequence of the emphasis on social integration as the basis of social order is that it leads to a rather one-sided picture of social conflict. Conflicts of interest between major social groups are not thought to play a very significant role in structuring social relations. Conflict tends to be interpreted as *the conflict between the individual and society*, rather than between one class and another.

The social upheavals of the 1960s are interpreted by action theorists as conflicts between individuals and society. Toby (1976:414) regards "the adolescent subculture of the high school, the subculture of the dependent gang, the hippies subculture, and the radical ideology of the New Left" as trying to protect "their adherents from feelings of personal inadequacy." These feelings have been generated by the pressure placed on individuals to achieve by the dominant value of instrumental activism. The individual defenses against "self-rejection" come "to the attention of the clinicians," while the collective defenses take a more public form. Each kind of "pathology" is the result of disintegration. Action theorists thus eliminate any possibility that movements like the New Left are based upon fundamental class, ethnic, age, or other group conflicts.

The third consequence of the emphasis on social integration concerns power. Action theory treats power not as a capability of one group to dominate another but as an attribute of the total system: "the capacity of the society to mobilize its resources in the interest of goals" (Parsons, 1967:225). Although power has to be divided or allocated, "it also has to be produced and it has collective as well as distributive functions" (Parsons, 1960:221). Power is therefore integrative rather than divisive. It is "applied against recalcitrant actors with the approval or consent of those other members of the community who are not themselves recalcitrant" (Wrong, 1979:241). The problem with this interpretation is that it treats power as legitimate by definition. The distinction between power and authority has collapsed.

Wrong (1979:214) argues that Parsons' view of power and conflict is in one other respect distorted by his assumption of consensus.

> Power, he insists, is primarily a facility that makes possible the attainment of collective goals to which normative commitment has been made ... it presupposes the existence of collective goals grounded in the shared values of a public that benefits from their attainment by means of an organized and established system of power. Neither the reality of the underlying consensus nor the process by which the system of collective power becomes organized and established are problematic to Parsons. He takes them for granted.

Parsons, while admitting inequalities of power, minimizes the dominance-submission aspect of power relations by suggesting that their asymmetry lies essentially in unequal rights to make decisions on behalf of collective goals.

The final consequence of this emphasis on social integration has to do with the primacy given to values in explaining social structure. The organization of social life is said to reflect dominant values. For example, formal organizations are classified and their operation explained by reference to the values they espouse. Schools will be organized differently from business firms because they espouse different values.

There is, however, little empirical evidence that formal organizations can be successfully classified or analyzed in this way. It is much more likely that technology shapes organizational structure and functioning. Schools are less bureaucratized than business firms, not because they espouse different values, but because the nature of the work involved is different. Work in schools is distinctive in "(1) the 'soft', uncodified, human relations technology of teaching activities; (2) pupil conscription; (3) the classroom as the basic ecological unit and (4) the weak occupational community of the teachers" (Dreebeen, 1976:870). Action theory *appears* to explain how schools operate (they do have different values and they do make different contributions to society), but values actually have little to do in a direct way with their social structure. It is influenced much more heavily by technology and conditions of work.

THE LOSS OF VOLUNTARISM

An issue of great concern raised by action theory is whether it is possible to constitute sociology "as a discipline which is not forced to understand itself in terms of either the models of strict causal explanation in the natural sciences or the pure ideographic methods of the study of arts and other cultural products" (Munch, 1981:713). Action theorists believe they have a frame of reference which allows room for both the determinism of the first and the voluntarism of the second. In this frame of reference, autonomous individuals and patterns of social order are both conceivable because the relation between the individual and society is conceptualized in such a way that the freedom of the individual enlarges as his bonds to society become stronger (Munch, 1982:780).

There are sociologists who dispute any claim to have achieved a synthesis of deterministic and voluntaristic approaches. They assert that Parsons' increasing preoccupation with formulating the necessary conditions for the existence of social systems has meant a loss of voluntarism and a drift toward more deterministic sociological theories. In the course of its development the voluntaristic aspects of action theory have disappeared in proportion to the emphasis placed upon systems theory. The unit of analysis is no longer the individual actor but the "person-in-role." The actor's behavior is interpreted from the point of view of the system and its needs. The person-in-role is the system's agent. The focus is less on the actor's intention and more on the structural and systemic consequences of what he does. The original unit act (in which one actor tries to ascertain the meaning of the conduct of the other and shape his conduct accordingly) gives way in *The Social System* to a cybernetic model in which "Ego" is "the delivery system" and "Alter" is the "receiving system." Ego's role expectations have become part of the "informational input" to Alter, and Alter's role performance part of his "informational output" to Ego. The rewards and sanctions Ego and Alter give each other have become "feedback mechanisms."

The "subjective component" is not ignored entirely. Parsons always attached great significance to norms and values. But it is possible to treat this subjective component more or less deterministically and, in the opinion of Parsons' critics, action theory became increasingly deterministic in its treatment of consciousness. Under the influence of systems thinking, the original emphasis on ideas and beliefs has undergone two kinds of change. First, social and cultural systems have been analytically separated. Social interaction has thus become divorced from the meaning attached to that action. Cultural systems take on a life of their own. "Science, religion, philosophy, and ideology are 'sub-systems'; they are differentiated, they 'interact' and so on" (Etzioni, 1968:82). This analytical separation only succeeds in reconceiving interpretive schemes deterministically, as if they were somehow separate from, rather than a part of, social interaction. An alternative view is to see ideology and other cultural systems as part of social interaction, as expressed in action. This is the view favored by sociologists who draw their inspiration from world views other than positivism.

Systems thinking has had a second kind of impact on our thinking about the subjective component. Action theorists maintain that, although people are free to make choices, they do so in ways shaped by the system. Norms are said to be "internalized" in such a way that the individual's wants are the same as the system's needs. This formulation demolishes voluntarism (Giddens, 1976:95; Wrong, 1970). Action no longer flows from human agency but from internalized norms. The "point of view of the actor" is now no longer different from the normative culture. If norms are internalized by the actor and constitute part of his sense of obligation, how can that actor stand back from those norms and interpret and modify them to suit different circumstances? The synthesis of determinism and voluntarism is no synthesis at all but a loss of the subjective component altogether (Dawe, 1978:405).

SOCIAL CHANGE

The adoption of systems models by Parsons facilitated the development of a theory of social change relying principally on evolutionary ideas. The reintroduction of evolutionary theory into sociology has occasioned considerable debate. There are many sociologists who think that the evolutionary perspective is not appropriate for human societies.

Superior adaptive capacity is an important aspect of theories about the evolution of natural systems, but its applicability to social systems is questionable. There is a tendency to treat as indices of heightened adaptive capacity only those innovations which stand in the direct line of Western modernization. Other innovations, however appropriate they might have been at the time, are not accorded this status (Smith, 1973:35). And it seems as if hindsight must always be used when considering and judging social innovations as preconditions for evolution. In short, it is not likely that ideas like "survival" and "enhanced adaptability" can be applied to human societies. Who is to say that a higher GNP at the cost of greater social inequality is evolutionary?

The evolutionary idea that development takes place in stages also causes problems. When we think in terms of stages we tend to think of the system before and after, but we pay no attention to the process of change itself, what happens to the system as it passes from one stage to the other. And the more attention we pay to describing the various stages the more likely are we to believe that by simply producing a sequence, we have explained it. By reading into historical sequences processes of differentiation and adaptive upgrading, we come to believe that we have explained those processes when all we have done is to identify them.

THE EPISTEMOLOGY
OF ACTION THEORY

Action theory is a research tradition in which an effort has been made to specify "the common structure of all systems of action" —the elementary units and their relations (Parsons, 1937:734). The "frame of reference," like any other research tradition, makes no formal, substantive claims about concrete social relationships. It states instead the minimum properties of social action.

And yet action theory is not merely a specification of *how* we should think about society. It is "a set of premises which have the character of postulates" (Munch, 1982:773). A frame of reference makes it possible "to describe phenomena in such a way as to distinguish those facts about them which are relevant to and *capable of explanation in terms of a given theoretical system* from those which are not" (Parsons, 1937:735). [My italics.] In other words, the action frame of reference comprises not only a logical framework in which to think about society, but a theory about how that society works.

If action theory is intended to be a causal theory, what kind of causal theory is it meant to be? Action theorists seek to distance themselves from "radical positivism" and its covering law model of causal explanation (Munch, 1981:713). While there can be no doubt that action theory does not simply treat social phenomena as equivalent to natural phenomena, this effort to create a distance from positivism has not been successful. Parsons seems to have shared with positivists "the idea of an abstract, context-free theoretical science from which one could deduce the laws of social life" (Bellah, 1979:455). And he also shared with positivists "a moderate version of the empiricist concept of explanation" (Rossi, 1981:59). It is appropriate to consider action theory, then, as a version of positivist sociology and judge it accordingly.

Is action theory really a set of law-like statements from which testable hypotheses could be derived? Black (1961:271) believes that, despite appearances to the contrary, there is "very little strict deduction in Parsons' exposition." Turk (1967:47) can find no propositions in action theory which postulate relations between social phenomena. If this is the case, why does action theory suggest itself as an explanatory theory?

Parsons' approach to theory building was neither inductive nor deductive. The predicated relationships in action theory (e.g. exchanges between subsystems) are not arrived at through empirical study, and neither do they distill the empirical findings of past generations of sociologists. Nor has the development of action theory been shaped by successive empirical tests. Its innovations (e.g. the reconceptualization of power) were instigated not by empirical research but by analogy or "derivation" from other parts of the frame of reference or from other sciences altogether, such as biology. Theory building has not been inductive.

The theory does resemble a deductive theory. However, there are no axioms and no propositions logically derived from them. The A-G-I-L scheme, which might appear to be an axiomatic statement about system requirements (from which propositions could be derived), is actually not an axiomatic statement at all. Rather, it is an example of *a priori* reasoning. It is an attempt to state the conditions necessary for the existence of something—in this case, system survival. Unfortunately, it is one thing to state the logical presuppositions which must organize our thinking about society and another thing to state a causal argument which states the conditions necessary for society's existence (Bershady, 1973). Action theorists frequently confuse the two. For example, in discussing socialization, Parsons argues that the maintenance of complementary role expectations is an essential aspect of social interaction. This conclusion is not reached as the result of empirical study. It follows from the solution to social order which Parsons assumes *must* have been achieved for us to think of social life in systemic terms at all. If we think about social life as a system, he seems to be saying, then it *follows* that there must be social cooperation, where people have similar expectations of each other. Furthermore, if the society is to survive as a system (if we are to continue to think of it as a system), parents must encourage their children to adopt prevailing normative standards. Parsons, having begun by formulating the logical categories (e.g. system integration, pattern-maintenance) necessary for thinking about social interaction, ends up by arguing that they actually describe necessary conditions for the existence of social life.

It is this habit of thinking which gives action theory its appearance of being a causal theory containing proposition statements. There are such statements but they tend to be used in a self-fulfilling way. The typical form is: If X is to remain in equilibrium, then Y has to occur. Having formulated this proposition, the action theorist sets out to show that Y has indeed occurred (Lopreato, 1971:323). Action theorists themselves acknowledge that this inability to move from the analytical framework to empirical theory without resorting to proof by example is one of the major weaknesses of this research tradition (Loubser, 1976:5).

CONCLUSION

The aim of action theory is to separate positivism from the radical empiricist tradition which sought to explain human behavior in terms of heredity, environment, or rational choice. Parsons and his followers have argued that a scientific sociology should be capable of dealing with sociocultural phenomena such as values and beliefs. For Parsons, social phenomena were similar in structure to the phenomena of the natural sciences. His frame of reference was a means of identifying and classifying this structure by means of systems analysis and functional explanation. Advocates of the theory of action have remained committed to the idea that a theory of functional imperatives and processes applicable to all empirical contents can be constructed. This commitment is the principal distinguish-ing mark of the version of systems theory I have described in this chapter. It distinguishes Parsons and his followers from other systems theorists, who would not accept the commitment to the idea of functional imperatives. In its positivist approach to sociology it is distinguishable from Marxian social theory, the other holistic theory to be described in this book. And in its image of the actor and the role of ideas in social action, it is distinguishable from the interpretive sociology to be described in the following chapter. To some sociologists, the theory of action in its most systemic form is an unconvincing and abstruse effort to incorporate sociology into a theory of all living systems, in which the benefits of breadth are outweighed by the costs of losing touch with what is essentially human about social interaction. To others, Parsons and systems theory in general have given direction and impetus to the search for general laws in sociology.

PART TWO

7

Idealism

What mental image of human societies is most appropriate for sociologists? Do the forms of social life resemble the forms found in nature, or does social life more closely resemble a text or work of art, a complex of meaning which must be interpreted before it can be known? Should social actors be treated as equivalent to physical objects whose behavior is determined by outside forces, or as free agents able to imagine and construct alternative futures? Should we think of society as being causally prior, a suprahuman, self-generating, and self-maintaining system which sets its stamp upon individual identity and purpose, or should we think of the actor as causally prior, active, purposeful, and creative, whose ideas and actions produce, reproduce, and occasionally destroy social forms?

What is the most appropriate strategy for learning about society? Should the methods of the natural sciences be used in an effort to discover the laws which govern the operation of social systems and determine the conduct of individuals? Or should the methods of the humanities be used to read and interpret social interaction? Is the sociologist a detached and objective observer of social life, or must she or he enter into conversation with all subjects in order to understand the language they speak and the acts they perform?

In Part One of this book I described research traditions in which the inclination was to assume that social life is, in all essentials, no different from the physical world, and that the methods of the natural sciences are appropriate for its analysis. In Part Two I will describe research traditions in which it is assumed that social life is different from the natural world and that entirely different methods are required for its analysis. I have singled out two prominent research traditions representative of this metatheory, which I have chosen to call idealism.

These research traditions could have been united under several other labels. Their common concern with human beings' unique capacity to choose and imagine new futures would warrant the label "humanistic." Their goal of understanding action "from within" would justify calling them "interpretive." However, I have chosen the term idealist because I wish to signify the importance they attribute to the power of ideas and their symbolic expression in social life.

Human beings are truly distinctive in their ability to use symbols. Symbols and clusters of symbols shape and direct human conduct. This symbolic dimension places demands on the social scientist which the natural scientist escapes. The social scientist must accord priority to the understanding of action. A way must be found for coping with the fact of human agency without abandoning the empirical search for pattern and order which makes sociology a rational enterprise.

Two Approaches to Roles

The difference between social life as seen by a positivist and social life as seen by an idealist can be glimpsed by contrasting two approaches to the analysis of an everyday encounter—the visit of a patient to a doctor. As we have seen, it is typical for a positivist to think of patient and doctor as performing complementary roles. Each knows how she should behave and how the other should behave toward her. The failure of either to respect these complementary expectations would seriously disrupt the relationship. The conduct of the respective actors in the encounter can thus be explained by analyzing the roles being performed. These roles are dictated by the larger structure (the hospital) in which the encounter occurs. The encounter follows a course predictable once the social structure is known.

From the idealist standpoint, this is a rather mechanical approach to the encounter. It presumes the existence of a social structure in which social forces (role obligations) operate to shape people's conduct. But is such an encounter merely the unfolding of predetermined outcomes? Not if roles are treated as *ideas* rather than *things*. In this case, roles could not be imagined as existing "ready-made" at the start of the encounter. Rather they grow and change during the course of the interaction. They might *appear* to preexist because we normally take role requirements for granted. But if we think about it, we realize that roles are but ideas in our minds about how people in certain situations should behave. The exact meaning of the role, the idea, is always being negotiated. Thus the doctor and the patient might well draw on a common stock of preexisting knowledge about how the patient visit ought to proceed, but the presentation of their behavior as being in accordance with these requirements—and the degree to which their behavior meets those requirements—is an outcome of their own efforts. They accomplish their role rather than "fit into it."

We can be more readily convinced that roles are ideas rather than things when their think-like quality is questioned. This happens, for example, when we are embarrassed, for it is at such times that the naturalness of roles is undermined (Goffman, 1967:99). Embarrassing episodes remove the veil which normally conceals the efforts we expend on making roles natural or "real": we are exposed. Such episodes are especially likely to occur during gynecological examinations by male doctors when women find it difficult to separate the physician's role from the role of lover, husband, or male friend. Heedful of this possibility, Emerson (1970) studied behavior in a gynecological ward in a large, general hospital. She observed that doctors and nurses do not simply enact organizationally prescribed roles when they deal with patients. Their roles are not simply donned like a suit of clothes. Doctors and nurses are especially sensitive to the possibility of embarrassment on the part of women patients, partly because it threatens the performance of their own role. Accordingly, the way the gynecological examination is performed is as important as the fact that it is performed at all. Doctor and nurse try to establish an understanding that "nothing unusual is happening." The doctor is casual yet professional, friendly yet not too personal. The nurse busies herself with the routine and mundane features of the examination. Each works to define the encounter as a medical rather than a sexual encounter.

What Emerson finds most important in this encounter is the meaning expressed and conveyed in the appearance and demeanor of the doctor, the mood of the setting, the posture of the nurse, and so on. The encounter does not exist apart from the meaning it has. Given a different meaning the encounter ceases to be an examination and becomes, perhaps, a sexual advance. Upon redefinition, the flow of interaction would take a different course. If meanings become incongruent, the flow of interaction will be impeded. If one party defines the encounter as an examination and the other as a sexual advance, one of the parties will be embarrassed. The embarrassment reveals the work which each actor has been putting into the production of meaning in that encounter.

Emerson's insights could not have been acquired at a distance. She could not have interpreted the gynecological examination by reading the organizational chart of the hospital. She had to learn the language used in the encounter. She had to watch doctor, nurse, and patient *play at their roles*. Her data were not things or objects but "the subjective intentions, feelings, attitudes, definitions of the situation and acts of human beings" (Brittan, 1973:13).

In summary, the idealist view takes as its fundamental premise the idea that the human social world is a world of meaning. Human actors have minds through which they categorize and order events, thereby giving meaning, rationality, coherence, and predictability to the world around them. Their experiences consist of applying meaning structures to events. The individual never confronts reality directly, but always through the use of interpretive schemes.

THE FOUNDATIONS OF IDEALIST SOCIOLOGY

The dominant influences on idealist sociology have been the theories of Max Weber, Georg Simmel, Edmund Husserl, and George Herbert Mead. Weber endeavored to create a nonpositivist sociology which claimed no capacity to generalize or establish final truth. He aimed instead at an interpretive understanding which would furnish only one of a number of legitimate vantage points from which to view social process. Simmel defined the subject matter of sociology as the forms of thought which people organize out of their experience and in terms of which they confront their environment. Husserl abandoned all problems of deciding what was real and concerned himself entirely with how the universe of phenomenal appearances is constructed. Mead sought to overcome the positivist's dichotomy of subject and object by conceiving subject and object as but phases of a single and continual process. These thinkers shared a concern with the power of ideas, with their symbolic expression, and with their impact on social action. They accordingly sought to develop a social science whose method would be as well suited to the task of understanding ideas as it was to the task of predicting events.

Max Weber (1864–1920) defined the subject matter of sociology as "all human behavior when and insofar as the acting individual attaches meaning to it" (Weber, 1964:88). The "specific task of sociology must be "the interpretation of action in terms of its subjective meaning." This explanation by interpretive understanding "as distinguished from external observation" would comprise the specific characteristic of sociological knowledge (Weber, 1964:210). A sociological account of social life must therefore be "adequate at the level of meaning." He accorded this kind of causal explanation greater importance than that used by the natural sciences.

In the opinion of some sociologists, Weber tried to modify his methodology of the social sciences to bring it into closer relation with the positivist tradition of empirical verification and deductive-nomological theory building (Coser, 1977:247). His work can thus be read as calling for complementary approaches to sociological analysis, in which understanding logically preceded but must be followed by causal explanation. But idealist sociologists do not accept this interpretation of Weber (Roche, 1973:287). They do not see the interpretive and the positivist approaches as complementary. They do not accept that these approaches refer to the same social facts. "They are not *additive* but *competing* explanations, employing different root images about the nature of man and the 'idea' of the social" (Brittan, 1973:21).

Like Weber, Georg Simmel (1858–1918) believed that social life was so rich in meaning that only a partial comprehension of it was possible. Any concrete social phenomenon could be studied from a variety of perspectives, each of them yielding part of the truth. Simmel's technique for dealing with this complexity was to concentrate on the forms of social life. He believed that people use a sense of form or pattern to impose order upon their world. Having thus conceived forms, people subsequently seek to realize them in their behavior (Rock, 1979:40). The form is therefore both a way of knowing and a way of being. It is both a mode of apprehending the world and a way of living in the world.

Simmel's forms included hierarchy, competition, friendship, and conflict. Each form comprises the essence of social interaction: it is what remains when all content is abstracted. The sociologist studying war and the sociologist studying divorce deal with very different contents but the form—conflict—is essentially the same, whether it be martial or marital.

This distinction between form and content is evident in any communication between human beings. The communication will have two aspects—what it is about and what it says about the relation between actors. In other words, it will have both content and form. Besides its content, it will tell us whether the communicants are friends or strangers, acting or serious, competitive or noncompetitive, equal or unequal, and so on. The form of the relation will affect the interpretation given its content, the meaning of the words exchanged; the content will, in turn, help validate (or invalidate) the form. The idea of forms was Simmel's way of dealing with the problem that society is both the creation of man (since it exists only where many individuals think and act) and the creator of man (since man's acting and thinking assume only a limited range of forms).

Edmund Husserl (1859–1938) is widely regarded as the founder of the phenomenological movement in philosophy. Husserl wanted to create a philosophy that would not be subject to the limitations of the empiricist account of the nature of knowledge, with its sharp separation of perceiving subject and perceived object. He was concerned that, by limiting science to those phenomena available only to direct observation, consciousness would either be rejected as a fiction or transformed into something physical. Accordingly he undertook an examination of the structure of consciousness.

Husserl argued that the mind is not the passive recipient of impressions from the outside world, but is an active process. To be conscious at all is to be conscious *of* something. Mental processes, (like naming) logically precede material phenomena. We should not wonder whether we really perceive the world—we must instead assume that the world is what we perceive. Accordingly, when we wish to make sense of the action of others (as laymen or sociologists) we must recognize that its meaning lies in what the actor intends by it. The act has meaning to us once we can see its aim.

Husserl's ideas, transposed into sociology by Alfred Schutz (1899–1959), reminded sociologists of the need to study carefully the structure of social knowledge. How is our conscious experience organized by the everyday world? How is our sense of social reality confirmed or denied by our experiences? What is the meaning of social categories like "male" and "female"? What techniques are used to construct and sustain these meanings? Husserl (and the phenomenological sociology he inspired) is possibly the most radically idealistic of all the research traditions in this group.

The fourth figure to shape idealist sociology, George Herbert Mead (1863–1931), was influenced by the pragmatist philosophy of William James and John Dewey. Pragmatism was a reaction to the deductive rationalism of positivist social science. James and Dewey, in their writings on consciousness, language, and the self, sought to improve upon the positivist's treatment of the relation between mind and matter, object and subject, individual and society. They argued that our experience of the everyday world is a dynamic, ongoing process of interaction in which "mind" and "matter," "individual" and "society" are merely different aspects or moments.

James and Dewey reversed the positivist assumption that human beings possess minds as original "givens" and that human actions consist of the response of these pregiven minds to preexisting objects. They said that mind is not a passive stage of cognition but an instrument for building knowledge and making adjustments. "Minding" (consciousness) consists of an active relation between knowing subject and known object.

Like Weber and Simmel, the pragmatist treated knowledge as partial and tentative.

> Knowledge as an experiential process had radically different implications from knowledge imagined to be a mirroring of some independent reality or an incision into an unchanging process. It suggests that men cannot grasp essences or absolutes because there are not such fixed noumena. Reality shifts as men build it up in their transactions with nature and with each other (Rock, 1979:70).

Knowledge was thus conceived as rooted in social interaction (an inherently social thing), changing as the interaction changes. Dewey believed that there could be no knowledge that preceded the interaction of thinking beings. Knowledge—what we take to be true—was therefore inherently social.

The pragmatists did not believe in a fixed human nature. They would not have agreed with the rational choice postulate of man as the eternal profit maximizer. They did not see the individual as a detached and unchanging monitor of events, much less in all-comprehending consciousness. In their view, human beings evolve as the events in which they are implicated unfold. The self is always "in the making." What is more important, human beings remake *themselves*. Rational choice theorists are correct when they argue that the individual monitors his environment. But they tend to overlook the fact that the individual also monitors himself. The self is reflexive.

What kind of social world makes a reflexive self possible? Mead did not believe that the social world described by positivists, with its structures, roles, and calculated exchanges, all governed by general laws of human behavior, left any room for reflexivity. Mead conceived of social interaction as a creative process in which, through the power of symbols, novel formations and new selves continually emerge as people adjust to one another in forming their joint acts. Mead did not deny the utilitarian's contention that people everywhere seek to be consistent in their beliefs and arguments and seek to make their actions rational, but he pointed out that what counts as consistency varies from one culture to another. We cannot simply assume that rational decision making stands in no need of interpretation.

ONTOLOGY—THE NATURE OF SOCIAL REALITY

The image of the social actor in idealist sociology is that of an active creator of his world. Man is a free, active, purposeful, and creative being. Humans have the unique capacity to imagine alternative futures and escape the overwhelming present. This is not to deny the existence of social restraint. "Rather, it locates constraint, not in an entity external to and superordinate over man but, quite simply, in the actions of other actors; that is, in humanly constructed structures of power and domination" (Dawe, 1978:373).

The voluntaristic nature of this image of man can be appreciated by contrasting the idea of "norm" or "rule" in positivist and idealist sociologies. Most positivists treat norms as constraints or determinants of social behavior. People sometimes disregard norms, but deviance is usually met with sanctions which deter future violations. Norms are rather mechanistically conceived. They resemble natural obstacles which direct the flow of human interaction.

Idealist sociologists dispute this image of the rules which govern social conduct. They rarely use the term "norm" at all, preferring to describe social behavior as "rule-guided" rather than "normative." "To say that interaction is rule-governed activity ... is to say that interactants are guided by, take note of, pay attention to rules in their production of action and utterance" (O'Keefe, 1979:187).

Rules are not abstract, fixed, and unchanging. They are open to continual reinterpretation, depending on the actor's goals, the setting in which the action takes place, and who else is involved in the encounter. Rules, then, do not exist independently of their use. Their precise meaning (their real meaning) is defined in use, as the action unfolds and the situation becomes more clearly defined. Thus, while "norms" are obeyed, "rules" are used chiefly to impart a sense of coherence and rationality to a course of action as it unfolds. A description of these rules constitutes "an explanation of how interaction comes to be, an account of the production of interaction" (O'Keefe, 1979:187). But the rules are not treated as determinants of action, as forces impinging on the actor from the outside. The rule-governedness of the interaction is something the actor helps bring about in concert with other actors.

This way of thinking about rules recognizes and acknowledges man's reflexivity. Rules are not stimuli which trigger automatic responses but resources which people use to make sense of their own and other people's actions. How they use a rule will depend on their goals, the situation, and on other people's demands. The idea of norm suggests constraint, determinism, and lack of freedom; the idea of rule suggests free will and human agency. There are limits to the possibilities of correct action but within these limits behavior is undetermined (Cheal, 1980:40).

Social reality often appears to be fixed and objectlike. But social reality is always the outcome of sustained interpretive efforts on the part of actors. The objectivity of social reality obscures the fact that humans have produced it. And this appearance of fixity conceals the real possibility of change contained in social reality. However tempted we might be to treat something as unalterable and objective (e.g. that there are two and only two genders), we must remember that this "objectivity" has been produced by humans, must be sustained by what people say and do, and can be destroyed by humans saying and doing something different.

The natural world is not as amenable to human modification.

> The natural world does not depend upon human recognition for its existence even if the latter imputes a structure of meaning to that world which it does not intrinsically possess. In contrast, a given social world would necessarily cease to exist if human recognition were withdrawn from it, since it has no existence apart from such recognition. In this sense, society is real (has objective facticity) because its members define it as real and orient themselves toward the reality so defined (Walsh, 1972:19).

The data with which the sociologist must deal are therefore *preinterpreted.* They already contain meaning in a way not true of physical objects. Many sociologists overlook this fact because they handle data which have the appearance of being natural or "raw" —although they have meanings concealed within them. Statistics recording voting, divorce, income, job turnover, and so on are the product of officials' interpretation of "what must have happened" and their judgements as to how acts should be classified and sorted. These data conceal meaning. Somewhere in voting records is hidden the meaning of casting a vote; divorce statistics conceal the meaning of the end of a marriage; an organizational chart is merely a schematic representation of the everyday interaction which goes on in an organization.

The subject matter of sociology as defined by idealist sociologists is not easily quantifiable. It is a world of everyday encounters in everyday settings, of people interacting in concrete, face-to-face meetings. Each encounter is an innovative accomplishment or reaccomplishment, "another first time" (Dawe, 1978:411). The data which record these happenings cannot be summed and averaged as easily as the data pertaining to physical objects. The subject matter is meanings, and meanings might well be ambiguous, shifting, and uncertain.

EPISTEMOLOGY—KNOWING SOCIAL REALITY

Natural events are not inherently meaningful. We do not ask what a volcano meant by erupting. We are free to sort and classify natural events without worrying about how well we have captured what they really mean. Social life is different. Social acts are intrinsically meaningful. Describing an act as an "insult" relies entirely on our knowledge of what the actor meant by it. We have to interpret the act before we can even say what it is.

What is the relation between interpreting actions and explaining them? Can an interpretation be an explanation? Positivists would say no. They would claim that an action is explained by pointing to the necessary and sufficient conditions for its existence. Idealists believe that this kind of causal explanation applies only to the natural world. What about treating intentions and motives as if *they* were antecedent conditions? Positivists would agree with this as long as the motive or the intention could be thought of as existing prior to and independent of the action—one "event" causes another "event." Idealists would reject this approach to motives and intentions because they do not believe that intentions and actions are separable in this way. Intentions and actions are not "cause" and "effect" because we cannot know one without knowing the other. We cannot determine the existence of an action apart from ascertaining its intention because the intention tells us what the action is. And we cannot ascertain the actor's intentions without thereby verifying that he acted in a certain way. Idealists conclude that the actor's intentions and his action are logically linked, "two aspects of the same thing" (Moon, 1975:164). Motives cannot be treated as antecedent causes of subsequent actions.

Idealist sociologists do not dispense with causal explanations altogether. There is a sense in which intentions explain actions, but the meaning of explanation is rather different from that found in the covering-law model favored by positivists. Actions can be explained by referring to the intentions of the actor if we make a "practical inference": we connect what the actor intended to do with the means he believes will be necessary to realize his intentions. We logically deduce the outcome (the act) from certain premises (the intention) in the light of the demands of the "outer world" (the means). The act of raising an umbrella is explained by referring to the intention of keeping dry, the available means for keeping dry being to raise a suitably shaped object over one's head. Or we explain why a person raises his arm at a political meeting by pointing out that he desires to cast a vote and knows that the means of doing so is to raise his arm. Cause and effect are not related in these examples in the manner in which cause and effect are related in the positivist model. In that model, cause and effect are contingently related: two independent events are in conjunction. In the case of the practical inference, cause and effect are logically related, and the effect makes sense given the cause. Cohen (1980:164–165) draws the distinction between these two kinds of connection very precisely:

> In nature there are connections between events which can be conceptualized as causation. In the world of human society and culture, on the other hand, there are connections between motives, meanings and assumptions about what is and what should be, all of which constitute reasons of which the subject is more or less aware, and, on the other hand, human conduct, which is commonly directed to other objects, most of them being other subjects: these connections can be conceptualized as implicative but not causal ... Thus, human activities, and the patterns which they form, cannot be explained in the sense that natural events can be explained; they can, however, be interpreted: and the logic of the interpretation is not the logic of science, but that of hermeneutics.

The relation between intention and action in the practical inference is thus implicative, a relation between ideas rather than a relation between objects, such that holding one to be true or binding entails holding the other to be true or binding. To explain is a matter of making sense of the logic people utilize when they make sense of settings of social interaction.

Epistemology thus flows from ontology. Having rejected the positivists' claim that social reality is composed of objects in space or events in time, idealists reject the kind of theory which encourages us to think in terms of "event causality." Instead, they recommend theories which encourage us to think in terms of "agent causality." Agent causality begins with a mental decision. Action is caused by "an agent's reflexive monitoring of his intentions in relation both to his wants and his appreciation of the demands of the 'outer world'" (Giddens, 1976:84).

Agent causality makes sense at the level of the individual, but how are macro-level processes like population movements, elections, economic recessions, and riots to be dealt with? Not only are they the product of millions of individual decisions, but they are often unintended by those who help bring them about. The answer is that, however complex the structure, however abstractly it is conceived by the observer, however far removed such processes might seem to be from the everyday intentions of the individual actor, macro-structural phenomena can only be adequately accounted for by reference to agent causality.

Patterns of behavior (e.g. the rate of theft in an organization), must ultimately be accounted for in terms of the interaction of purposive actors:

> the rate of theft in a group may not even be known to the members of the group; nevertheless, an individual act of theft is behavior meaningful to the members, and the rate expresses a regularity in these actions that can be taken as a phenomenon for sociological investigation. Thus, complex social phenomena are seen as patterned arrangements of interactions among individual actors. The process of interaction, then, is at the logical core of sociological interest, even though for some purposes, particularly of a macrosociological sort, this is often left implicit (Wilson, 1971:59).

Far from agent causality being irrelevant to macro-sociology, we see that theories at the macro-level are actually reconstructions of the practical inferences of the relevant individuals. Links between variables are made by inference about actors' intentions which make the covariation intelligible and reasonable. The relation is mediated by a practical inference.

The positivist approach to sociological investigation either ignores the process of practical inference altogether or "smuggles in" such inferences during the course of an explanation which rests on event causality. A well-known example of this is Durkheim's study of suicide. Durkheim discovered that suicide rates vary with factors like religious affiliation, social mobility, and marital status. He used this information to propound a theory which used social structural conditions rather than individual pathologies to explain suicide. But in order to make sense of the correlations, he made a number of practical inferences. He had to translate his statistics into meanings. Why should self-destruction be more common among one social group than another? Why should marital status make a difference to suicide rates? Durkheim surmised that widowers have a higher rate of suicide than widows because the woman has only a "rudimentary" sensibility whereas the widower, "a more complex being," feels his loss more keenly. Durkheim's "theorizing" rests entirely on what he supposed his subjects were thinking and feeling. Although he specifically rejected psychological explanations of suicide and sought the social facts which would explain it, he tacitly acknowledged his reliance on knowledge of the meaning of widowhood and how that meaning relates to the meaning of suicide. He "smuggled in" his practical inferences (Douglas, 1967). The idealist, in criticizing this kind of sociology, is not arguing that we need to know what each suicide meant to each actor. But we do need to know the socially acquired rules or conventions defining suicide: we need to know the proper way of carrying it out, of justifying it, the circumstances under which it is expected and excused, the kind of response thought appropriate, and so on. We would also need to know much more than Durkheim tells us about what it means to be deprived of one's spouse.

The idea that understanding and accounting for suicide means learning the rules for carrying it out suggests that interpretation means much more than learning motives or intentions. If we could rely only on knowledge of motives we could never achieve more than a fragmentary and imperfect knowledge of people's actions. But we can learn more than motives. Actions have both subjective and objective meaning. Intentionality is not the only meaning actions have. An actor can be raising a flag while thinking about something completely different, but the raising of the flag still means the same thing. His thinking about something else does not change the meaning of raising the flag in that society, its objective meaning.

Objective meaning is no less part of consciousness than is subjective meaning. The difference lies in the extent to which it is fixed and shared. Therefore, it, too, can only be ascertained by interpretation. Objective meaning is ascertained by the application of a rule or "convention." Rules describe what shall count as an action of a certain type. They stipulate what shall count as performing an action—what counts as an apology, a promise, an agreement, a joke, a game, and so on. Interpretation in this sense means uncovering the rule which constitutes the action. The rule is what makes the action what it is. A sociologist might thus interpret an act by attributing motives, but he must warrant this interpretation by making more explicit the rule or convention the motive presupposes.

Interpretive explanation becomes richer and deeper as we make the interpretive scheme more comprehensive. Just as motives presuppose rules, so rules presuppose yet more general patterns of meaning. These more general patterns tell what, for the actor, is "seeable in a particular situation" (Goffman, 1971:185). These "constitutive meanings" (Taylor, 1971) are usually taken for granted by the actors involved, treated by them as "natural." The whole complex of meanings having to do with romantic love and its "natural" consummation in marriage makes sense of the rules defining marriage and the motives of the marital pair. It is these constitutive meanings that Weber (1964:96) had in mind when he described the act of interpretation as "placing the act in an intelligible and more inclusive context of meaning."

Lofland (1973) furnishes an example of this method of interpretation. In her work on city life, she focuses particularly on the ways in which city dwellers (who must often venture out alone in a world of strangers) use a variety of techniques for reducing the tension this causes. For example, the various actions of people thrown together in public waiting rooms are motivated by people's desire to create private spaces for themselves. This is their reason for "hiding themselves in a book." Lofland warrants this interpretation by reference to the social conventions or rules which are attached to behavior in public places, including the rule that people must remain open to contact and yet have rights of autonomy. These rules, in turn, make sense once we understand what public as opposed to private life means in Western society. The meanings of public and private are constitutive. Taking them for granted, we fail to recognize how important they are in shaping and guiding behavior. We are unaware of how different public and private life is in other societies, or that some societies make no such distinction at all (Sennett, 1974).

Lofland adds power to her interpretive account by generalizing in a manner different from that dictated by the deductive-nomological model. Goffman (1971:226) provides instructions on how to follow her method of generalization.

> ...start with a particular practice, in this case hand-holding, and move from there to a consideration of a class of practices of which it is an example, a class then can be defined naturalistically in terms, say, of function or role and accorded the status of a concept. Thus, hand-holding can come to be seen as a 'tie-sign', and interest can then shift to a general consideration of this broad class of events.... The other strategy is to try to assemble all of the environments in which the particular practice is found and then attempt to uncover what these various contexts have in common. Here the 'meaning' of the practice is whatever co-occurs with it.

Goffman finds the act's meaning by locating it in a stream of behavior, by situating it within a complex of meanings. He makes sense of the part by relating to other parts in the whole, "reading" the whole meanwhile by making sense of its partial expressions, as we would interpret a text. The overall concern is to understand people's ordering of experience in order to step outside it so as to reveal the process through which human activities acquire their meaning. The sociologist thus stands back from common sense in order to understand the logic that underlies it, to reveal its typicality rather than its uniqueness, its form rather than its content.

CONCEPTS

Positivists place great emphasis on making their concepts precise, unambiguous, and context-free. We do not need to know who is using them or on what occasion they are used in order to grasp their meaning. This is why a sharp distinction is drawn between "common-sense language," which is context-dependent, and scientific language, which is universal. A concept provides a "literal description": an assertion that "on the basis of [certain] ... perceived features the phenomenon has some clearly designated property, or what is logically the same thing, belongs to some particularly well-defined class of phenomena" (Wilson, 1971:72). The deductive form of explanation depends entirely on concepts which purport to provide literal descriptions. Each description entering into a deductive argument must be treated as having a stable meaning that is independent of its use.

Where the subject matter is the natural world (or the social world conceived as if it were part of the natural world), literal descriptions are quite appropriate. The scientist is free to formulate concepts at will. He imposes human significance on a subject matter otherwise devoid of meaning. Furthermore, he is free to reject one conceptual scheme and replace it with another if he feels it will advance the cause of exact description and accurate prediction.

The idealist cannot follow this strategy. His subject matter is not meaningless, for its shape and flow has preconstituted meaning. He must respect this meaning in his description. "If he ignores these ideas, he is, so to speak, no longer studying the same subject" (Moon, 1975:181). There is no way of correctly describing action without identifying the underlying pattern of meaning in terms of which it "makes sense." When a sociologist classifies the behavior of an actor on a given occasion as an instance of a particular type of action he is not basing this judgement on a limited set of specifiable features of the behavior and the occasion. Rather, he must depend on the context as he sees it being relevant, a context which is infinite in its zones of relevance (Wilson, 1971:75). For this reason there can be no final, correct description: concepts must be tentative, open-ended. Abstract and formal conceptual schemes must be avoided. No description, however detailed and substantial, must be supposed to be complete. All descriptions are open to modification as new contextual relevances are uncovered.

TESTING THEORY

Max Weber simultaneously endorsed two types of sociological explanation and thereby indicated two ways to test theory. One the one hand he recognized explanation in terms of causality and statistical correlations. This is validated by the accuracy of its predictions and the ability it bestows on the scientist to control events. On the other hand there was explanation by means of the attempt to understand the motivation of actors. How is the validity of this interpretation judged? It is clear that one does not proceed by discovering empirical generalizations, for these merely state a fact of association and do not necessarily explain anything. Sociological explanation must be "adequate" not only as a prediction but at the level of meaning as well. Adequacy at the level of meaning cannot be secured by repeated experiments or replicated surveys.

> Suppose that somehow an empirical-statistical demonstration in the strictest sense is produced, showing that all men everywhere who have ever been placed in a certain situation have invariably reacted in the same way and to the same extent. Suppose that whenever this situation is experimentally reproduced, the same reaction invariably follows.... Such a demonstration would not bring us a single step closer to the 'interpretation' of this reaction. By itself, such a demonstration would contribute nothing to the project of understanding 'why' this reaction occurred and, moreover, 'why' it invariably occurs in the same way (Bauman, 1978:70).

Interpretation is not validated by the assessment of probability, although repeated occurrences of a given act in a given setting might well aid in the work of interpretation itself.

Why is it not possible to test interpretive accounts by predicting outcomes? The success of prediction in the natural sciences rests on the fact that all states of the system (past and future) can be described using the same concepts. We do not suppose that a concept like "energy transfer" would somehow have no meaning in the physical world of the future. We can use it in our predictions about the future state of the physical world with confidence. In sociology this is not the case. "The very terms in which the future will have to be characterized if we are to understand it properly are not available to us at present" (Taylor, 1977:129). Future social worlds will produce new meanings (i.e. new realities) and we will need new concepts to describe that world.

The kind of prediction found in the natural sciences can therefore never be achieved in the social sciences. Human beings are reflexive. The data of sociology are the self-definitions of human beings, how they describe what they are doing. As these self-definitions change (frequently under the impact of sociology itself), social life changes, such that it has to be understood in different terms. For this reason, it is much easier to understand social life after the fact than predict its future course. "Human science is largely *ex post* understanding" (Taylor, 1977:129).

How is an *ex post* understanding validated? Idealist sociology is "hermeneutical"—concerned with "making sense" of social life in much the same way a scholar reads a text. In the physical sciences, skepticism about a theory might prompt a search for more facts—a recapitulation of the survey, a new and better experiment. In the social sciences, the rejection of an interpretation can only be countered by an appeal to understanding on the part of the skeptic. "The superiority of one position over another will thus consist in this, that from the more adequate position one can understand one's own stand and that of one's opponents, but not the other way around" (Taylor, 1977:127).

There is a further means of validating idealist theories which prevents their becoming merely the speculations of armchair sociologists. It is assumed that interpretations are adequate only if the sociologist is thereby better equipped to communicate with his subjects: "only when the observer and the actor ultimately come to talk about the actions and beliefs of the actor in the same way is it possible to claim that a correct account has been given" (Fay, 1975:82). If we impute intentions we must ascertain whether or not these were what the actor had in mind. If we invoke rules, we must be confident of our own ability to use those rules properly if placed in our subject's circumstances. Finally if we articulate constitutive meanings (which are usually taken for granted by our subjects), we must be sure that our subjects would agree that their actions could be understood in this way, to the extent that they would modify their own account of what they were doing if there were a discrepancy (Fay, 1975:82).

The research traditions described in Part Two reflect these ontological and epistemological commitments. They accentuate man's free will, agency, self-consciousness, and his ability to reinterpret and modify social arrangements. They refuse to treat as fixed and final the social constraints which shape the flow of social interaction. They pay close attention to what people actually think and how they actually behave. They avoid grand conceptual schemes, formal theories, and quantitative analyses. Theory is designed less to aid prediction and more to increase the self-understanding of all actors. There is less emphasis on testing preconceived theories and more upon the use of careful observation to generate theory. These approaches to sociology are committedly humanistic and interpretive—sociology is a dialogue, a conversation, as much as it is an experimental science.

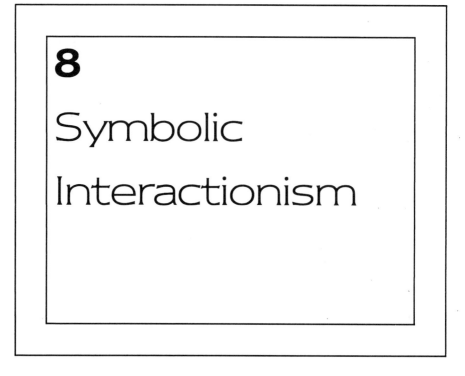

8

Symbolic Interactionism

The term "symbolic interactionism" was coined by Herbert Blumer in 1937. The label indicates precisely what is distinctive about this research tradition. It concerns itself with the process of social interaction itself rather than with its causes or consequences. And it focuses upon the way in which social interaction is shaped and guided by symbols. How we respond to the action of another depends on the relationship in which that action is embedded, and how we see and feel about it. A gesture will not be "an insult" unless we see it as symbolic of the intention to offend. And we make this interpretation only during the course of interaction with the other. The meaning of acts thus emerges during the process of social interaction.

Symbolic interaction is located within the metatheory I have called idealism. Society consists essentially of ideas. More precisely, society consists of ideas in action. Each social interaction is a meaningful encounter in which actors assign purposes and significance to each other's conduct and adjust the meaning they give off accordingly. The sociologist's task is to read and interpret these meaningful encounters.

THE FOUNDATIONS OF
SYMBOLIC INTERACTIONISM

Some of the most renowned pioneers of American sociology were responsible for laying the groundwork for symbolic interactionism. Charles Cooley (1864–1929) contributed the idea of "the looking glass self," extending William James's argument that a person's consciousness of himself as an object is partly a reflection of the ideas he thinks others have of him. William Thomas (1863–1947) is best remembered for his investigation of how people's conduct is shaped by their definition of the situation. Thomas criticized sociologists who ignored the process of interpretation through which the impressions of the natural and social worlds are filtered. He pointed out that, if men define situations as real, they are real in their consequences.

George Herbert Mead (1863–1931) was influenced by William James as well as other pragmatist philosophers like John Dewey. They taught him that the mind is not a passive spectator of the passing scene. Contrary to the impression conveyed by positivists, the mind is neither a ready-made product of nature (instinct) nor a blank sheet that passively receives the imprint of the natural and social environment (conditioning). Rather, the mind is an activity. "Minding" is a process of interaction between the individual and his social environment. On the basis of certain goals he has in mind, the individual deliberately selects the environmental stimulus to which he responds (Mead, 1934:11). The social world should not, therefore, be thought of as consisting of objects or stimuli which have fixed meaning or significance. Social objects change their meaning—and their consequences—according to our purposes. Our purposes, in turn, are shaped by our experiences. Thus the same "thing" (e.g. my present salary) can exist in the past, present, or future, in each case with a different meaning. Meaning is therefore a relationship between an individual and events in the environment: "existing meanings are utilized to interpret events and events are simultaneously utilized to evaluate the adequacy of meaning" (Lauer and Handel, 1977:17).

Mead's contribution to symbolic interactionism can be summarized in the form of three postulates. First, the world of reality becomes known to human beings only in the symbolic form in which it is perceived by them. Second, social reality changes as human beings develop new perceptions of it. Third, the world is objective, capable of resisting efforts to change it. Mead's contribution was to help overcome the dichotomy between thinking actor and social forces characteristic of positivism.

Blumer's (1969) programmatic statement of the principal tenets of symbolic interactionism closely follows Mead's ideas. First, social life is shaped by the human being's unique capacity to use symbols. Second, man is an agent, capable of spontaneous action. Third, social interaction is a continuous stream of action, a process with no natural beginning or end. This chapter will elucidate the meaning of these tenets, describe the kind of theorizing favored by symbolic interactionists, and comment on their contribution to sociology.

SYMBOLS

Symbolic Order and Social Order

The human world is inherently symbolic.

> Humans respond to a classified world, one whose salient features are named and placed into categories indicating their significance for behavior. In short, humans do not respond to the environment as physically given, but to an environment as it is mediated through symbols—to a symbolic environment (Stryker, 1978:326).

What does "mediated by symbols" mean? The act of symbolizing is creative. By symbolizing we reach out and impose a sense of unity and coherence on sensory inputs which are otherwise chaotic and formless. The imposition of form onto chaos is evident in all symbolic forms—in the language we speak, the stereotypes we use, and the art forms we find attractive.

Social order is equivalent to symbolic order. The patterns of social life are essentially symbolic patterns. Social order is an "all-embracing frame of reference in a society that its members know as social reality" (Scott, 1972:18). Symbolic interactionists are therefore just as interested as other sociologists in describing and accounting for social order. But they see this order as existing at the level of meaning rather than physical form.

Sociologists other than symbolic interactionists acknowledge that human beings use symbols. But in research traditions other than those included within the idealist world view, symbols are treated as if they were merely labels which people affix to a preconstituted reality. This is to assume that the reality to which symbols are attached already possess meaning. The actor has only to select the right label by which to tap this meaning and interaction will proceed smoothly. Idealist sociologists, as we have seen, do not subscribe to the notion that the actor who attaches the label and the labeled object are separable. They believe that symbols help create the objects of the social world. They are a means of constructing the world as well as a means of reflecting on it.

Mead believed that objects exist for us only because we attend to them. We turn our attention to and thus create social objects because we have certain plans. These intentions determine the meaning the object will have. An object is a pencil only if we plan to write with it: it becomes a missile if we throw it in anger. We also decide what an object means for other people by imagining what they intend to do with it. Included in the category of objects are ourselves. We imagine what we must mean to others by deciding how we fit into their plans. We might complain that they regard us as merely a "sex object," if sexual fulfillment is their primary aim.

Symbols include not only written and spoken languages but also symbols of appearance, such as gestures, clothes, body posture, and manners. Each kind of symbol is part of a code by which others can read our meaning. Each code provides a tool for people to ascertain our identity, to determine our significance for them (Stone, 1962:90).

We are not free to use symbols or symbolic codes in any way we choose, of course. Symbols are the product of social interaction. Their meaning is given to us by the way we see others using them. Our social existence and our purposes therefore shape the meaning objects have for us.

The Definition
of the Situation

The capacity of human beings to use symbols to impart a sense of order and coherence to their social world is most evident in the practice which William Thomas called "defining the situation." Thomas argued that, if men define situations as real, they will be real in their consequences. This was his way of saying that it is more important to know what people think is happening than it is to know what is really going on. People only can act on the basis of what they perceive. The panic which ensues when someone in a crowded theater jokingly shouts "Fire!" will have consequences just as tragic as if there were a real fire.

To most symbolic interactionists, examining how people define situations is more important than observing "non-situational factors" (Douglas, 1980:8). The definition of the situation is more than a simple description of what already exists. It is not merely a response to what is already "out there." Rather, the definition of the situation is an active process of reality construction in which people are authors of their own experiences and of the realities they inhabit" (Hewitt, 1976:117).

In what sense is the definition of the situation "an active process of reality construction"? First, situations seldom present themselves unambiguously. They "vary in the degree to which participants view them as clear, structured, known and unambiguous on the one hand, versus unclear, unstructured, unknown and ambiguous on the other" (Lofland, 1976:34). The actor must make sense of what is going on in the situation. This decision will be based on past experiences and plans for the future. A woman might refuse to acknowledge the words and gestures of a man which could have sexual connotations if she is intent on negotiating a business deal and concerned to see the situation as a business lunch.

Second, because the actor has to use a variety of resources of information to make sense of situations, variations in the information to hand will influence the definition of the situation. For example, we use information about roles to give meaning to situations. If we decide that the individuals in the group are students, then the situation must be a seminar. If we decide the individuals are devotees, then the situation must be a worship service. Often, we decide what is going on by first determining what roles are being played.

All those involved in a situation play some part in determining its meaning. However, their parts are not equal. "True, we personally negotiate aspects of all the arrangements under which we live, but often once these are negotiated, we continue on mechanically as though the matter had always been settled" (Goffman, 1974:2). We frequently decide what the definition of the situation ought to be on the basis of social rules we have learned. Our freedom to choose a definition is restricted by social convention. And occasionally, we will be obliged to act in such a way as to sustain a definition of the situation we have not chosen and do not particularly like. Many settings are staged by others in order to control our actions. The pomp and ceremony of a courtroom is intended to establish the seriousness and consequentiality of the proceedings. In mental hospitals, the definition of the situation is almost entirely in the hands of the custodians. Nevertheless, while there are many occasions on which we have to acquiesce to a definition of the situation others have made, it remains true that we must either agree or disagree with this definition. Otherwise our behavior would be meaningless to the others involved.

The role played by the definition of the situation in shaping conduct is the focus of much of the research conducted by symbolic interactionists. They are concerned to show that definitions emerge out of the purposes of the people involved and to demonstrate that the definition, once made, affects social conduct. Cavan (1966) found that San Francisco bars have a variety of meanings depending on the purposes to which their customers put them. "Convenience" bars are used simply for getting a drink: they are treated much like public washrooms. A "nightspot" is primarily a place for watching entertainment. A "marketplace" bar is used chiefly for the exchange of commodities such as illicit drugs. And a "Home territory" bar functions like a social club, catering to a regular clientele. Each bar will have its own symbolic code consisting of decor, lighting, seating arrangement, body postures, and interaction pattern of customers. Cavan discovered that interaction between customers differed according to how a bar is defined. She points out that most of us "read" a bar before we enter it in order to see what kind of situation we are entering.

Learning how to read and adjust to situations is an important part of early socialization. Children must acquire this capability in order to "fit in" (Fine, 1981:269). As they move through life and mature, they learn new roles and acquire greater role flexibility. But the ability to make situational determinations must also grow. People regard situational information as of equal importance to role information. They will be disturbed if their attribution of role and definition of the situation do not match. If this occurs, they are as likely to change their mind about roles as they are about situations. Police officers have a keen sense of what kinds of roles are being played in what kinds of situations. Any person whose apparent role does not fit the situation in which he or she is spotted is likely to have that role "checked out" (Goffman, 1971:241).

The definition of the situation is important to the actor because it tells him what "vocabulary" he should use to describe and make intelligible other people's actions, and how he should describe his actions to them. Each setting has its own vocabulary, consisting of both verbal and visual symbols, not only language but objects, clothes, and gestures as well. Ball (1972:130) shows how illegal abortion clinics contain their own "rhetoric," which functions to enhance parallels with conventional medicine and make it easier for the client to see herself in the role of "patient" rather than in the role of criminal conspirator.

Each setting also contains its own phraseology for interpreting conduct. Appropriate reasons for action are stipulated by the setting. Thus motives will vary according to the definition of the situation. Marijuana smokers are likely to offer an *excuse* for their conduct in the parental home but more likely to provide a *justification* to skeptical friends in the street. They might tell their parents that their smoking results from the pressure of peers but they tell their friends that they smoke "just to get through the day."

Motives are treated by symbolic interactionists as part of a situation's vocabulary. A motive is a situationally specific "justification for present, future or past programs or acts" (Mills, 1978:303). Motives are not thought of as causes of action. They are not forces that impel behavior. In assigning a motive to an action, the actor is not merely describing what she did or ascribing an antecedent cause. She is creating a new act. Thus we should "not treat an action as discrepant from 'its' verbalization, for in many cases, the verbalization is a new act" (Mills, 1978:304). What we say we are doing and what we do continually interact during the course of the encounter (Deutscher, 1973). Someone accused of violating a law is not automatically subject to control and punishment, because the reality of what she has done can change during the course of an encounter. All kinds of remedial actions are open to her. By giving an "account" she can show that she either did not commit the offense or did so blindly; by "apologizing" she can disavow the person she was; by making a "request" she can transform the act from an offense into a favor (Goffman, 1971:350). As the act is redescribed it becomes something different.

AGENCY

Reflexivity

Symbolic interactionists assume that humans are creative, innovative agents. They are reflexive, capable of standing back and reflecting on the social forces in the environment which impinge upon them. They comment on their own actions and comment on their commenting (Goffman, 1971:341). They are therefore self-aware in ways which make the rather passive imagery fostered by positivist sociology unrealistic (Lofland, 1976:41).

Mead located the basis of reflexivity in the human being's unique capacity to use symbols. This capacity makes it possible for us to stand outside our stream of consciousness and reflect upon our behavior. The maturation of the human individual consists in large part of acquiring this reflexivity. At first a child does not differentiate itself from its mother and its actions are simply imitative. In the subsequent "play stage" the child begins to play at being mother and, from that standpoint, becomes capable of treating itself as an object, as its mother would see it. In the "game stage" the child is able to assume a number of roles simultaneously (i.e. all the other players in the game). He learns that he must take into account the collective wishes of the group. Later still, the child learns that collective wishes become institutionalized in the form of abstract rules, the rules of the game. These rules, and the group consensus on which they stand, enable the child to view himself from a consistent standpoint and to acquire a stable definition of himself, to the point where he can carry the same self from one game (or situation) to another. He thus acquires a unique but socially formed personal identity.

The Self

The self is not a thing. It is not a fixed attribute of a person. The self is a process, a constant movement between two analytically distinct phases. The first phase of the self Mead called "the I." It is the impulsive phase of the self, the spontaneous and unpredictable aspect all individuals possess. The "I" is not experienced directly because it is part of the stream of consciousness. When we reflect, we stand outside the stream of consciousness to make sense of our action and plan for the future. The second phase of the self has already begun. At the moment of reflection, the "I" is already doing something else and the "me" has begun to consider how the "I" will be received by others. The "me" is the product of the inferred attitudes of other people. The individual puts herself in the position of others to see how they would view what the "I" has done. The "I" and the "me" are continually adjusting to each other. The "I," spontaneous and creative, is constrained to some degree by the "me." "The attitudes of others constitute the organized me, and then one reacts toward that as an "I" (Mead, 1934:175). The "me" responds to the prodding of the "I." As Goffman (1971:185) puts it, "the individual does not go about merely going about his business."

The "me" phase of the self is the product of the generalized other. This is the individual's perception of the general expectations of the group to which he belongs as to the behavior expected of him. Mead coined another term, "the significant other," to describe those people with whom the individual interacts who are particularly important to his socialization.

> What the individual is for himself is not something that he invented. It is what his significant others have come to see he should be, what they have come to treat him as being, and what, in consequence, he must treat himself as being if he is to deal with their dealings with him (Goffman, 1971:279).

A boy's father is especially significant for his identity as a son. The strength of his self-concept, "son," is a function of the extent to which his father defines him as a son.

Each of us, then, has a sense of self, of who we are. This self-attitude provides an initial behavior tendency in any situation. Manford Kuhn (1954) attempted to measure individuals' self-concept by means of a Twenty Statements Test, in which subjects were asked to provide twenty answers to the question "Who Am I?" and to write their answers in the order they occurred to them. Kuhn found that most people identify themselves primarily in terms of social categories—their sex, age, race, religion, occupation, family role, and social group membership. Subsequent research has shown that self-concept does have a strong association with the judgements others make of us (Charon, 1979:75). If we think others think well of us we tend to think well of ourselves (Rosenberg, 1981:597). And we tend to act in ways consistent with our self-concept: in school, the higher our conception of our abilities, the better we tend to perform (Shibutani, 1961:260).

Turner (1968:94) acknowledges the existence of a self-concept, but he sees this as relatively fixed, while a "self-image" tends to vary from one situation to another. We modify our self-image according to the situation. We therefore have many self-images, not all of them consistent. Our self-concept, on the other hand, does not form and dissolve with each encounter. This is "the real me." It becomes so fixed that we are inclined to excuse our actions by saying "that's just the way I am." We are likely to be thought vain if we have a weak self-concept in relation to our self-image, if we change our self with each new encounter. The self-concept testifies to the power of society; the self-image testifies to the autonomy of the individual.

By making conceptual distinctions such as these, symbolic interactionists create logical space between the socially determined "official self" and the actual performing self. The official self is "at once coherently unified and appropriate for the occasion" (Goffman, 1967:105). It is institutionally defined. Underlying this official self is a self capable of distancing itself from the demands of institutions. We have our own "personal standards" we will not allow other people to violate in the demands they make on us.

Self-Presentation

The self is not simply "present" but must be presented to others. Self-presentation is "a performance." The impressions we give others must be managed. In an illegal abortion clinic, patrons and staff engage in mutual "face work" as they help in the presentation of selves. This self-presentation is intended to downplay the disrespectability of the encounter and highlight themes such as hygiene and decorum. "Patrons cooperated with staff by evading or ignoring information in contradistinction to the medical model that the staff emulated; similarly, the staff treated the patrons 'as if' they were persons with, or with persons with, a legitimate medical complaint seeking a conventional, legal course of treatment for their dilemma" (Ball, 1972:179).

Once we become sociologically aware of the significance of self-presentation in the maintenance of orderly social interaction, the kind of role analysis described in earlier chapters begins to seem inadequate. We recognize that people do not passively respond to roles imposed on them by the social structure. Even physical characteristics undergo interpretation. People defined "officially" as physically handicapped do not passively conform to this categorization. They play an active role in "becoming" physically handicapped by presenting a self which meets their needs. They have the freedom to decide how much of their identity is to be caught up in this "official self." They can work at presenting a different real self which fits more comfortably with their self-conception. They can manage the impression that their handicap is only temporary or, if permanent, that it has brought with it compensations. "What one becomes is determined not only by others but also by the self" (Levitan, 1975).

PROCESS

Social interaction is a continuous process, without clear beginning or end. Each episode of interaction, each act, is temporary, continually in a state of becoming something else (Stryker, 1980:125). All talk of social action as a sequence of cause and effect must therefore be avoided. Social action is not an outcome or consequence of prior actions. Thus, present actions are not caused by prior roles or norms. Roles and norms are not things which determine our behavior; they are processes.

Roles

How is it possible to conceive of a role as a process rather than a thing? First, instead of simply assuming that people occupy roles, we examine the degree of roleness of an encounter (Weinstein and Tanur, 1978:142). We treat roles not as positions people must fill in order to be social but as a set of expectations or understandings which they can invoke, ignore, manage, or change. The expectations which comprise a role are more or less clearly articulated, more or less forcefully imposed on us by others, more or less abstract. Rather than imagining that the actor "puts on" a ready-made role, we can think of the actor using a role, choosing which aspect of the role to accentuate, how closely to identify himself with it, and so on.

Second, we see role as process if we shift our attention away from "maps" of roles (as if they were different locations) and begin to think about roles as typifications. Roles are nothing but "socially shared, abstract categories of 'types of persons' that humans employ in organizing their dealings with one another and with themselves" (Lofland, 1976:174). If we think of roles as typifications, we have to acknowledge that role behavior is nothing more than "a basic tendency for actors to behave *as if* there were roles" (Turner, 1962:22). Thus we speak of someone performing a role if there is some theme or consistent line of action toward others in their conduct. This line of action can wax and wane in strength and clarity. We will not always be sure whether it is consistent or not. The role seems to come and go.

Third, role is process if we recognize that people help create the very role we think is "governing" their conduct. People create roles as they search out the line or theme in others' actions and as they try to convey a sense of consistency in their own actions. For example, a part of the physician's role is "detached concern." But conduct which meets this criterion is not obvious, especially in a crisis. Both physician and patient must work at establishing what acting with detached concern means.

Role creation is evident in the way roles are continually being revised during the course of interaction episodes. Shame occurs when we are forced, as part of our attempt to take the role of the other, to see that other people do not accept us for the role-players we claim to be. We will be embarrassed if we become confused about the roles being played (Shott, 1979:1325).

Fourth, role is process if we recognize that we do not merely respond to the role expectations others impose on us. We actively engage in creating those expectations. We try to ensure that a desired role is made for us by others. We "coach" or educate others in the performance of a role which will be satisfying for us (Stryker, 1980:63). This, again, is one of the social skills all humans must learn (Fine, 1981:261). This ability to "altercast" depends a lot on a person's power. It is more important for the subordinate to act according to the desires and orientations of the power-holder than *vice versa* (Thomas et al., 1972:606). Whites find it easier to altercast blacks than *vice versa.*

This treatment of roles as process is clearly illustrated in the symbolic interactionists' approach to deviance. The role of the deviant is treated as a process. Deviance is not a personality predisposition, nor is it the outcome of antecedent social factors. Deviance is built up during the course of social interaction. A marijuana smoker gradually becomes deviant in a process during the course of which the meaning of the drug changes, as does the meaning of the feelings it generates and the image of one's fellow smokers. From the symbolic interactionist's standpoint, people do not become marijuana smokers because social forces impel them. Only those exposed to the drug become users, and of these, only those who learn to smoke marijuana properly continue to use it, and of these, only those who come to appreciate being high think of themselves as marijuana users (Becker, 1953:242).

Deviant roles are not, therefore, simply "occupied." The individual has to define herself as deviant. She has to manage her role as an abnormal person. This requires training. Conversely, she can deny the deviant label. Elderly people protect themselves from the stigma associated with aging by various processes of "deviance disavowal." They suppress information about their age, they avoid situations in which age is likely to be a disadvantage, and they draw parallels between their own behavior and the same behavior among younger people (Matthews, 1978).

Structures

Symbolic interactionists treat clusters of roles (e.g. kinship networks, occupational structures) as processes. They assume that social structures continually change. It is impossible to define what structure is "without taking into consideration the temporal dimension and the kinds of objects and activities for which a given structure is a 'structure'" (Maines, 1977:249).

To some extent, structure is always invisible. By defining the performance of specific roles in a specific setting we are usually implying the larger structure of which that interaction is an expression.

> By defining role relationships during an interaction we are typically defining obligations that must be fulfilled at other times and in other situations, often when we will not be present. For example, in reaching

an agreement with a repair person we will be concerned with his or her performance in actually doing the repairs as well as with how he or she acts during the interaction with us (Lauer and Handel, 1977:121).

However, this structure does not "precede" and determine action. The structure is "achieved in and through interaction" (Blumer, 1975:60). Structures simply refer to "persons redirecting their actions into those activities which support and reproduce ... routines" (Glassner, 1980:12). For these reasons, symbolic interactionists prefer to call the coordination of lines of action "organizing action" while other sociologists refer to it as "the organization of action."

Social structure might have the appearance of fixity and rigidity, but it is actually a set of tacit and usually fragile agreements to cooperate which actors have worked out (and continue to work out) in a continuous process of negotiation (Strauss, 1978). Where structure is conceived as a continuous process of negotiation, studying structure will involve getting to know this process as it happens. It means finding out what it is like to work in this factory, to be a student in this school, or a patient in that hospital. Seen from the point of view of the actor, social structure assumes "a much looser and less determinative character" (Maines, 1981:472). Thus an organization's written rules and regulations do not constitute its structure but a resource for negotiating that structure. They "provide guidelines for interaction, but they do not control the interaction itself: they are topics for negotiation" (Fine, 1981:263). Such rules are neither consistent nor final. They are points of negotiation between actors, to be ignored or reinterpreted according to the organizational needs and specific interests of those involved in their implementation (Gusfield, 1981:160). Rules make things possible, but we use them rather than obey them. Simple rules governing when to begin and end work provide the basis for often tacit negotiations about when work time actually begins and ends. Whether or not putting away tools, clearing up the desk, or washing up are included in work time is negotiated in daily bargaining sessions. Organizations comprise a host of such sessions.

The relations of the organization to its environment are no more fixed and rigid than the social relations within it. An organization, like a person, must negotiate a suitable relationship with the outside world.

> The appearance of complying with the rules has a similar effect on organizational survival as the adequate protection of self in everyday life has on social survival. In both cases (individual and organizational) fronts are erected to legitimate selves and action irrespective of what one really thinks or feels and irrespective of what the organization really is or is not doing (Altheide and Johnson, 1980:38).

The boundaries, purposes, and identity of an organization are thus constructed during the course of interaction. Many modern organizations, including police departments, the armed forces, business corporations, universities, and government agencies, routinely deploy information for the purposes of constructing a public front with which to conceal unappealing "backstage" operations.

Social movement organizations must also present an acceptable image to the public in order to be recognized as a genuine political body. The growth of social movements is a continuous interaction between protestors and those who oppose them. "Each action provokes a counter-reaction, which in turn produces a modified situation—a new basis from which decisions regarding subsequent action must be taken" (Schur, 1980:199). Changing perceptions and social definitions will prove crucial in this interaction. "Protest organizers must actively seek to influence conceptions regarding the nature of the 'problem', the justness of the cause, the necessity of their tactics, and the consistency of the movement's own priorities" (Schur, 1980:212). The movement, like an individual, seeks to establish an acceptable identity, but is not free to create any identity it chooses.

When writing about structures, symbolic interactionists are extremely wary about using concepts like "society" or "the state." They believe that such concepts exaggerate the degree of coordination and consensus in society and convey a deterministic image of social life. They maintain that social institutions must always be described from the point of view of the actors involved, and these actors rarely think of their life in such abstract terms. In studying city life, for example, they would avoid much of the conceptual language of ecology and urban sociology. They would prefer to know what various images of the city were prevalent: how are the various symbols of city life learned and used, and what effect do they have on social action?

Symbolic interactionists are not uninterested in macro-social processes. They are interested in public as well as private realities.

> A 'crime wave' is not a matter of personal, private experience. What is happening to 'the community' or 'society' enters into the assessment of the person about the public experience. What is true about society is more than a reflection of individual experiences; it is also a set of beliefs about the aggregated experiences of others (Gusfield, 1981:52).

Thus, although most of their work focuses on face-to-face interactions, symbolic interactionists believe that their research tradition is useful at the macro-level.

In the case of a pattern of behavior like racial conflict, structural forces (e.g. economic competition) are not considered sufficient to account for what actually happens. Race relations are interactions between groups of people in which one racial group, in defining another racial group, defines itself. The manner in which the people of one group consistently treat those in another will depend largely on the estimate placed on that group. Various groups will be ranked and opposed. Each social encounter and each social circumstance will encourage typical orientations to out-group members. Race relations are but another manifestation of the general rule that people interact on the basis of assumptions they form about each other (Shibutani and Kwan, 1965:96).

Thinking of race relations simply as the interplay of structural forces impoverishes our understanding. The argument that black migration into formerly all-white neighborhoods causes the flight of whites can be supported statistically. But what do we learn about social interaction from these statistics? We learn nothing of the meaning whites assign to the influx of blacks and even less about the process of interaction itself. We see only the beginning and the end of the process and not the actual sequence of action which connects black in-migration, perceived threat to property values, and flight response.

In the symbolic interactionist's view, it is a truism to state that patterns of behavior—social structure—are shaped by other patterns of behavior and that these patterns shape individual conduct. Their unit of analysis is interactional, not structural: "we must understand action before we can methodologically be said to have observed institutions" (McHugh, 1968:11).

The subject matter of symbolic interactionism is individuals "managing co-presence." "Matters of structure and process, on the one hand, and causes and consequences on the other, are decidedly background and enter only to the degree they bear on the qualitative, strategic thrust of immediate concern" (Lofland, 1976:47). It is the micro-processes of encounters which attract the attention of most symbolic interactionists:... "Drugstore purchases, hallway conversations, job interviews, baseball batting, radio and TV broadcasts, doorstep sales pitches, public place entrances, waiting in public places, single meetings of college classes or laboratories, sports events, Nazi rallies, and evenings out" (Lofland, 1976:28). This concern with "the small crises of the moment" is more apparent than a concern with the world crises of international conflict and economic exploitation (Becker, 1981:310).

THEORY BUILDING

Some symbolic interactionists regard their work as but an adjunct to more positivist sociology, a kind of prefatory stage of interpretation before the more formal work of hypothesis testing begins (Stryker, 1980). However, the majority of symbolic interactionists follow Blumer (1975:62) in claiming that symbolic interactionism is better suited to understanding social life than any version of positivist sociology. And, indeed, it is true that "no major sociological paradigm is so little influenced by the natural sciences as a model for the study of society" (Adler and Adler, 1980:20).

Symbolic interactionists believe that the positivist approach to sociological explanation, with its reliance on deductive logic and its use of variable analysis, distorts social reality. Voting, which is frequently studied positivistically, is conceptualized in terms of the interaction of variable factors. "Voter turnout" might be correlated with "income level." In this process, the act of voting is singled out and standardized for the purposes of quantification. But voting "is not an abstract isolated piece of behavior that can be dissected from life and examined separately, but is something that takes place in real situations, interspersed with other acts and conduct that may well have different meanings to different voters" (Hewitt, 1976:236). Voting has meaning only in the context of other actions. It is not possible to interpret this act outside of this context nor read its meaning in aggregate data. The tabulation of data into frequency distributions not only hides meaning, it also obscures the process of interaction that takes place in actual social circumstances. It destroys any sense we might have of the relationship of action to its practical concerns. "The correlation of discrete variables does not reveal the interactional activity between people that produces the social structure that discrete variables presumably index" (Mehan, 1979:8).

Symbolic interactionists reject both deductive and inductive methods of theory construction. Neither manages to sustain "a continuing interaction between guiding ideas and empirical observation" (Blumer, 1977:286). Stating theory in propositional form tends to "freeze" it: concepts and propositions cannot be modified as the research proceeds. Inductive "head counting" (in the hope that generalizations will suggest themselves) encourages us to treat the "facts" too seriously. These "facts," however, must be treated as if they were social constructions. The facts we are provided with in official statistics, for example, "are not records of individual events but are rather aggregates of data, amassed and presented" by officials and their organizations. "Fact gathering" is actually a process of social organization. In every stage of the recording, aggregating, analyzing, and transmission of statistical data, human choices of selection and interpretation operate (Gusfield, 1981:37).

Symbolic interactionists accordingly regard the relation between theory and fact as a process. Theorizing begins with a question which has been raised with regard to the empirical world, "and seeks through persistent and flexible examination of that world to progressively clarify the problem and to progressively cut out and refine the empirical data that are relevant to the problem" (Blumer, 1975:62).

How are data "progressively cut out and refined"? This is accomplished largely through the use of types or forms. A type or a form is an abstraction from a situation or sequence of interaction which describes only part of what is going on. The form describes that part which is relatively enduring. It provides the sociologist with a generalized grasp of what is taking place.

The writings of symbolic interactionists abound with forms abstracted from observed human behavior. We find types of "accounts" people give to justify what they are doing, types of "territories" people occupy in social space, types of "readings" people make as they enter strange situations, types of "recruitment strategies" used by religious sects, and many others. These forms proliferate in bewildering fashion, with little sense of accumulation or consistency (Lofland, 1980; Manning, 1976). In only a few pages of *The Presentation of Self in Everyday Life,* one of the most popular and influential symbolic interactionist works, Goffman describes three types of "face," four consequences of being "out of face," two kinds of "face work," five kinds of "avoidance processes," three kinds of "corrective processes," and five ways of making an "offering." These types seem not to be aimed at deriving discrete and finite classification schemes, which is the purpose of positivist typologies. Symbolic interactionists are more interested in staying "close to the data" and letting their material dictate their categories than with formulating exhaustive and complete classification schemes (Lofland, 1980:31).

Finding social forms requires a methodology which is neither deductive nor inductive. Forms will not be made clearer by the multiplication of cases nor the analysis of covariances. Forms will not be indexed by frequency distributions. Forms of "managing" deviant identities are seldom recorded or officially recognized and cannot be reduced to matters of quantity. Multiplying the number of cases we observe or trying to ensure the representativeness of our sample will not improve our understanding of these forms.

The analytical usefulness of forms depends on how well they draw interactional similarities between seemingly disparate social situations. Goffman (1971:80) talks about saying "hello" as but one instance of the more general form of "access rituals." These access rituals are ways in which individuals regulate access to self-territory. In order to make these generalizations, the symbolic interactionist must think comparatively. In their study of terminally ill hospital patients, Glaser and Strauss (1965) differentiated between patients according to who knew that they were dying. In some cases both the doctor and the patient knew and were open about it; in other cases, the doctor but not the patient knew; other cases were found where both suspected the patient was dying but neither would admit it to the other. During the course of thinking about these various types, Glaser and Strauss realized that nearly all social relations are like this. They all have an "awareness context" about the true identities of the people involved. Some contexts are open, some closed, some filled with suspicion, and some based on pretense. Filtering our perceptions through this conceptual scheme might help us understand not only terminally ill patients but used car salesmen, couples on a date, or students taking an exam as well.

The most fruitful form of comparison in symbolic interactionism allows the content of the interaction to vary in order to permit the form to emerge. We could observe different settings (e.g. customer interaction in different bars), different times (e.g. husband and wife interaction on different days), different organizations (e.g. patient-doctor relations in different hospitals), or different encounters (e.g. body posture in interviews, on dates, and at work). An example drawn from Glaser and Strauss (1967:106–107) will illustrate this "controlled comparison" at work.

Glaser and Strauss begin their analysis with a set of real-life problems. How do nurses handle the death of their patients? What variations are there in the way in which dying patients are treated? What accounts for this variation? Nurses tend to think of a patient's death in terms of "social loss." This is the nurses' appraisal of the degree of loss that their patients' death would be to their family, their profession, and to society at large. Some patients were defined as great social losses ("She was to be a doctor") while the death of others was discounted ("He had a full life").

Glaser and Strauss begin to build on this notion of social loss by noting all incidents in which nurses respond to the potential social loss of a patient, constantly comparing one incident with another. They begin to entertain the possibility that there are different types of social loss, to speculate whether there are specific conditions under which a death might be classified as this or that type of loss, and to investigate the consequences for patient treatment of the classification. They notice that high social-loss patients receive better treatment.

Progressing to more abstract levels of conceptualization, Glaser and Strauss (1967:115) formulate a "discussional theory" which sets patient treatment within its larger context: the specific treatment setting (cancer ward), the relations nurses have other than those to the patient (e.g. physician, other nurses, family), the organizational structure (e.g. hospital rules and regulations), and the cultural milieu (e.g. values associated with death and dying). The form "social loss" has thus been abstracted in such a way that it can be used to help observations in a variety of social settings, but its precise meaning in the case of the treatment of the terminally ill is given by its location within a broader context of meaning. The symbolic interactionist thus pursues the strategy of generalization outlined in Chapter Seven.

CONCEPTS

Each research tradition will formulate its own concepts and its method of generating and means of assessing the utility of concepts. We have seen that idealists and positivists differ in their epistemology of sociological concepts. Idealists are reluctant to employ abstract conceptual schemes derived from a few logical options. They are committed to the view that the reality with which sociologists deal has a preconstituted meaning. Sociological concepts must capture this meaning. Therefore it is important to adhere as closely as possible to the language of everyday actors in formulating sociological languages. In categorizing cabdrivers' strategies for extracting tips from passengers, Davis (1959) remains very close to the categories used by cabdrivers themselves. He distinguishes

> Fumbling in the making of change
> Giving the passengers a hard luck story
> Making fictitious charges for service
> Providing a concerted show of fast, fancy driving
> Displaying extraordinary courtesy

Davis thus describes in somewhat more generalized terms categories of action which each cabdriver could easily recognize. In the process, however, he is suggesting that these strategies represent forms of social interaction. With only slight changes of content (e.g. cutting hair rather than driving a cab) the same forms could probably be detected.

The concepts of symbolic interaction resemble but are not the same as the concepts of everyday language. Concepts like "social loss," "face work," and "awareness contexts" are sociological. They are unlikely to be used in everyday speech. They are second order constructs, having been built upon the constructs (or concepts) already in use in everyday speech. Instead of "gay," the sociologist might use the term "homosexual" or even "deviant," in each case trying to make more general controlled comparisons. However, he would want never to forget that it is not he but his subjects who decide what is gay, homsexual, or deviant. If the first difference between sociological and common-sense concepts is their self-conscious generality, the second is their self-conscious usage. The sociologist makes greater efforts than does the layman to make use of his concepts consistently, to establish a common understanding as to their precise meaning. He will also be sensitive to how much they help him understand other people's worlds, and he will reject them if they impede this understanding. His use of concepts as tools is therefore much more self-conscious.

COMMENTS

SYMBOLIC INTERACTIONISM AND SOCIAL STRUCTURE

The most common criticism of symbolic interactionism is that it is a micro-sociology which concerns itself only with the ephemera of social life. Symbolic interactionists seem to be much more interested in how workers in massage parlors treat their customers than in the broader issues of economic and political conflicts (McNall and Johnson, 1975:62). Gouldner's (1970:379) comment on Goffman's work could be extended without injustice to symbolic interactionism in general. "It is a social theory which tends to dwell upon the episodic and sees life only as it is lived in a narrow interpersonal circumference, ahistorical and noninstitutional, an existence beyond history and society, and one which comes alive in the fluid, transient 'encounter'." Alluding to Goffman's preoccupation with "impression management," Zeitlin (1973:196) asks if there is "not more at stake in everyday life than merely avoiding embarrassment and 'off-key' performances." And it is certainly true that symbolic interactionists have concentrated almost exclusively on "the intended effects of actors on the decisions of other actors," seemingly uninterested in the interplay of social structures which is often hidden from view (Kanter, 1972:78).

We do not have far to look for the reasons for this reluctance to deal with social structures. They are to be found in the very qualities which make symbolic interactionism so appealing to its practitioners. First, in reminding us of the meaningfulness of social interaction, symbolic interactionists imply that orderly social relationships arise exclusively out of the mutual accommodation of the individuals concerned. Social order is the result of "individuals fitting their lines of action together" (Blumer, 1969:7). The macro-phenomena of social life—the division of labor in society, patterns of economic inequality—are portrayed as the result of actors pursuing their individual aims and purposes. Social structure is thereby relegated to being a shadowy outcome of individual decisions. The reasons that actors have various purposes and are unequally endowed with the resources to fulfill them are not investigated. Something like labor-management wage negotiations thus receive rather impoverished treatment. Impression management is part of these negotiations, true enough, but an analysis which ignores the fact that the participants' legitimacy, their resources, and the constraints under which they bargain (e.g. labor laws) are predetermined by the social structure, will be inadequate (Weinstein and Tanur, 1978:140).

Symbolic interactionists probably grant too much autonomy to the individual. Roles are said to shape individual behavior only in the sense of being options or tools for optional use. This rules out the possibility that an individual's actions are grounded in norms which have been thoroughly internalized, so that what he *wants* to do is also what he *ought* to do. This does not necessitate a more functionalist model of man. George Herbert Mead, after all, believed that individual conduct would be shaped in part by the generalized other, which is nothing other than the internalization of the expectations of others (Lewis and Smith, 1980:174).

Granting too much autonomy to the individual is one reason why symbolic interactionists deal inadequately with social structure. A second reason is their tendency to adopt a position of extreme idealism. The more importance sociologists attach to people's ideas about their world, the greater their temptation to write as if there are as many different worlds as there are ideas of it. It then becomes possible to assert that the social organization, of which a number of people might be members, is not a single, fixed entity because each of them, arranging their perspective on the organization in a slightly different fashion, will create a different organization. "In a sense ... there are as many versions of an entity as there are people to construe it" (Rock, 1979:132). This argument can easily lead us to the conclusion that there is no such thing as *the* organization.

This kind of argument is surely too idealistic to be a realistic view of social life. Social organizations can and do impose meanings on their members. And even if individuals see the organization differently, it is because they occupy different positions within it. In other words, their perceptions have been structurally determined (Glassner, 1980:18).

A third reason why dealing with social structure is difficult for symbolic interactionists is that the more stress placed on the idea that social action is process, the more difficult it becomes to account for structural change. If we look at the social order as being continually renegotiated, always being constructed anew, we lose sight altogether of the fact that certain things in social life change only slowly. Processes may not be at all significant compared with the fixity of structures. "They may just be shifting around the same goods among the same set of players, providing the illusion of change while more general conditions remain the same" (Kanter, 1972:85).

SYMBOLIC INTERACTIONISM AND POWER

Another common criticism of symbolic interactionism is that it misrepresents the basis of social order. Chiefly, it tends to overestimate the extent to which social order rests on negotiation and underestimate the extent to which it is based on domination. Charon's (1979:156) definition of society clearly rests on the assumption that the existence of social order depends on consensus rather than coercion. "Society is people acting in situations cooperatively, either through working together for common goals, or through helping one another achieve individual goals, or both."

This image of society exaggerates the degree to which role playing and mutual understanding are necessary for social order. It also exaggerates the extent to which people know their true selves and are able to make themselves intelligible to others. "Our social life is only a deformed and rudimentary one: we are fragmented, alienated, mutually isolated from each other and ourselves" (Lichtman, 1970:80).

Symbolic interactionists are not ignorant of the fact that power influences role playing. However, for a number of reasons, their treatment of power is less than satisfactory. First, the distribution of power is assumed rather than explained. "Given that the social world is massively determined in a hierarchical fashion and thoroughly divided into superordinates and subordinates, attention turns reasonably to how encounters are handled between subordinates and superordinates" (Lofland, 1976:108). Other sociologists do not see this as so reasonable. Looking at how power is used rather than why it exists in the first place is a misplacement of priorities.

A second problem with the symbolic interactionists' treatment of power is that it is conceptualized as an attribute of individuals. "Power is reduced to one-upmanship, conflict to keeping one's cool, political domination to personal embarrassment" (Dawe, 73:248). Power is thus trivialized. Third, power is treated by symbolic interactionists as an idea. But symbolic manipulation—threats, ceremony, drama—is not the only and perhaps not the most effective form power can take. "Power is also involved in the use of force, the bringing to bear of great financial resources, the withholding of resources and decisions, or the invoking of legitimized authority to control others" (Kanter, 1972:86). While it is true that the exercise of power often involves symbolic manipulation (e.g. dress, display, rhetoric), this power rests upon a more material base.

Fourth, power tends to be neglected by symbolic interactionists because they emphasize the fragility of social structures. It is ironic that, in stressing the power of the individual to manipulate and redefine social relations, the symbolic interactionists are led to neglect the real exercise of power. A fragile social order would be fragile to powerful and powerless alike. It would always be open to renegotiation. But many social issues are non-negotiable. Powerful groups can remove certain issues from the bargaining table.

During the 1960s, symbolic interactionists did begin to pay closer attention to the manner in which definitions of the situation are shaped by power differences in society. Power was recognized as determining the designation and treatment of deviants and as playing a part in determining the ability of certain groups to avoid stigmas which others were trying to impose on them (Schur, 1980:175). Symbolic interactionists became much more aware of the political aspect of deviance. It was obvious that politically powerful actors could punish the violation of those rules most important to them and ignore violations of rules of lesser importance (Becker, 63:18). However, recognizing the role played by powerful actors in defining social problems and their solution is not the same as explaining how those actors gain power and why they have the interests they do.

SYMBOLIC INTERACTIONISM
AND EXPLANATION

Symbolic interactionism is not itself a theory but a research tradition. But do the theories spawned by it conform to conventional models of explanatory theory? Does symbolic interactionism make possible an empirical science of society?

From a positivist standpoint, symbolic interactionist accounts of social life are not real explanations. Instead of asking why things happen they are more likely to ask how things happen. "Whatever it is that people feel they want, need, are striving for, are coping with, how do they do it?" (Lofland, 1976:1). While a positivist might ask why an individual commits a deviant act, a symbolic interactionist is more likely to ask how the person acts deviantly. Rather than asking why a person is prejudiced, he might ask how a person prejudices (Glassner, 1980:93).

Symbolic interactionists want to be able to describe how social interaction is "brought off." They provide descriptions of how arrests are made, how religious conversions happen, how terminally ill patients are treated, how abortions are performed, how the passage through medical school is accomplished, how confidence tricks are pulled off, how physical handicaps are dealt with, how embarrassment is overcome, and so on. The way people do things is more important than what they do: "the manner, style, and nuance 'laid over,' 'on' or 'around' the sheer what of their doing" (Lofland, 1976:55).

To many sociologists less convinced by idealist principles, this heavy emphasis on "reading" what is happening, often with the help of an elaborate metaphor (e.g. life is a stage play), resembles more closely the work of a literary critic than that of an empirical scientist. This kind of interpretive thinking must be the starting, but not the stopping point of sociological analysis. It ought to lead to a more formal statement of propositions using unambiguous and consistent concepts. By these criteria, all symbolic interactionist theories are deficient. Not only do they rest on many untested assumptions (e.g. about our ability to take the role of the other), they also multiply new concepts with every new study with little sense of parsimony or cumulation (Burr et al., 1979).

CONCLUSION

In common with other research traditions, symbolic interactionism contains a variety of sociological approaches: "the methodological stances of symbolic interactionists range from a thoroughgoing rejection of the ordinary conventions of science as commonly understood to a complete acceptance of these" (Stryker, 1981:3). The kinds of criticism with which I have concluded this chapter tend to have their greatest impact on those symbolic interactionists whose training and predilections are closest to positivism. Other symbolic interactionists reject the holistic assumptions which seem to inform these criticisms. They reassert their idealism to argue that, for all its appearance of facticity, "society" and the larger structures it contains are nothing but "an imaginative construction which is built up inferentially" (Rock, 1979:226). The workings of society do not represent naturelike forces at work but the workings of its interpreters' minds.

The argument that social life must be recognized as a symbolic phenomenon, as a drama or a game, does not deny the possibility that social life has a utilitarian component. But it does assert the need, as yet unmet in sociology, for an understanding of the intrinsic satisfactions gained from social interaction. The play of symbolic forms in social relations must be recognized as a central part of the subject matter of sociology, and should not be excluded by the models of explanation we choose to use.

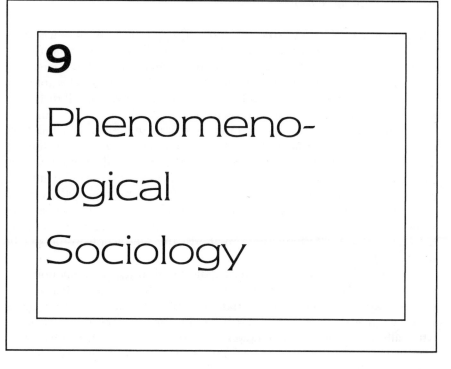

9

Phenomeno-
logical
Sociology

The sociologists who work within the research tradition to be described in this chapter share certain sympathies with the movement in philosophy known as phenomenology. More than other sociologists, they are preoccupied with the study of ideas and thinking, with the study of consciousness. Their subject matter is the world of conscious experience (Freeman, 1980:114).

Phenomenological sociologists reject the idea, inherent in positivist sociology, that the social world constitutes an object world divorced from the interpretive procedures of its members. The social world must be treated as the product of human thought and activity. That world might appear to be a domain of objects but this appearance is produced by human beings and is continually reaffirmed by them through the "readings" or "accounts" they give of their own and other people's actions. These accounts must be the subject matter of sociology.

The focus of phenomenological sociology is how actors assemble their social world, or the procedures and methods they use to make their lives coherent, consistent, and methodical. The best-known form of phenomenological sociology, ethnomethodology, literally means the study of folk methods. Phenomenological sociology is therefore more idealistic than the research tradition described in the previous chapter. Symbolic interactionists acknowledge the precarious and negotiated character of social interaction. But they nevertheless stop at the question "What is going on here?" They still treat the social world as "real" and "out there." Phenomenological sociologists do not take for granted that people can decide "what is going on." They question how anyone understands what is going on anywhere, as well as what methods anyone uses to assure himself or herself that anything is going on at all (Freeman, 1980:139).

The ethnomethods, the accounts and interpretations which people use to create a sense of facticity, are not applied to social interaction already in process. Ethnomethods are constitutive: they help make the interaction what it is. To use an analogy, the rules of a game like chess are not formed to apply to a game already in progress which needs regulating. Without these rules the game would not be chess in the first place, it would be some other game. Likewise, ethnomethods are not superimposed on interaction but help constitute it. Without these methods, the interaction would not be considered real.

By now it should be clear how radically idealistic phenomenological sociology is. All sociologists would go along with the argument that rules or norms shape the flow of interaction. But phenomenological sociologists refuse to treat this idea as the starting point for sociological investigation. After all, norms derive their power from their appearance of objectivity. They exert constraint because we cannot wish them away. But how do they acquire this property of objectivity? That question is the starting point of phenomenological sociology. Rather than seeking the causes and consequences of social norms, phenomenological sociologists ask how the idea that social norms exist is caused, and what consequences that idea has.

PHENOMENOLOGICAL FOUNDATIONS

The "ordinary language" philosophy of Wittgenstein and Austin has exercised a strong influence over the sociologists working in the research tradition described in this chapter. This is evident in the fascination with language, with speech, and with the creative power of words. However, its chief philosophical debt is owed to the phenomenological philosophy of Edmund Husserl and Alfred Schutz.

Edmund Husserl (1859–1938) rejected the idea that science should eliminate the subjective or introspective element from its analysis. He believed that this idea ran contrary to the inescapable fact that what we take to be real or objective must be grounded in everyday, common-sense knowledge. The "factual descriptions" we give of the "object world" are inescapably embedded in the language of everyday life. A pure, formal, impersonal language providing a true picture of a world unaffected by our way of talking about it was an impossibility.

Husserl thus rejected a central tenet of empiricism, a commitment to the object world as the first and most basic source of certainty and truth. Empiricism glossed over the constitutive role of consciousness. To Husserl and other phenomenologists the only realm of certain and unquestionable knowledge is that of immediate experience. The task of phenomenological philosophy should be to trace all understanding (including scientific understanding) to its origins in immediate experience. The term "phenomena" refers to that which is given or indubitable in the consciousness of the individual.

In his philosophical writings, Husserl

> sought to eliminate all presuppositions, the greatest obstacle to clear understanding, by confining all claims to truth to that which is disclosed within the realm of consciousness. He regarded consciousness not merely as a product or receptor of some feature of reality, but as an active force in the constitution of that reality. He used this recognition of the formative character of consciousness as a basis for criticizing sciences that naively accepted their subject matter as well defined and ordered (Freeman, 1980:121).

Husserl maintained that the scientist could not take the appearance of reality as reality but must question how that appearance came to be. He urged that the scientist "get back to the things of consciousness themselves." Phenomenology thus came to focus on "the ways in which individuals construct in their own consciousness the meaning of things" (Douglas, 1980:17). What others chose to call a "fact," what they treated as "real" Husserl treated as an accomplishment. Phenomenology became the task of revealing this accomplishment and describing its consequences.

In order to investigate how phenomena are constructed, Husserl advocated the method of "reduction." This involves the suspension of belief in the thing-like status of the object under investigation and directs our attention to how the belief in objectivity was formed. We concern ourselves with what the world claims to be rather than with what it really is. We treat things as "mere phenomena." Rather than asking "what is real?", we ask "under what circumstances do we think things are real?"

The method of reduction is a frontal attack on the methods of positivism, which assume a clear distinction between what is subjective and what is objective.

> Husserl said that consciousness is neither objective nor subjective, but is at once both. Husserl expressed this dual nature of consciousness as intentionality. Intentionality refers to the fact that consciousness is always consciousness of something, that consciousness always points beyond itself—it intends some object. One is never just conscious, but conscious of things or feelings or thoughts. At all times awareness has an object. The corollary of this is also true: there is no apprehension of the world that is not evident in consciousness, since consciousness is the experiential form in which the world appears (Freeman, 1980:119).

The world of social objects comes into "being" only as we turn our attention to it, as we select discrete impressions from our flow of experiences and assemble them to form phenomena. "The world does not appear to us in an even glow; it presents itself to me in zones of clarity and imprecision that shift with the changing locus of my practical concerns" (Freeman, 1980:117).

Normally, we are unaware of the constitutive role that consciousness plays. We naively assume that there must be a preconstituted world of social objects which we will naturally perceive, albeit with varying degrees of accuracy. Husserl called this "the natural attitude." While in the natural attitude we do not question the facticity of the world itself. This is "naive" because we are treating as natural that which has been humanly constructed. By the method of reduction we step outside the natural attitude and ask how this sense of naturalness is brought about and what practices sustain it. We begin to examine the "seen but unnoticed" features of social life. Thus, the layman might reflect on the fact that what it means to be ill and what it means to be in good health shows some variation from one society to another, but he never questions the "fact" that there is such a state as illness. If we step outside the natural attitude, we question the facticity of illness and of health and ask how this phenomenon has been constituted. What methods are used in any society to establish a sense of the reality of illness as opposed to health, however these states are defined?

Husserl did not concern himself with the application of his ideas to sociology. Alfred Schutz (1899–1959) was familiar not only with Husserl's phenomenology but also with the sociology of Max Weber. Schutz agreed with Weber that social action must be defined as meaningful experience, but he did not think that Weber had really shown how action comes to have meaning or how actors understand each other.

Schutz took from Husserl the idea that the beginning of inquiry should be the process whereby the social world is constituted as a meaningful entity. Rather than assuming that the social world has meaning and investigating its consequences, Schutz understood that we should look at the process of meaning-attribution itself. The "idealizations" and "formulations" of the social world should not be taken for granted but treated as human constructs. "The first task of the methodology of the social sciences," Schutz (1962:59) wrote, should be "the exploration of the general principles according to which man in daily life organizes his experiences, and especially those of the social world."

Schutz's own writings were largely taken up with exploring the properties of the natural attitude. All of us believe that the object world existed before our arrival and will persist after our departure. We also believe that the object world remains there even though we are not attending to it. How do we come to believe this?

THE NATURAL ATTITUDE
AND THE SOCIOLOGICAL
ATTITUDE

Schutz's phenomenology pointed the way from the natural attitude of everyday life to a sociological attitude which would show how that attitude is constructed and maintained. Schutz pointed out that people respond not simply to the content of other people's actions (what they say or do) but also to the manner or form in which those actions are carried out (how they say or do). His phenomenology thus struck a familiar sociological chord. For instance, in the classroom, the content of the interaction (what is taught and learned) is important, but also important is how the teaching and learning are carried out so as to sustain the reality of the lesson. "Although it is incumbent on students to display what they know during lessons, they must also know *how* to display what they know" (Mehan, 1979:169).

In the natural attitude, we rarely notice that any of this is going on. The more typical, probable, and familiar actions are, the more likely we are to think of them as real. We would not be likely to question their authenticity. For example, in a court of law, a great deal of this attention to the form of the interaction goes unnoticed. Sudnow (1965:271) reveals, however, just how much is being taken for granted.

> For the Public Defender and the District Attorney it is a routinely encountered phenomenon that persons in the community regularly commit criminal offenses, are regularly brought before the courts, and are regularly transported to state and county penal institutions.... The morality of the courts is taken for granted. The Public Defender assumes that the District Attorney, the police, the judge, the narcotics agents and all others conduct their business as it must be conducted and in a proper fashion.

As a sociologist, however, Sudnow steps outside the natural attitude and asks how this appearance of normality is sustained. How is the existence of routine criminal offenses confirmed? How are offenders "brought before" the court? How are sentences decided?

While in the natural attitude we assume that the object world (e.g. normal people and deviants) is simply there. By stepping outside the natural attitude we learn that people are constantly at work to *make* things appear normal, typical, or routine. If they are uncertain as to the reality of something (if it is abnormal, untypical, outside of routine) actors will usually work to make it real.

Sociology should therefore recognize that the social world is what actors have "brought off." The most simple and basic aspects of society must be considered from this standpoint. Even the fact of there being two, and only two, genders must be "reduced." Indeed, there is no list of items which "always and without exception" would distinguish males from females. The fact that there are only two genders results from interpretive work on the part of social actors. We are conscious of these efforts only when actors are confronted by ambiguous stimuli, such as a "man" speaking with a high-pitched voice or a muscular "woman," in which case they will set to work to reestablish the authenticity of gender and we can watch what they do (Kessler and McKenna, 1978).

In order to distance herself from the natural attitude, the phenomenological sociologist declares her indifference to the actual status of the assumed world and asks how the appearance of reality of that world is maintained. The layperson rarely engages in this kind of reflection. He has the "know-how" to produce an event or social situation through his action but he does not know how he does it (Psathas, 1980:110). Because the method whereby the social world is constructed is usually invisible, "a special motivation is needed in order to induce the naive person even to pose the question concerning the meaningful structure of his life-world" (Schutz, 1970:138).

The natural attitude is most likely to be questioned when normal routines are radically disrupted, when a disturbance breaks fundamental interactional rules. The sociologist can use this method to question the natural attitude.

> ...start with familiar scenes and ask what can be done to make trouble. The operations that one would have to perform in order to multiply the senseless features of perceived environments; to produce and sustain bewilderment, consternation, and confusion, to produce the socially structured effects of anxiety, shame, guilt, and indignation; and to produce disorganized interaction should tell us something about how the structure of everyday activities are ordinarily and routinely produced and maintained (Garfinkel, 1967:37–38).

The sociologist might observe what happens when people treat their friends as if they were strangers, when children treat their homes as if they were boardinghouses, and so on. Any study of deviance will achieve the same purpose, since it throws light on what ordinary people do to maintain their ordinariness.

We have already noted how symbolic interactionists treat social categories like deviance as relative, their precise meaning changing from one social situation to another. Phenomenological sociologists pursue this line of argument somewhat further, "holding in suspension" even the most basic building blocks of our sense of social order. Time and space are treated as social constructs. They are regarded as ordering schemes actors place upon the world. There will be as many worlds as there are ideas of time. Once these ideas of time acquire objectivity they act back upon individuals and shape the flow of interaction. A number of social times can be identified, each with its own "zone of relevance." There is "self-time," in which biographical events are sequenced; there is the "encounter time" of fleeting interactions and passing acquaintances; there is "interaction time" for exchanges of longer duration, like a job interview or a shared meal; and there are longer "times" such as the day, week, or season. Each time is defined socially (e.g. the typical duration of a meal), each has to be learned (e.g. when to break off a greeting), and each can be violated (e.g. judging a person lazy, incompetent, rude, or irresponsible) and so on (Weigert, 1981:207).

Not only time but timing is an important device for creating social order. We acquire a sense of the reality of social life if it is predictable and routine. This is facilitated by proper sequencing and spacing of interactional responses. The taking of turns in conversation, the use of tact and diplomacy, rules of lining up and waiting all demonstrate the importance of timing. It is noteworthy that only human beings can wait. Only humans create a temporal structure to conflict with their natural desires.

SOCIAL ORDER AS AN ACCOMPLISHMENT

Schutz's phenomenology encourages sociologists to think again about the bases of social order. Positivists think of social patterns, the orderly arrangement of the constituent units of society, in terms of social structure. This structure is akin to a natural force, "exterior" to and "constraining" the individual. From a phenomenological standpoint, positivists have failed to step outside the natural attitude. They take for granted that structures are real. They assume that the sociologist is always in a position to specify "how day-to-day activities continually generate 'normative stability'" (Cicourel, 1972:147).

Phenomenological sociologists treat social structure as a product of consciousness. Rather than describing structure as an object, they talk of "a sense of social structure." This is evident in Weigert's (1981:169) description of the family, a unit which in positivist sociology is likely to be described in terms of roles.

> Family members share a common time which is unique to themselves; they share a common space or at least have rights of access and spatial closeness denied to nonmembers; they possess a private pool of knowledge about each other and the affairs of the family which occasionally need to be protected against the prying eyes of outsiders; and they present, bestow, and validate identities in the unity of a biography created and maintained in the little world which the family continually recreates.

Two features of this account of the family make it distinctive. First, "familiness" is portrayed as a matter of common perceptions, ideas, and relevances. I am a member of the same family as you if we treat the same things as relevant, if we "speak the same language." Second, the family, as an object, must be sustained or reaffirmed by the actions of its members.

ETHNOMETHODS

People develop a sense of social structure by using certain "interpretive methods." These methods make interaction possible in the same way that the rules of grammar make speech and writing possible. They specify the form, rather than the content, of the interaction. As a child matures, these methods must be learned. The child must become familiar with the basic rules which make it possible to "'pass' as a 'boy' or 'girl' and someone's 'son' or a 'normal six-year-old' and the like" (Cicourel, 1972:148).

These methods make it possible to interpret, understand, and use the more explicit "blueprints for living" such as roles, norms, and values. These blueprints specify in a general way what is to count as normal and acceptable but they are given meaning by the interpretive methods which underly them. Thus, if we were to observe the behavior of police officers on the beat charged with sorting the normal from the deviant, we would notice that much more goes on than the simple application of the norm. The police officer must decide what the norm means in that context, what the observed action means, and so on. To account for his action we "would need some idea of how the officer goes about recognizing the phenomenon he considers to be 'deviant' or in violation of the law, and how much information is processed so as to transform it into 'evidence' that can then be described to others by the officer and accepted as 'fact' or indices of 'real or actual' events" (Cicourel, 1972:145). In other words, we would need to know what methods he uses to create a sense of social structure.

There are three categories of ethnomethods. Some methods involve the use of rules, others the use of social types, and a third category involves the use of "practical reasoning."

Rules

Phenomenological sociologists assume that social action is guided by rules. This sounds like the argument common among positivist sociologists that patterns of social behavior reflect conformity to norms. But "rules" is not simply another term for norm: it is an entirely different concept. Phenomenological sociologists reject the argument that social action is determined by norms on the following grounds. First, it assumes that we can first describe the action to be explained, then describe the norm thought to explain it, and then identify the setting in which the causal connection was made. To the phenomenological sociologist this argument overlooks the fact that all three are phenomena of consciousness, not objects. We cannot know the meaning of an action until we know the meaning of the norm being invoked and we cannot know the meaning of either unless we know the meaning of the setting. It is therefore nonsense to claim that the norm is the cause and the action the effect (Wieder, 1974:187).

The second reason why phenomenological sociologists reject the theory that patterns of behavior reflect conformity to norms is that it requires that norms be described literally. If we seek to use norm as an "antecedent condition" as part of a causal argument, it must be specifiable as either present or absent, that is, described literally. But norms cannot be literally described (Heap, 1980:92). Consider what would be necessary for this to be so. At a minimum we would have to be able to state who is expected, and by whom, to do or refrain from doing something, and what the circumstances are. We would have to specify the penalties forthcoming if the norm is violated, or the rewards earned from obeying it, the circumstances surrounding a violation regarded as extenuating, and who will administer the penalties or give the rewards. A norm cannot be abstracted from its context and used as an independent variable. Its meaning is contextual.

Phenomenological sociologists recognize that there are shared guidelines which prescribe the behavior that is appropriate in given social situations but these guidelines delineate only general possibilities. They are ideas about order which can be used in various ways to give social interaction the appearance of naturalness and objectivity.

Norms do not simply "act upon" the individual. They must be interpreted and used. They are interpreted according to certain basic interpretive methods. It is these methods which enable the actor to develop a sense of structure, a sense that there is order, pattern, and predictability in social encounters. Phenomenological sociologists have discovered a number of these methods in common use.

Reciprocity of perspectives. The actor's assumption here is that he and others would have the same experience should they trade places. For present purposes, differences in personal biography are irrelevant.

Normal forms. The assumption in this case is that people's behavior will be normal or "what everyone knows" (Cicourel, 1974:52). In the typical sequence of interaction "subjects and their others have a like concern—to appear normal" (Goffman, 1971:279). In ambiguous cases people will accomplish normality by redefining the cases as typical or routine, altering what they see. They search for and select features of social settings which make them seem normal.

The et cetera principle.   The assumption on the part of the speaker is that the hearer will fill in unstated but intended meanings. "To make sense of the give-and-take of an ordinary conversation, we must appreciate its laconicity, that is, the tendency of the participants to assume, and correctly so, that allusions to items of common experience will serve effectively as full reference" (Goffman, 1971:168).

Indexical expressions.   The assumption here is that the full meaning of communications can only be understood in context. The meaning of utterances cannot be decided without knowledge of the context in which they were made and the biography and purposes of the person making them. Without context, messages have equivocal and multiple meanings. When attributing meaning to the action of another, we assemble a context for which that meaning seems appropriate. We treat the action as a key to the context. Conversely, once we know more about the context, our interpretation of the act may change. The relation between act (or expression) and context is reflexive. This is revealed in a startling way in Atkinson's (1978:116) study of suicide. The notes which suicides leave could indicate the intention to commit suicide, but the meaning of these notes is not fixed. "The identification of a note as a suicide note may certainly make it easier to view the other features of the situation as 'suicidal', but it is also the case that it may not be possible to identify a note as a 'suicide note' without reference to those other features of the situation."

These four rules of interpretation are considered essential in forming a sense of social order. They structure the flow of interaction. Actors must be able to invoke these rules in order to analyze the flow of interaction and take part in it. Although people will unhesitatingly point out when we fail to use them properly, these rules are tacit and learned informally. In this respect they are like the "deep structure" of grammatical rules which we tacitly follow in speaking and writing a language. They are transformational procedures for adapting the sense of social structure to the innumerable differences encountered by actors among the concrete situations in which they participate. They enable actors to process a limited set of rules to gain orientation to the open-ended, creative quality of social interaction.

These basic rules therefore underlie and give meaning to the norms with which other sociologists are preoccupied. They are used to give norms the appearance of reality that is essential for their effectiveness. Phenomenological sociologists are consequently as much interested in how norms are used as they are in whether they are used at all. The norms contained in a penal code, for example, cannot be applied in a direct and straightforward manner. A penal code will contain many categories of crime which are actually shorthand references to knowledge of social structure. It is only by studying *how* the penal code is used that we can explain *why* it works the way it does (Sudnow, 1965).

In his study of "the convict code" in a halfway house, Wieder (1974) was not interested in treating the code as a codification of norms which could be used to predict behavior in the house. He was more interested in "the telling of the code," the manner in which it was used to create a sense of structure. The code was not obeyed but used to make equivocal acts unequivocal, and to make actions otherwise puzzling part of a familiar class of actions of inmates and staff. This telling of the code did not exist outside the setting it was being used to describe.

In the telling of the code, in a single utterance even, a great deal of "work" is accomplished. During the course of his fieldwork, Wieder (1974:168) frequently found that a relatively friendly line of conversation would be terminated by a resident's saying, "You know I won't snitch." Part of the convict code was being told in this utterance, but the social structure of the halfway house was also being reproduced in a number of ways. This utterance

(a) told what had just happened—e.g., 'You just asked me to snitch!'. It (b) formulated what the resident was doing in saying that phrase—e.g., 'I am saying that this is my answer to your question. My answer is not to answer'. It (c) formulated the resident's motives for saying what he was saying and doing what he was doing—e.g., 'I'm not answering in order to avoid snitching!' Since snitching was morally inappropriate for residents, the utterance, therefore, formulated the sensible and proper grounds of the refusal to answer the question. It (d) formulated (in the fashion of pointing to) the immediate relationship between the listener (staff or myself) and teller (resident) by re-locating the conversation in the context of the persisting role relationships between the parties— e.g., 'For *you* to ask *me* that, would be asking me to snitch'....It (e) was *one more* formulation of the features of the persisting role relationship between hearer and teller—e.g., 'You are an agent (or state researcher) and I am a resident-parolee. Some things you might ask me involve informing on my fellow residents. Residents do not inform on their fellows. We call that snitching'.

The convict code thus helps determine what actions mean, and its meaning is in turn determined by those actions, the agents involved, and the setting. The code is used reflexively. The rule against snitching is used for different purposes in different relationships. For a fellow inmate it might convey reassurance and reaffirm the solidarity of the inmate group. For a member of the staff it might be a show of defiance and a reaffirmation of the essential conflict of interest between staff and inmates. The rule is not a blueprint which can be followed with precision and certainty. It provides no unequivocal criteria for deciding right and wrong behavior. Because of the "et cetera" clause, the full meaning of the rule must be filled in on each occasion of its use, its meaning elaborating as action unfolds. Rather than learning the code as a series of dos and don'ts, inmates learn how to use the code to create a sense of social order.

Social Types

The use of rules establishes a sense of the structuredness of life by imparting to the actions of people a reasonableness. A sense of social structure is also engendered by the use of social types. Typing is a device used to order and place people so that their conduct makes sense.

The idea that human beings respond to each other as instances of broad categories of actors rather than as unique individuals is not an idea of phenomenological sociologists alone. It is widely acknowledged that we cannot hope to know more than a few people as they really are and must rely on our ability to type people in order to be able to form relationships with them. During socialization, we learn types and we learn how to type. We learn to use types to make our world predictable, familiar, and understandable. Phenomenologists have pushed this line or argument much further, however, reminding us that types are not things or objects but human constructs, *ideas* we use to give our world the appearance of being orderly and objective. Typing is thus a means we employ to create a sense of social structure, rather than the appearance which social structure has for us.

Social types accomplish a sense of social structure in this way: other people do not present themselves to us in a clear and unambiguous manner as an instance of this or that type but need to be "sorted out" into types. Typing is an active process in which social reality is produced. What the other person is doing, who that person is, is determined in the act of typification. Types are tools used to impart a sense of order and routine. Behavior which might seem strange and disorderly to bewildered parents will seem routine and orderly to the child psychologist (Gorman, 1977:41).

In the natural attitude, our active engagement in typing is concealed from us. We assume we are uncovering categories of behavior which already exist, that acts must really belong in this or that category. Stepping outside the natural attitude, we see how much effort goes into typing, effort designed to impart a sense of routine to social life. We see how types are used to make actors and actions more reasonable, more real (McLain and Weigert, 1979:171).

Sudnow (1965) shows how Public Defenders in the California court system determine the adequacy of their client's version of "what happened" by the extent to which it struck them as typical. Sudnow noted that in most interviews "the public defender interrupted when he had enough information to confirm his sense of the case's typicality and construct a typifying portrayal of the defendant."

Emerson's (1969) study of the workings of juvenile courts uncovered the same typing behavior. A juvenile court is routinely presented with a wide range of youthful misconduct. It is required to categorize this misconduct into degrees of "seriousness," differentiating those cases which can be "let go" from those where "something has to be done." The court thus formulates various types of delinquents—"normal," "hard-core," and "disturbed" types. Court officials assume that there are patterns of behavior and social circumstances associated with the juvenile which can be used to place his actions into one or another of the types.

In the normal course of events, there will be no question about the right and proper way of handling the case, and the work of typification is implicit. If the facts of the case are out of the ordinary or ambiguous, however, the work of typification will become more explicit. It becomes possible for the sociologist to observe attempts to establish a correspondence between a delinquent's moral character and the kind of person for whom a given outcome (e.g. incarceration) is typical (i.e. "He is that type of person").

To establish the delinquency of a juvenile, the prosecutor routinely endeavors to "(a) establish that the present act is of a kind typically committed by a delinquent or criminal-like character and (b) construct a delinquent biography that unequivocally indicates someone of such character" (Emerson, 1969:105). The delinquency of the juvenile must be constructed by selecting from a variety of cues which tells the prosecuting officer what "must have happened." These cues are contained in secondhand reports which must be truncated and selective. If the cues provide no clear information about the act itself or its circumstances, the court must try to build up a sense of the character of the juvenile. Is he a "hopeless case" or a "good kid"? The juvenile's moral character must be constructed, often by an outside "knowledgeable" authority.

> Two Puerto Rican boys, ages 13 and 14, were brought into court for shooting a BB gun across a public way. They had been apprehended by chance; four policemen cruising by in a police car had noticed them on the roof of a project firing the gun. Probation officer then reported that both boys had been in court once before, both on larceny from parking meters; the complaints had been dismissed after successful probation. Judge then asked the priest accompanying the families and serving as interpreter.... "Basically, what kind of boys do we have here? I have not seen them before". Priest replied: "I think we have a boyish bit of follishness here. These boys are not guilty of malice.... It's a case where they arrive home and there is not a great deal of supervision, at that time" (Emerson, 1969:133).

The character of these boys is being "prepared" so that a given type of action makes sense.

The more general point is that act, setting, actor, and others all must be meaningfully congruent for action to make sense. Types are used to achieve this congruency. Thus, a death will not be a suicide unless it takes place in private because suicidal acts do not occur in public—typically, that is (Atkinson, 1978:130). Conversely, types of actor and action are used to make sense of setting. A police officer's knowledge of criminal types (known

by their style of dress and comportment) is used to determine the setting—
"what is going on" (Cicourel, 1968:67).

Typing is also the focus of attention in Kessler and McKenna's study of
gender attribution. Most people take gender for granted. That a person is
either a man or a woman is assumed, and gender is soon decided.
Transsexuals cannot assume that their gender is obvious. By means of
appropriate talk and physical appearance, transsexuals must "manage"
themselves as male or female so that others will attribute the desired
gender. They must induce others to type them. They might have to go so
far as to reconstruct their biography: "I am a woman because I have had a
typical woman's biography."

Transsexuals adopt the natural attitude toward gender. They assume
that there are two and only two genders and use this to make their behavior
seem rational.

> This is demonstrated in the ways transsexuals refer to themselves, their
> bodies, and to the surgical operations they request. A male-to-female
> transsexual, being interviewed on NBC's "Tomorrow" television pro-
> gram was asked, "How was your beard taken care of?" The transsexual
> answered, "I was fortunate. I never had much of a *facial hair growth
> pattern*" (emphasis ours). The fact that she used this particular language
> is evidence of her belief that real women do not have (and never did
> have) beards. If they have anything, they have facial hair. Since she was
> always a woman, she never had a beard (Kessler and McKenna,
> 1978:121).

The transsexual shares the attitude of the layperson that the types—male
and female—really exist, that all human beings must therefore be examples
of one type or the other, and that, if any ambiguity exists (as is true in their
case), the ambiguities must be cleared up by proper placement. The
ethnomethodologist steps outside the natural attitude, suspends belief in
the reality of gender, and observes the methods used to attribute gender, to
make gender seem real.

Practical Reasoning

The final method of achieving a sense of social order is practical
reasoning. Any means the actor uses to render social acts and settings
recognizable and familiar qualifies as practical reasoning. It is in one sense
description, a means of reporting "which renders objects and events
observable, objective, and rational" (Leiter, 1980:163). But it is much more.
The account which an actor gives of his conduct becomes part of that
conduct. It creates and sustains a sense of that action as being normal and
routine. It "is a vehicle through which members create both a setting and
their understanding of that setting" (Freeman, 1980:142). If we greet an
acquaintance and our greeting is not reciprocated we will give an account

(e.g. "She is probably not feeling well") which reaffirms the reality of the encounter as an orderly interaction between acquaintances (Mehan and Wood, 1975:14). This account, more than a description of what happened, helps bring what happened into being.

Phenomenological sociologists are less interested in the content of accounts than they are in their form. They are more concerned with accounting practices, the methods used to make social objects and events part of the object world. When accounts are given, the chief aim will be to achieve a sense of social order. The content of the account is incidental. For example, social workers are obliged periodically to account for the use of their time by filling out reports for the benefit of higher personnel. Not only must social workers complete a number of such reports, each with its own intended purpose, but each report will contain ambiguous and sometimes conflicting demands for information. The account provided by a completed report could not be anything like a true description of what "really" happened. The social worker is obliged to fill out the report with an eye to what the higher authorities would regard as reasonable conduct. The reporting thus consists of various accounting practices, procedures for ensuring that the report makes sense and appears rational to the super-visor. The social worker will routinely "fudge" time-use reports by over- or underestimating various time uses, changing time uses to make them consistent, clarify ambiguous categories on the form, and so on. The concern is less to give a "truthful" description than to preserve and enhance a sense of social order the supervisor expects to see (Altheide and Johnson, 1980:116).

Accounts and descriptions function as "documents of" or "point to" an underlying social order. "Talk" is therefore "documentary," connecting the here-and-now of action with the larger social structure. Talk among family members is both an account of what is being done and a method of "doing family."

> A son routinely taking out the garbage in the presence of his father is not immediately doing family; it is the removal of the garbage that is relevant. If, however, the grandmother is present and witnesses the balking son who grumbles, moans, and resists the task of garbage removal, and if she then begins to wonder out loud whether she was an inadequate mother that she could not bring up her own son to be a responsible father, so that he in turn appears to be unable to raise a responsible son of his own, the family is immediately being done.... No speech, but a simple, self-accusing statement by grandmother accomplishes family, e.g. "Doesn't he usually take out the garbage when you ask him?" (McLain and Weigert, 1979:184).

The social structure of the family is "contained" in the talk. The symbolic exchange is not merely a gloss upon the "real" interaction. It constitutes the action: without the talk, the action would be something else.

THEORY BUILDING

Phenomenological sociologists do not believe that there are universal laws of social behavior. They reject the notion of "event-causality." Social action is "caused by an agent's reflexive monitoring of his intentions in relation to both his wants and his appreciation of the demands of the outer world" (Giddens, 1976:84). The explanation for human actions is to be found in the reasons agents provide for their actions. These reasons (e.g. accounts) will make actions "reasonable" or intelligible in the light of the actor's environment.

The first step in an explanation of social action is, then, to investigate what order actors impart to their actions. The second step is to describe the methods they use to accomplish this sense of order. "How do people come to see forces like norms, values, social classes, and institutions as objectively real and as the cause of behavior?" (Leiter, 1980:25). What are the taken-for-granted and socially sanctioned monitoring procedures actors use to impose order on the flux of events?

Explanation thus consists of a movement from the context of subjective meaning (how the actor makes sense of her actions) to the context of objective meaning (how the sociologist makes sense of the actor's making sense). An objective context of meaning is a set of related statements which could be understood "apart from the special perspective of the person making the statement" (Freeman, 1980:128). The objective meaning yields a "radical description," making intelligible observations and actions which are unintelligible so long as we remain in the natural attitude.

The creation of a more objective context of meaning in which to situate and make sense of actions is not an activity unique to sociologists. All of us organize our experiences into types, and some of these types are quite abstract and anonymous. Sociologists merely pursue this goal of abstraction more systematically. They want to understand their subjects' ordering of experience, but their ultimate purpose is to understand the process whereby this ordering takes place. The sociologist must come to terms with the "first order" of categories which laypeople use and then try to place those categories within a broader framework of meaning.

The sociologist's categories are "second order constructs." They must reflect the subjects' logic and reasoning, beginning in the ordinary language of everyday speech and returning to that level when theory is put to use (Coulter, 1979:22). Although grounded in common sense, the concepts of phenomenological sociology are distinguishable from it. They have been formed with a specific purpose of understanding how any kind of social action is accomplished. They have a different "system of relevances." They are also set within a larger "stock of knowledge" than common-sense categories, which are usually specified only for the "purposes at hand." The sociologist's concepts must be more consistent, more complete and provide a total framework of thought. The prime requirement of sociological concepts, however, is still "a direct and demonstrable continuity between sociological concepts and the linguistic typifications men use to index their social experiences" (Phillipson, 1972:109).

Phenomenological sociologists are very critical of positivist methods of conceptualization and theory building. In their view, positivists make little effort to ensure that their concepts derive from or can be translated into a language that has meaning for their subjects. Positivists are likely to impose their own meaning on the social world. They are screened from that world by techniques of data gathering (e.g. survey questionnaires, structured interviews, official statistics) which contain their own ordering schemes dictated by technology.

The responses to items on a questionnaire have no self-evident meaning: they are not "raw data." They tell us little about how the respondent accomplishes the answer, what is considered relevant in the question, whether the question uses terms familiar to the respondent, whether the respondent feels a moral obligation to give a certain answer, and so on. Questionnaires impose their own rationality on respondents. They "tidy up" reality by their use of forced-choice items. Forcing choices assumes that accurate, clear, unambiguous, and consistent choices can always be made—and phenomenological sociologists do not believe this is true (Cicourel, 1964).

Official statistics also belie their appearance of objectivity. They are not literal measurements. They rest on the tacit, common-sense under-standings of those who compile them. They should be regarded as accomplishments of record-keeping agencies. For example, statistics on juvenile delinquency rest ultimately on decisions made by the officer on the beat. At some point the officer has to decide (perhaps on the basis of something so intangible as tone of voice) whether an act is a sign of a "bad attitude" and thus a documentation of a typical juvenile delinquent, or simply a kid "goofing off" and having fun (Cicourel, 1974:3). The statistics on automobile accidents are no less subjective. Records of automobile fatalities record the "artful practices" of the coroner. "Thus the coroner's sheets reporting auto deaths occasionally include statements that the body was found in or next to the auto, and given the damaged character of the car, that the death was presumed to be due to an automobile crash" (Gusfield, 1981:68).

Without some appreciation of the routine processes of categorization engaged in by record-keeping agencies, the improvisation which neces-sarily enters into the amassing of official statistics is overlooked and their objectivity exaggerated. Official statistics are merely estimates of "what must have happened." They are the result of applying organizational rules for making sense of what seems to have occurred. They are nothing more.

Phenomenological sociologists are not interested in improving the accuracy of such statistics, however, for this would be to assume that there is a knowable, "real" phenomenon which the statistics approximate. The phenomenological sociologist's project is confined to investigating how these statistics come to be treated as referring to the real world. Their "radical description" has to do not with the world as such but with the facticity of that world, with the methods by which that world is made real.

Interviews are less prone to distort actor's meaning, but they nevertheless rely heavily on tacit, shared understandings between interviewer and interviewee. The interview is itself a social encounter. It is a form of conversation and is replete with inconsistencies, ambiguities, and indexical expressions. The story the interviewer hears might be one of several versions the subject tells of the same incident. A lot remains unspoken and understood between interviewer and interviewee. We would be naive if we treated the data gathered in an interview as "raw."

TESTING THEORY

Phenomenological sociologists take the view that their work, like any other "account," must be reflected upon and analyzed as an "artful practice" (Psathas, 1980:16). Their concepts must be regarded as indexical expressions. They are developed with a certain purpose in mind and depend on their context for their precise meaning. For example, the concept, "accounting practices" is defined as "any method of observation and reporting which renders objects and events observable, objective and rational" (Leiter, 1980:163). But no formal criteria are provided for recognizing and distinguishing accounting practices. The meaning of the concept, like the meaning of other indexical expressions, is the product of the organized occasion of its use.

The status which phenomenological sociology claims for itself is thus different from the claim made by positivists for their theories. If all accounts are "irremediably indexical," then so too are the accounts given by sociologists:

> ...like everybody else's accounts, they are glosses of the experiences which comprise their world. In this sense they carry no special privileged status as being more 'objective' or nearer the 'truth' than the accounts of anybody else (Phillipson, 1972:107).

The sociological world is just as much an accomplishment as the social world (Cicourel, 1974:3).

If the sociologist's account is just another accomplishment, how can a good or truthful account be distinguished from a bad or untruthful one? First, the account must be faithful to and consistent with the experiences of the sociologist's subjects (Psathas, 1973:12). Second, the account must enable someone else to understand what is going on when they are confronted with the events the sociologist is interpreting. It must render transparent the reasoning and communication contained in the interaction (Coulter, 1979:25). Finally, the account must specify rules in such a way that anyone following them could "pass" among the observed subjects.

Phenomenological sociology is validated not by appeal to the community of scientists, not by appeal to "hard data," but by appeal to the subjects of the sociology. "Researchers must be able to demonstrate to the natives that they can talk as they talk, see as they see, feel as they feel, do as they do" (Mehan and Wood, 1975:228).

COMMENTS

Phenomenological sociologists do not believe that their problems can be approached using the normal methods of sociology. They are convinced that positivist sociology suppresses "whole classes of data" (Zimmerman, 1974:21). Their own work is characterized as "a paradigm shift," in which accustomed ways of studying social life are "suspended," because they take for granted what should be made problematic (Zimmerman and Pollner, 1971:93). Phenomenological sociology thus regards itself as a distinct research tradition, dealing with a world of hitherto only dimly perceived facts and tackling problems other sociologists have not even thought to raise (Wieder, 1974:41).

Not surprisingly, these claims have aroused considerable controversy within sociology. Some sociologists working in other research traditions regard the close scrutiny given to concept formation and data gathering as very invigorating for the discipline (Goldthorpe, 1973:452). However, most conventional sociologists would probably agree that the preoccupation with mundane reasoning seems rather "trivial" and that the conclusions arrived at by phenomenological sociologists are little more than "common sense" (Coser, 1975b).

THE PROBLEM
OF NOMINALISM

The most searching criticisms of phenomenological sociology focus upon its phenomenological foundations. Phenomenology is charged with having a nominalist bias. It encourages us to believe that social phenomena are real only insofar as the individual's actions and interpretations routinely confirm them as such. Society is "in the mind."

The charge of nominalism is tantamount to saying that phenomenological sociologists have failed in their effort to transcend the subject-object dualism which characterizes positivism and have lapsed into subjectivism. Alfred Schutz himself encouraged this tendency to subjectivism. He described the social world as "strictly speaking, my world." The social world is "in the mind," the social structure is real only insofar as the actor forms an idea of it.

The emphasis on practical reasoning and on the constitutive role of "talk" and "telling" exemplifies this nominalism. Ethnomethodologists,

> instead of seeing order in purportedly objective patterns of stable interaction between people ... see order ... as created in the accounts (talk) members exchange with one another. Instead of treating orderly social life as a fact, something in the world out there, ethnomethodologists view order as an accomplishment of members' practical reasoning process—a constructed appearance (Anderson, 1977:174).

Phenomenological sociologists tell us a great deal about ideas like "deviance" and about how deviant categories are constructed, but we get only the vaguest notion of what deviants actually do. The deviant world has become a linguistic world, a world not of action but of ways in which action is made accountable. And it is true that action itself is not the primary focus of phenomenological sociology. More interest is shown in the way in which actions are received and accounted for than in the actions themselves.

The nominalistic bias in phenomenological sociology is not something easily remedied. It stems not only from Schutz's phenomenology but also from the ordinary language philosophy of Wittgenstein and Austin in which it is argued that the meaning of a word (and, by extension, an action) is determined by the way in which it is used. To abstract from usage would be misleading because it would suggest that meaning lies behind or transcends usage. Phenomenological sociologists thus come close to denying the objective character of social situations and the possibility of the existence of decontextualized objective meanings. If all social meanings depend on usage, if all social meanings change with context, how can we speak of social structure and social relationships at all (McSweeney, 1973:148)? The activities which produce the settings of everyday life are not the same as the actors' procedures for making those settings intelligible. The mind is not self-sufficient, consciousness is not autonomous from social, political, and economic conditions (Gellner, 1975:434; Giddens, 1976:40).

THE PROBLEM OF SOCIAL STRUCTURE

These nominalistic tendencies are especially evident in the phenomenological sociologists' treatment of social structure. They prefer to talk of a "sense of social structure" rather than refer to social structure as if it were a thing. Structural phenomena like roles, norms, and values are treated as fragile accomplishments. The problem with this manner of conceptualizing social structure is that few tools are provided for dealing with the interplay of social forces of which the actor is unaware. The result is an exclusive concentration on small-scale, delimited areas of inquiry and an absence of any sociological analysis of macro-social processes (Wagner, 1973).

Ironically, the result is that phenomenological sociologists are hardly less guilty of reifying social structure than the positivists they criticize. They tend to fall back on their subjects' knowledge of social structure to make sense of the subjects' behavior. And in the course of analyzing a particular pattern of behavior, they are obliged to treat other aspects as constant in much the same fashion as the sociologists they criticize. For example, Wieder's study of the halfway house draws upon implicit assumptions about the structure of the facility and the logic of the correctional system of which it is a part—including the structure of power and control (Law and Lodge, 1978:380).

The result of treating social structure as "background" is that phenomenological sociologists are unable or unwilling to provide an explanation of why this or that account, type, or rule is used as it is. Focusing all their attention on the way in which facticity is accomplished, they ignore the question of why one set of facts rather than another is taken seriously.

> ...what can studies of police or teacher typification on the beat or in the classroom tell us other than just *how* interaction takes place. Is it not possible to situate the contexts of such interaction features in relation to 'structural' features such as poverty, resource allocation, unemployment, political decision making, work, professional training and historical factors? (Gleeson and Erben, 1976:481).

This preoccupation with accounts of everyday situations and face-to-face encounters, coupled with the argument that all relationships are fragile, leaves us with the impression that in social life "anything goes" (Mehan and Wood, 1975:23). But this is not true. People have different resources, different amounts of power, which makes it possible for the more powerful to establish their facts as real (Collins, 1975:115).

Because phenomenological sociology contains no structural analysis of power, it provides no explanation of why certain facts are constructed and others not. Nor does it make allowance for the possibility that meanings might be false, perhaps deliberately falsified. Thus, the phenomenological sociologists might be right in arguing that social interaction relies on there being intersubjective understanding among the parties involved. But this understanding might be false, and the actors suffering from false consciousness (Bauman, 1978:190). We can also agree with phenomenological sociologists that human beings act only on the basis of some understanding of their social world, but it does not follow from this that their activity (or the world at large) possesses the character they understand it to have. The phenomenological sociologist refuses to order "accounts" in a hierarchy of adequacy, preferring to assume that all are equally valid versions.

PART THREE

10

Realism

Realism furnishes an ontology and epistemology of social life quite distinct from both positivism and idealism. It asserts, like positivism, that the objects of which scientists seek knowledge exist and act independently of human actors and their thoughts. But it rejects the positivist's empiricist assumption that those objects are only knowable with certainty by means of direct, human sense experiences. It asserts, like idealism, that social objects could have no existence apart from the conceptions which humans possess of them. But it does not support the idealist position that society is nothing but the product of these conceptions. Such a view would render sociology incapable of dealing with those features of society which operate as unconscious determinants of social behavior (Keat, 1981:3).

Philosophers use the term "realism" in a number of ways. Indeed, some positivists would claim to be realists because their theories provide statements about a theory-independent "real world." But the version of realism I describe in this chapter differs from positivism in not restricting scientific ontology to the domain of what is observable. In this nonpositivist version of realism (variously referred to as "theoretical realism" or "transcendental realism"), scientific theories make claims about the nature and the existence of unobservable items. The positivist's attempt to define theoretical terms in an observational language "is seen to be misconceived" (Keat, 1981:20).

How can two philosophies, each claiming to be realist, differ so fundamentally in their implications for sociology? The reason is that each uses a different criterion to ascribe reality to a posited object. Using a "perceptual" criterion, by which an object is considered real if it is perceived, positivists exclude from scientific relevance anything that cannot be readily observed or is not in principle observable. Using a "causal" criterion, by which an object is real if it brings about a change in material things, nonpositivist or theoretical realists are willing to include in the scientific domain entities which cannot be observed and perhaps will never be observed.

All that the theoretical realist requires is that it is possible to make observations that could count in some way for or against the truth or falsity of their theory. Their concepts are not built upon phenomenal categories, but refer to the forms which must be supposed to exist if the world described in phenomenal categories is to be possible. The realist's theory will simply state that "it is because an entity of some kind exists, or has some property, that when the specified test conditions are carried out, the predicted results occur" (Keat and Urry, 1975:38). It does not detract from the reliability of the theory that the entity or property cannot be observed.

A number of research traditions have developed in which the ontology and epistemology of theoretical realism dominate. In the social sciences, these include a research tradition in anthropology (e.g. Levi-Strauss, 1963), in social psychology (e.g. Harre, 1980), and in psychology (Freud, 1954). For example, Freud followed realist procedures in arguing that the manifest forms of consciousness are the effects of an underlying structure he called "the unconscious." The unconscious is invisible but real in its consequences.

The most "clear-cut example of realism in the social sciences" is historical materialism, the theory developed chiefly by Karl Marx (Keat and Urry, 1975:2). And this chapter is designed more as an introduction to historical materialism than as a comprehensive treatment of realism. I will accordingly draw my illustrative examples from the work of Marx and contemporary exponents of Marxian social theory. I am aware that "there is a great deal in Marx which is humanist, and not a little that is positivist" (Benton, 1977:139). I will introduce some of the nonrealist versions of Marxian social theory in the final chapter.

The limited aims of this chapter and of the third part of the book it introduces should by now be clear. In addition to positivist and idealist social sciences, there exists a third variant which I have chosen to describe as theoretical realism. Historical materialism has proven to be the most popular of the several research traditions which rest on realist assumption and will constitute the sole topic of this third part. However, a realist interpretation of Marx and his followers is by no means the only interpretation possible. Accordingly, some of the contributions of other interpreters of historical materialism will be presented in the final chapter.

ONTOLOGY

Realists reject the argument that a scientist must be an empiricist, if that means that science must confine itself to abstraction and empirical generalization from the immediate experience of reality. This confuses the level of observable social relations with the underlying structure of those relations (Rossi, 1981:55). The realist distinguishes several layers of reality. First, there is the level of immediate sense impressions, the level of our everyday life in all its flux and variety. Then there is the level of phenomena, of the "objects" which appear as we stand back from the chaos of sense impressions to create a pattern or a sequence. And finally there is the level of the structures which generate these phenomena, a deeper reality which, not being observable directly, can only be known by its effects (Bhaskar, 1975; 1979).

Relations

The deepest level of reality consists not of things or atoms but of relations and relations between relations. As we shall see, the concepts of historical materialism all refer to relations, despite the fact that conventional usage would suggest that a thing is being referred to. In historical materialism, a commodity is not a thing but a relation between buyer and seller: a good cannot become a commodity unless a relation forms between buyer and seller. Nor is "class" a thing, a social group formed independently of other groups. A class is a relation. Without the capitalist class there would be no proletariat; without the proletariat, there would be no capitalist class. Neither class could exist nor its conduct be understood outside the relation of which it is a part. The "state," too, is a relation rather than a thing. It should be treated "neither as a specific institution nor as an instrument, but as a relation—a materialized concentration of the class relations of a given society" (Therborn, 1978:34).

This ontology of relations is different from the structural and functional research traditions associated with positivism. Positivists treat structures as visible in or inferable from social relationships. Structures can be described and classified by observing the interactions between categories of people. It is assumed that the structure can "read off" observable social relations. "Reality and appearance are coterminous" (Glucksman, 1974:20). Realists believe that structures underlly social relations and are neither reducible to social relations nor directly inferable from them. Abstractions and empirical generalizations based on social relations merely formalize manifest properties of social life and are unable to disclose its inner structure. "Phenomenal forms may be such as to mask or obscure the relations of which they are forms of manifestations" (Sayer, 1979:9).

Totality

Structures are comprised of elements or entities which form a totality. In other words, the whole is more than the sum of its parts. The entities help form the whole but are at the same time transformed by it. This method of conceptualizing part-whole relations is different from that found in positivist research traditions. In the latter, parts and wholes are treated as causes and effects of each other. For example, the family is "caused" by the larger society of which it is a part. The family, in turn, helps create the larger society, being one of its constituent units. This manner of talking about the family and society leaves us with the impression that the family is a "pre-existing object on which the structure imposes its imprint" (Blackburn and Jones, 1972:372). A realist would regard this as a reification of the family and an incorrect conceptualization of part-whole relationships. A realist would not think it proper to talk about "family life" being shaped by social processes like industrialization, or about the "contribution" the family makes to a society's industrialization, because this linear, cause and effect thinking is too mechanical.

> ...there is no 'family' in general upon which another social process such as 'industrialisation' has effects. 'Industrialisation' no more deprived the family of its productive economic functions than the development of the family as a unit of consumption caused the 'spread of industrialisation'. To speak of one change presupposes the other, and neither can be understood in isolation (Harris, 1977:84).

The family is part of the whole and, because it exists within that particular whole, contains within itself the logic which ties together the whole. Conversely, the whole would not be what it is were the part not to assume that form. Thus the family in capitalism is organized along capitalist lines (e.g. the division of labor between husband and wife): the family also functions to reproduce capitalist social relations.

Contradiction

The elements which constitute underlying structures form relations of both combination and opposition (Burris, 1979:6). The relative autonomy which each element enjoys creates a clash of discrepant elements. Structural relations are contradictory in the sense that the existence of the parts is both necessary for and yet destructive to the relation. The opposing elements or processes "share a common causal condition of existence" (Benton, 1977:160). The mechanism which generates the two elements also generates their opposition. For example, the mode of production called "capitalism" includes the proletariat and the bourgeoisie among its components. These classes both presuppose each other and contradict each other. The mode of production created their combination and their opposition. This dialectical approach to structure distinguishes historical materialism from other research traditions within realism (Blackburn and Jones, 1972:379).

A contradictory relationship is much more than a conflict relationship (Frank, 1974:349). The ability to locate and describe social conflicts is therefore not a necessary indication of dialectical acumen. Most social conflicts have "no more 'contradictory' significance than the chance encounter of two particles or the clash of two wills" (Heilbroner, 1980:39). Contradictions exist at the level of underlying structure. They might or might not find expression at the level of social relationships in the form of social conflict.

To conceive structural relations dialectically is to think of them as being in constant motion. Their parts are better described as "moments" or "instances." Contradictions are resolved only when the opposition is transcended and subsumed within a new unity. The factory system initially enhanced the power of the capitalist class and brought into being the capitalist system. It also produced a new class (the proletariat) and this class eventually formed the basis of resistance to the capitalist class. The conflict expressed a contradiction between the continued private ownership of the means of production and their increasingly socialized form. This contradiction cannot be resolved short of a dissolution of the relationship itself, that is, with the overthrow of capitalism. The successor to capitalism will have taken something from both capital and labor, although more from the new class than from the old.

A realist social science will thus regard history as a succession of structures, each with distinctive characteristics and laws of internal functioning. The purpose of sociological investigation is to establish the distinctiveness of separate structures, indicating the main lines of development within each, positing the central elements of the processes of change each structure possesses. It is not the aim of realist social science to develop a set of categories of universal applicability (after the fashion of Newtonian physics) but to enlarge our capacity to perform specific analyses.

EPISTEMOLOGY

Realists have their own ideas about how reliable knowledge about the social world can be achieved which set them apart from both positivists and idealists.

Causal Explanation

Positivists think of cause in linear terms, as that which usually comes before an event or thing. A cause is a stimulus which impinges on the event or thing from without. A causal law expresses the idea of a constant conjuncture of externally related events or things. Using this idea of cause, we can never say there are necessary connections in nature. We can only say that there appear to be regular successions of phenomena.

Realists subscribe to a different idea of causal explanation. They believe there are necessary connections, that the relation between cause and effect is real rather than a matter of convention. The relation between events or states that are related causally "is internal to them, the cause and effect are not independent of each other, and the effect could not happen without the cause" (Harre, 1972:116).

Realists do not deny that it is possible to observe regularities in social life. Nor do they discount the value of empirical generalizations. They do deny, however, that positing a law to "account" for an empirical generalization is sufficient to explain these regularities.

> If we discover a regular relationship between two kinds of phenomena, this gives us some reason to believe that they are causally connected: the existence of the regularity is strong, though not conclusive, evidence for a causal connection. But this is not all we mean in claiming that one thing is the cause of another. In addition, we commit ourselves to the presence of some intervening mechanism which links them together, and it is the scientist's task to discover and analyse the nature of such mechanisms (Keat and Urry, 1975:29).

Causes are therefore mechanisms or structures which, upon being stimulated, produce an effect. The nature of these mechanisms is determined by the internal constitution, or structure.

The idea that a thing comes to do something by virtue of its having a certain structure is called "natural necessity." A description of the structure simultaneously explains the event (Glucksmann, 1974:146). Realists draw a sharp distinction between an antecedent event (which might trigger a mechanism) and the mechanism itself (which is the true cause). The molecular structure of glass makes it brittle such that, if it is hit by a flying rock, it will break. The rock seems to cause the glass to break but the molecular structure of the glass is actually the mechanism which generates the break. We explain the breaking of the glass by discovering this mechanism rather than the rock.

Theories which invoke causal mechanisms, so-called "generative theories," do not assume that phenomena are related in terms of linear causality. Cause exists only in the totality of the elements and their relations contained in the generative mechanism. Causality is conceived synchronically, as an aspect of a particular structural configuration at one time, rather than diachronically.

What is distinctive about the use of generative theories in historical materialism is that the mechanism generates *antagonistic* processes and tendencies. The key to any society is believed to be the mode of production, the specific combination of and opposition between the forces of production and the social relations of production.

Laws

Realists do not deny that the regularities which social life displays can be described in terms of laws. The laws of supply and demand do enable us to predict market behavior with some accuracy. But these laws, far from sufficing as explanations, themselves need to be accounted for. To explain such laws, it is necessary to penetrate to the level of the structures which generate the patterns to which they refer. "Experience" is an infallible guide to observing regularities in social relationship but a poor guide to finding out what determines them (Marx, 1962:846).

Realists often use the term "law," but they do not use it to refer to higher-level empirical generalizations. They refer, instead, to the tendencies, or powers, which structures possess. A tendency statement should not be confused with a statement of probability. It does not say that a sequence of events has a certain probability of occurring. A tendency might rarely manifest itself in practice. A tendency statement is not, therefore, a prediction either. It simply asserts that a mechanism has the power to bring about a certain outcome. Whether or not this happens depends on other mechanisms which impinge upon it.

There is a further difference between positivist and realist laws. Positivists treat social laws as equivalent to natural laws. Human actors can know and use them but not alter them. Realists believe that the parameters which "contain" laws (i.e. the conditions under which they apply) can be modified by human action. Humans have the power to alter the structural conditions surrounding the mechanism and thereby the working out of the tendency. Social laws cannot have the same status as natural laws.

Concepts

The social world is not like the natural world in that new social "realities" are constantly forming. Each new reality demands a new set of concepts. Realists are closer to idealists than positivists in arguing that sociology should not aspire to a fixed and formal scientific language. However, realists are different from idealists in acknowledging the social determination of concepts.

The social determination of sociological knowledge means that the appropriate conditions for correct sociological knowledge must pertain before valid concepts can be formulated. "A more advanced society will offer a better vantage point for comparing the different forms, and so constructing the concept of their common features" (Benton, 1977:168). Thus, to be able to conceive of "labor-in-general," we must have lived in a society in which the division of labor is highly developed and in which one particular form of labor is not dominant over others. This experience throws more light on the concept of labor itself. Similarly, a concept like "authority" has no fixed and final meaning. Its full meaning is determined by the social conditions in which it appears. We can only speak of particular forms of authority (Braverman, 1974:16).

Method of Analysis

The realist maintains that there is more to the world than appears immediately. There is a world of appearances and a world of underlying structures which generate those appearances. It is the object of analysis to uncover these hidden structures. Although analysis begins with concrete reality, with phenomena as they appear to us, it must move from these phenomenal forms to the real relations which underly them.

Underlying structures are revealed by the method of abstraction. The analyst thinks away the concrete details of the phenomena to reveal the general forms beneath. Abstraction is used in all sciences, whatever their philosophical foundation. The distinctiveness of the realist method of abstraction can be grasped by contrasting it with that used in positivism.

Positivists begin their inquiry with what they consider to be the level of reality, the world of "raw data" or "brute facts." This is the level of observable social phenomena—people giving gifts, robbing banks, going to class—summarized usually in some statistical form. The characteristics these phenomena have in common are revealed by thinking away the details, by abstracting the particulars. For example, we might observe people shopping in a supermarket and think of what they are doing as "making a purchase," although they might also be doing many other things in the shop. Ignoring the idiosyncrasies of purchases (e.g. what was bought) and generalizing to other retail transactions, we create a class of acts we call "consumer behavior." This class of acts might be abstracted further by abstracting the details of purchasing and creating the general category of "rational choice behavior."

In this positivist method of abstraction, individual and particular features are eliminated in order to reintroduce them at a later stage, when specific predictions are made (e.g. about the chances of a given commodity selling). The assumption is that the abstraction contains all the essential elements of the phenomenon being studied, albeit in a much simplified form. An abstraction is therefore a simplifying model of the real thing.

Realists, distinguishing between the level of appearance and the level of reality, argue that these levels rarely coincide and frequently are "inverted." Abstractions cannot simply be simplifications of appearances. Their function must be to penetrate reality, not simplify it. Abstract concepts must "designate the most fundamental determinations within a given process" (Wright, 1979:25). In positivism, the concrete is real and the abstract a fiction, in the sense of being removed from empirical reality

(Hopkins, 1978:201). In realism, the abstraction is not fiction but has a real existence (Rosdolsky, 1977:47). The concrete is merely the level of conceptualization, not the level of reality.

The realist method of abstraction relies heavily on the use of analogies or models. They are used to postulate the existence of structures that cannot be directly observed. Models are used in all types of science. But the realist use of models is different from that found elsewhere. Positivists use models to suggest covariances. Models are treated as heuristic devices, as aids to thinking about the relations between events or states. These models are fictions, quite dispensable once a law has been discovered (Benton, 1977:67). Realists, on the other hand, anticipate that the mechanism their model describes actually exists and explains the level of appearances. Their models are not so much useful or useless (as in the positivist usage) but more or less accurate. If the model correctly represents the underlying mechanism, the surface phenomenon will be causally explained. And it is possible to find out if the model is accurate or not by working out the further implications of the model—what it "predicts" about the world of appearances in addition to those with which we began. If we test these predictions and the predictions are accurate, "this gives good reason to believe in the existence of these structures and mechanisms" (Keat and Urry, 1975:35).

Realist theory building does not end with and is not conducted for the purpose of abstraction. The goal of realist social science is not a set of formal principles applicable to all times and places. Analysis is complete only when abstractions have been rendered more concrete. This provides a new description of social phenomena based on new knowledge of the underlying structure. Thus, it is common practice among historical materialists to "think away" fluctuations in the demand and supply of goods in order to think more clearly about the underlying structure of labor exploitation. Once the underlying relations of production have been revealed, fluctuations in demand and supply (and the effect they have on labor exploitation) can be reintroduced (Meek, 1967:94).

TESTING THEORY

Realists reject the positivist idea that the social order is akin to the natural order. They assume that, if the social order has been made by humans, it can be changed by humans and is not a force which stands against their will.

> Men by their very nature work on the constituent parts of the world—
> the world they find and the world they find made for them by other
> men—and thereby change the material world and the human world at
> the same time. This view is quite irreducible to a scientific view of man
> confronted by an external world not of their own making, a world with

its own immutable laws which merely human agency is powerless to deflect (Thomas, 1976:14).

Social reality is shaped by humans through their conscious practices. By their very nature, humans work to transform natural objects to fit their own purposes. At the same time, human beings come to know more about those objects and make use of this knowledge by incorporating it into practice. This applies to theory building also. Theorizing is a kind of practice, and practice part of theory building. Theory and practice presuppose and define each other.

The second reason why realist theory testing differs from that of positivism has to do with the distinction between appearances and reality. In the realist view, positivist theories are ideological, not in the sense of being deliberate distortions, but in the sense that they confine themselves to the level of appearances. At this level, they might be accurate. For example, role theory is true because in our everyday life we tend to have significance only insofar as we act in accordance with the positions we occupy or expect to occupy in the future. But role theory does not itself explain why this should be so or suggest that this kind of existence is anything less than permanent. A theory must be judged, not simply by how accurately it predicts outcomes, but by how revealing it is of the structures which determine those outcomes.

Finally, realist and positivist theory testing attribute different meanings to "better theory." Positivists see theory developing through successive empirical tests leading to refinements which render the theory more powerful and precise. It is assumed that the world to which the theory refers remains the same and only knowledge of that world changes. Realists believe that the world to which theory refers can also change, perhaps in response to theory. Testing theory in practice means that validation comes not from agreement among a community of scholars that the facts fit the theory but from agreement among the sociologist's subjects that they now understand their circumstances well enough to change them. Theory has made social life "transparent" (Bernstein, 1978:215). Theory development thus consists of people becoming aware of the structures which determine the concrete details of their lives. Errors in theory will be caused, not by weakness of intellect, but because social conditions encourage us to treat the false world of appearances as reality. If theory guides practice, practice shapes the development of theory. The resolution of theoretical difficulties will be a practical problem. And true theoretical understanding will be possible only when the practical conditions in which this understanding is possible have been created (Bauman, 1978:54).

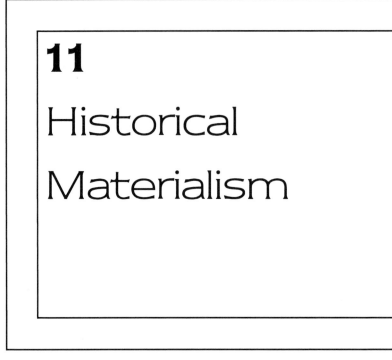

11

Historical

Materialism

The research tradition described in this chapter is "materialist" in the sense that the social world is explained in terms of the interaction of human beings and inanimate nature in the process of producing goods to meet material needs. It is "historical" in the sense that it is a theory of how social formations change. It sees human history as a sequence of social formations, from primitive to capitalist, each of which encapsulates a level of development of productive forces and a particular set of social relationships. The object of historical materialism is to analyze the laws of motion of these social formations. The bases of this research tradition are clearly realist.

One way of looking at historical materialism is as a comparative sociology of different modes of production, such as feudalism and capitalism. Each mode of production consists of forces of production and relations of production. The forces of production include the means of production (e.g. raw materials), technological equipment, and the labor power and skills necessary to use the equipment. The relations of production include the

> conditions and forms of ownership and control of the means of production as well as the means of administration, political control and violence; the forms of exchange, circulation and distribution, and

consumption of the social product; the forms of the division and control of labor, including especially the authority relations associated with these forms ... (Heydebrand, 1977:89).

Historical materialism assigns primacy to the forces of production in social change, but it is in no sense a theory of technological determinism, in that it conceives of the relation between the forces of production and the relations of production dialectically. Each is a "moment" within the development of the mode of production as a whole.

The unit of analysis in historical materialism is not, then, the abstractly conceived rational actor (as in exchange theory), nor the formally defined role player (as in structural functionalism). Nor is it "the social system." The unit of analysis is the mode of production. A mode of production is an abstraction from concrete societies. In some cases, a society may approximate a single mode of production, but this is rare. Any given society or "social formation" is called "feudal," "capitalist," or "socialist" according to which mode of production is dominant. The dominant mode of production is said to contain a certain "logic" which determines the conduct of social relations in the society as a whole.

The forces and relations of production are concepts fundamental to historical materialism. They are "transhistorical," in the sense that a full and correct understanding of any society without them is inconceivable. However, it is not possible to derive knowledge about specific social formations from these categories. They are abstractions and need to be made specific before they can throw light on concrete social phenomena. Following realist principles, historical materialism has as its object the goal of accounting for concrete phenomenal forms by revealing the abstract categories which underly them. This inspires no general theory of society, no elementary principles of social behavior. Rather, it inspires a search for the laws of transformation, the generative mechanism, which underlie each social epoch. The historical materialist, in contrast to the positivist, is more interested in what is distinctive about an epoch.

What is distinctive about the capitalist mode of production? The answer cannot be labor or capital because each can be found in other modes of production. What is distinctive about capitalism is the commodity form, and particularly the commodification of labor power. This insight is the kernel of contemporary historical materialism. In the precapitalist world, goods are produced primarily for use. They are valued for their utility. They are said to have "use-value." Of course, barter and exchange of goods exist, but if goods are exchanged and if cash is used, it is simply to expedite the acquisition of other needed goods. In the capitalist system, goods are sold primarily for their exchange value. The aim is no longer to sell in order to buy but to buy in order to sell, or rather, resell. Economic life is directed not toward the production of objects to be used by those who actually make them, nor toward the fulfillment of some direct human need, but toward objects designed for sale in the market place for the sole purpose of generating profit. Goods which cannot be sold will tend not to be produced (Gamble and Walton, 1976:115).

A commodity has both use-value and exchange-value. Its use-value lies in its power to satisfy a human need. Use-values are limited by the physical properties of the product. Exchange-value is an expression of a product's capacity to exchange against other products and of the proportions in which it will do so. Bread baked by a baker and consumed by him has use-value; it acquires exchange-value if he brings it to market and exchanges it for other products. The exchange-value of a commodity is not fixed (as it may seem) by supply and demand of different goods, but by the amount of labor that went into its production. Hours of labor (or some equivalent measure of labor) is the only common yardstick with which to compare usually disparate goods. Goods which have taken the same length of time to produce will be of equal exchange value.

The use-value and the exchange-value are not just two different aspects of a commodity. The relation is dialectically conceived. A commodity has both use-value and exchange-value, and without either would cease to be a commodity. On the other hand, use-value and exchange-value contradict each other. Use-value means that the good must be immediately useful to whoever has it. A commodity has exchange-value to the extent that it is not immediately used but is exchanged for something else.

The distinction between use-value and exchange-value did not originate with Marx, but Marx rejected the idea current in his time that exchange-value is determined in the process of circulation, in the ratio of supply and demand of different goods. Instead, he located the origin of exchange value in the amount of value that had gone into its production, in the production process. When Marx argued that labor time determines exchange-value he did not mean by this the actual time taken to produce a good, for this would have meant that slow workers create more value than fast workers. Rather, he saw value as reflecting "the socially necessary labor time" for the production of a good, the average amount of time necessary to produce a given article at a particular stage of human development and technological progress.

LABOR POWER
AS A COMMODITY

The capitalist practice of buying raw materials, hiring labor, and selling the transformed material would make little sense if value were not added in the process. If the capitalist cannot resell what she has bought at a price high enough to more than meet her total costs, the transaction will not yield a profit for her. Marx did not accept the argument that this added value derived from the process of circulation. Instead, the value derives from the labor which enters into the production process.

When he enters the employ of the capitalist, the worker sells his labor power, his capacity to work. Like any other commodity, labor power has both use-value and exchange-value. The exchange-value of labor power is determined in the same fashion as the exchange-value of any other commodity, by how much labor time went into producing it. In this case, the labor time necessary to produce it is the value of the means of subsistence necessary for the "reproduction" of the worker. "The value of labor power is a sum of the labor of others required to keep the laborer continuously appearing in the market and of the labor required to train and maintain his children, who are his future substitutes" (Smelser and Warner, 1976:215). In reality, the labor costs of the reproduction of labor power are determined in complex ways: not only does the definition of the value of the means of subsistence vary, but the costs of reproduction will also be influenced by "various technical considerations (training costs, transportation costs, etc.) as well as by class struggle over wages" (Wright, 1978:118). However, the important point remains that the exchange-value of labor power is determined by what it takes to make that labor power.

When she purchases the labor power of the worker, the capitalist tries to pay only enough to ensure the reproduction of that labor power. If this were equal to the value of the product the worker creates, no surplus value would be realized and the capitalist would not make a profit. However, the worker actually works longer than it takes to reproduce his labor power, and the resulting surplus value is expropriated by the capitalist.

The capitalist has two kinds of costs which must be offset in order for surplus value to be realized. Constant capital is the value of the means of production used up during the production process, primarily the depreciation value of machines, buildings, and raw materials. This capital is constant because it adds no value during the production process. It is simply consumed by the labor power and its value preserved as part of the new commodities produced. Variable capital is the cost of labor power applied in the production process. It is variable because it not only reproduces its own value (i.e. its subsistence wages) but creates new value, a value which need not be constant.

It might be that neither worker nor capitalist is fully aware of the fact that the wage contract is anything less than an exchange of equivalents. It appears that labor power is sold freely on the labor market and that workers get a fair day's pay for a fair day's work. But in fact the capitalist production process is inherently exploitative. It contains both necessary and surplus labor. Some labor is necessary in that it furnishes the means of livelihood for the worker. However, some labor is surplus, in that it is "beyond the requirements of simply reproducing the direct producers themselves, a surplus which is appropriated by the non-productive classes" (Wright, 1978:114).

The progressive extension of the domain of surplus labor is the essence of the capitalist mode of production (Rosdolsky, 1977:225). The concept "exploitation" thus has a very precise meaning in historical materialism. It refers to the process whereby the dominant class extracts from the subordinate class amounts of surplus labor (Gough, 1979:18). Wherever jobs are capitalistically organized, this kind of exploitation will occur. For example, a hairdresser who sells her services directly to a client has created no surplus value to be appropriated by another; a hairdresser who is hired by the owner of a hairdressing salon and paid a wage is exploited. It is this transformation of labor power into a commodity, and the part it plays in the extraction of surplus value, that distinguishes the capitalist mode of production from other modes, not the rise of markets, not the development of money economies, and not the industrialization of manufacture.

The labor theory of value is intended to explain how it is possible for the owner of the means of production to get more value out of the production process than he puts in. It solves the riddle of how a person with money can multiply it by lending it at interest to a manufacturer who hires wage labor. The theory is only indirectly relevant to the question of what determines the actual price of a good or what determines the profit margin of a particular capitalist or the interest paid to a lender. It simply states that, if an understanding of the dynamics of the social relations of production under capitalism is desired, a measure of value based on hours of human labor embodied in commodities is the most useful.

> ...the degree of exploitation is not measured by the rate of profit but by the rate of surplus value, i.e. the ratio of surplus value to variable capital only: for it is this which shows how much of the value produced by the worker accrues to him and how much he forfeits to the capitalist by the sale of his labour power.... There is no linear relationship between the rate of profit and the rate of surplus value; one may rise while the other falls and vice versa. The realisation of surplus value depends, in reality, on circulation as well as production (Kolakowski, 1978:294).

During the process of circulation many other factors beside labor will intervene to determine the profit rate.

The labor theory of value is important because it alerts us to the fact that profits originate in production rather than in exchange relations. It is a sociological more than an economic theory, less suited to predicting the price of goods or the profit margins of firms, and more suited as a model of the social and political structure of the capitalist enterprise, where the domination of capital is a condition for the existence of profits. The theory leads us to expect that decisions about what to produce and how to produce it are based on the ability to extract surplus value from the wage-laborer. It is a means of explaining the social relationships of the workplace rather than the economic theory of supply and demand for goods.

CLASS RELATIONS

Every mode of production implies an ordering of people into groups with competing economic functions and claims. The relations into which people enter in the production process are the basis for class relations. In every society where the means of production are private property there will be at least two contending classes, those who own the means of production and those who do not.

When the capitalist system is defined at the highest level of abstraction, the fundamental antagonism is that between the capitalist and the worker. Capitalists are the owners of the means of production and purchasers of labor power. Workers are forced to sell their labor power to the capitalist in return for a wage. Capitalist development means the increasing polarization of society into these two classes as a larger share of the labor force is proletarianized. More and more workers become employees of someone else, depending for their living on selling their labor power.

In historical materialism, classes are not "things" or mere aggregates of people.

> Classes are not defined simply *relative* to other classes, but in a social *relation* to other classes.... In a gradational view of classes, lower classes are simply defined as having less of something that upper classes have more of—income, wealth, education, status—but within a relational view, the working class is defined by its qualitative location within a social relation that simultaneously defines the capitalist class (Wright, 1980a:6).

Class relations are defined primarily by the social relations of production. The capitalist is the purchaser of labor power and the owner of the means of production; the worker must sell his labor power in order to survive. Even a worker who owns his own means of production (e.g. a plumber and his tools) is part of the proletariat if he must support himself by contracting with a capitalist.

At the most abstract level of conceptualization, when all historical, concrete details have been thought away, only two contending classes are discerned. However, it is quite apparent there there are more than two contending economic groups in real life. There are a number of reasons why the phenomenal forms of social relations are more complex than the structure which underlies them. First, all societies contain more than one mode of production. The class structure of any society will therefore be more complex than the simple dual model because there will exist classes belonging to different modes of production (e.g. an aristocratic element in capitalism). Second, there are three aspects to the relation between capital and labor: capital can control the physical means of production, control investments and resources or control labor power. Only when the same group directs investments, decides how the physical means of production are to be used, and controls the authority structure within the labor process will there be only two contending classes (Carchedi, 1977). Anything less than this will produce "contradictory class positions," consisting of occupational groups like salaried managers, professionals, technicians, and small shopkeepers, which are capitalist in some respects and proletarian in others (Wright, 1980b).

The third reason why a simple dual model of class is rarely applicable to concrete societies is that divisions exist within each class. There are divisions within the capitalist class according to the kind of productive force controlled (e.g. land, business, or finance) and there are divisions within the proletariat according to the kind of labor power sold (e.g. skilled versus unskilled, white collar versus blue collar). It should be borne in mind, however, that these intraclass conflicts are secondary to the principal contradiction between the owners of the means of production and those who must labor for them (Jalee, 1977:51).

Finally, the simple dual model must be complemented by an understanding of the role of "unproductive labor." There are many workers in capitalist societies who neither own the means of production nor sell productive labor power. Labor power is productive if it adds value during the production process. Workers in occupations like schoolteacher, soldier, professional athlete, advertising executive, and so on do not directly create surplus value but live off the surplus value created by others. Although they perform a necessary function in the total creation and realization of surplus value they are not part of the true proletariat. Also included in this category would be the expanding number of workers not employed by capital at all, those employees of the state who produce goods and services that are not sold, hence do not assume the form of commodities, "employees in the social services as well as the administrative, judicial and repressive apparatus of the state" (Gough, 1979:104). This distinction between productive and unproductive labor reveals one of the bases for the exploitation of women. Women who work exclusively in the home are not producing exchange-value. They are producing use-values and transforming commodities into use-values for immediate consumption. One result is that housework is regarded as having no social value although in reality it does indirectly produce surplus value through the reproduction and maintenance of the male labor force (Benston, 1969).

CLASS RELATIONS AND
INDIVIDUAL LIFE CHANCES

The theory of class relations at the core of historical materialism is different from that found in other research traditions in sociology, particularly those which draw upon the work of Max Weber to formulate a "gradational" theory of social inequality. Weber conceptualized social classes as groups possessing different "life chances," or opportunities to obtain material rewards (e.g. income) and social benefits (e.g. prestige). Inequalities in life chances were explained by pointing to the individual's differential perform- ance in the market for labor. Those who have the greatest life chances are those who have competed most successfully in the market for their labor skills. In this Weberian model, adopted most enthusiastically by positivist sociologists, social inequality is seen as comprising a series of strata or ranks.

In this model, people are distributed along continuous strata, with a bulge in the middle to indicate the middle class. The consequences of adopting this gradational image of class are at odds with the theory of class relations suggested by historical materialism:

> ...[the] empirical description of 'socioeconomic standings' became independent of any historical understanding; the vision of classes as historical actors became replaced by statistical analyses of distribution of income, education and prestige; the analysis of social differentiation became separated from the analysis of conflict (Przeworski, 1977:364).

The reason for this different mode of conceptualization is that Weber saw the origins of classes in market relations, in the process of distribution and exchange, whereas Marx saw the origins of class and social inequality in the relations of production. Labor market processes were considered important but seen as operating only within the constraints imposed by the dominant mode of production.

Occupations (and other measures of labor market competitiveness) are not used by Marxian theorists to empirically ascertain class boundaries. Occupations reflect the technological division of labor and tell us nothing about the social relations of production (Wright, 1980b). We can see the difference between an occupation and a genuine class by contrasting capitalists (a class) with physicians (an occupation).

> ...the capitalists have a direct operating relationship to the mode of production, while the physicians do not; the capitalists have distinct economic interests (the size of their profit) based on these relations which place them in conflict with the proletariat and landowners, the other two groups directly involved in capitalist production, while the economic interests of physicians—though leaning toward those of the capitalists in present society—are really compatible with the interests of any of the three great classes; the capitalists are conscious of their uniqueness as a class with interests that are opposed to those of the two other main classes in society, while physicians, even if they are conscious of themselves as a distinct group, do not view their interest as being opposed to those of others; the capitalists are organized in one or more political parties, which work to promote their interests, while physi-

cians—despite their pressure group activity—have no such organization; and finally, capitalists exhibit a general cultural affinity, a way of life and a set of social values, which mark them off from the proletariat and the landowners, while physicians as a group have no such distinguishing features (Ollman, 1979:39).

Conceptualizing social classes as relations, rather than as aggregates of individuals, emphasizes the structural nature of social inequality. Income differences are caused less by individual inputs of "human capital" (e.g. education, training) and more by location of an occupation in the realm of production.

The American occupational structure is properly conceived against a background of sectoral divisions within the American economy which have created a dual or "split" market for labor. The monopoly sector creates a "primary" market for labor. It consists of rapidly growing industries making use of new raw materials and productive technology. Industries in this sector are capital intensive, highly productive, and pay high wages. The competitive sector generates a "secondary" labor market. In this sector, firms are typically small, highly competitive, and labor intensive: pay tends to be low and jobs insecure.

A historical trend toward economic segmentation has produced two major sectors. Income differences follow from this economic segmentation. "Workers in the monopoly sector generally have higher earnings, more stable employment and better non-wage benefits than their counterparts in the competitive sector" (Kalleberg, Wallace, and Althauser, 1981:653).

But the segmentation of the economy into monopoly and competitive sectors is not sufficient to explain income inequalities. All capitalists would prefer cheap labor, but the working class resists this. Its resistance meets with mixed success, depending, in part, on the nature of the production process concerned. Efforts to resist exploitation (e.g. labor laws) will apply unevenly across the economy, perhaps benefiting monopoly sector workers more than competitive sector workers. The competitive sector, with low rates of unionization, weak labor laws, low wages, and job insecurity, is testimony to the weakness of the working classes' efforts in that segment of the economy.

Bonacich (1979:24) has combined dual economy theory with a theory of class conflict to explain income inequalities by sex and race. She distinguishes three classes in contemporary capitalism—capital, high-priced labor, and cheap labor. The cheap labor is concentrated in the secondary sector. The two groups of labor rarely compete for the same jobs. For reasons of oppression and late entry into the urban labor force, blacks, women, and other socially oppressed minorities have been concentrated in the cheap labor competitive sector. Both capital and labor have thus become fragmented. There are big labor and big capital segments in the monopoly sector, small capital and small labor segments in the competitive sector. Big labor is dominated by white males.

What is true of the economy as a whole is true also of the causes of inequality *within* organizations. Treated by other sociologists as the result of technological development, changes in the organization of work are regarded by historical materialists as reflecting the ongoing struggle between capitalist and worker over the distribution of surplus labor. The evolution of new work practices, of new job categories, and of new occupational groups and hierarchies is interpreted as part of an effort on the part of each capitalist (beset with competition from other capitalists) to cheapen labor, and as part of the struggle of the workers to resist this.

The employer, who purchases in labor power only the *capacity* to work, finds it necessary to organize and direct very carefully the way in which this capacity is realized. The search for "efficiency," which is the stated purpose of the division of labor in the workplace and of the system of rewards and punishments used in incentive schemes, is therefore inherently political, part of a drive for more reliable and efficient forms of control: "the functions of management and administration are inseparable from those of oversight and oppression" (Jalee, 1977:55). The very structure of work—the separation of planning from execution, the grading of occupational levels, the system of incentives, are part of the class struggle (Braverman, 1974; Burawoy, 1979; Edwards, 1979; Noble, 1979). The precise nature of the distribution of opportunities in a work organization and the resulting distribution of rewards is a "moment" in the struggle between capitalist and worker for control over the labor process.

ALIENATION

Only in societies oriented chiefly to the production of commodities does the labor power of the individual have to represent itself as its opposite, as impersonal, abstract, and general. The commodification of labor power reduces the relation between employer and employee to the abstract form found in the exchange of equivalents. This is the root of alienation.

Beginning with the transformation of labor into a commodity, historical materialism shows how things come to rule the people who have created them, governing the way they perceive and treat each other.

> For the capitalist, the worker exists only as labour power, for the worker, the capitalist exists only as capital. For the consumer, the producer is commodities, for the producer, the consumer is money (Geras, 1973:293).

Commodification means that humans take on the appearance of objects and objects take on the powers of humans. The means of production (which are actually "dead" labor) confront the worker as a hostile power.

When any object is transformed into a commodity it loses its concrete meaning. Its value is determined solely by that for which it can be exchanged. Marx called this "commodity fetishism" because it amounted to investing in a thing powers it did not have. The impression that most of us have that an object has exchange-value because of its inherent qualities (what it is worth) conceals the reality that its value has been imparted by the human labor that produced it.

In the world of work, the commodification of labor has consequences of great significance. The labor of one worker becomes related to the labor of others as if the relation were between things; the producer becomes less important than what is produced; machines become more valuable than humans; efficiency and profits are more important than human values; and what the worker produces is no longer his or directly useful to him.

These conditions are alienating because man's most basic need is to conceive a project in his imagination and execute it in reality. To be fully human is to act to further a preconceived project. If the worker does not own the means of production, if her labor power is a commodity, if she has no responsibility for planning work, if her products are designed above all to realize exchange values, and if she has come to treat herself and her fellow workers as objects, she has lost her humanity, she has become alienated. Workers who cannot sell their labor power are made to feel useless, no matter how much society might be in need of what they are capable of producing. To be useful is to have "marketable skills."

Alienation is manifest not only in the concrete conditions of work which have been reduced to mindless detail tasks, but also in the belief that economic events are the working out of "blind" economic forces or "the hidden hand" which no human being, not even the capitalist, can control. Alienation therefore affects both worker and capitalist. And it refers not only to a structural condition but to an image of the world.

Marx did not believe that alienation was simply a state of mind, an illusion which would disappear once his writings became known. He was aware that the conditions of alienation were all too real. People had forgotten that their fellow human beings were human, that they all contributed to the making of society and could also contribute to its remaking. Marx also understood the illusory power of money, but he did not treat this as a delusion, because the illusory power of money lay in its ability to create the very conditions of which it is the fantasy.

> ...to conceive of money as having the power to buy everything is indeed to have money which has the power to buy everything.... For all practical purposes, that is for purposes of life in capitalism, reification brings about the very mistake it embodies (Ollman, 1976:199).

Freedom from alienation could be achieved not by getting people to think differently, but by getting them to act so as to abolish the system of private property on which it is based.

BASE AND
SUPERSTRUCTURE

Fundamental to historical materialism is the division of social systems into a material base (or mode of production) and a superstructure, along with the claim that the mode of production determines the general character of the superstructure. The superstructure includes political and legal institutions; legal, religious, and moral codes; ideologies; scientific and philosophical systems of thought; and the arts.

The relation between base and superstructure is dialectical. Social relations determine the mode of consciousness, but consciousness also acts as a determinant of social relations (Sumner, 1979:12). The superstructure, once established, acquires a life of its own and thereby has a secondary impact on the movement of history.

The dominant ideas in the superstructure will reflect the interests of the dominant class. This class controls not only the means of material production but also the means of mental production. Through its control of mental production, the dominant class is able to supervise the construction of a coherent set of beliefs which penetrates the consciousness of the subordinate class. That class thus comes to see and experience reality through the conceptual categories of the dominant class.

The superstructure does not consist simply of ideas. Education is part of the superstructure, not only as manifested in ruling ideas of what education ought to be, but also in the form which educational institutions assume in capitalist society. A sociological analysis of education from a historical materialist standpoint is different from that found in a research tradition like functionalism. Functionalists argue that "organizational hierarchy based on educational certification practically assures occupational placement and reward according to merit" (Antonio, 1981:49). Schooling is believed to serve as a selection and training mechanism, ensuring that the skills and aptitudes requisite for an increasingly complex society are available.

The interpretation of schooling given by those who work within the tradition of historical materialism is rather different. Schooling reproduces the labor power essential for the process of accumulation and for the reproduction of the social relations of production. The process of accumulation is ensured by the transmission of cognitive skills and appropriate motivation. The social relations of production, however, are reproduced by transmitting inequalities. These inequalities are transmitted "not so much through the conscious intentions of teachers and administrators in their day-to-day activities but through a close correspondence between the social relationships which govern personal interaction in the workplace and the social relations of the educational system" (Bowles and Gintis, 1976:11). The school is transformed into a training and selection mechanism for an increasingly bureaucratized and alienating work world.

> Schooling prepares students for alienating labor by substituting grading for wages. In school, as in the factory, persons lose control of the work process and product. In both cases satisfaction derives largely from sources external to work (grades, money). Also, students and workers have little or no input into the organization of their activities. In both cases the administrative structure demands submission to authority, regulated by calculable, externally imposed rewards and punishments (Antonio, 1981:53–54).

The form or structure of education thus manifests the form of the capitalist system as a whole.

The family is also part of the superstructure. The family is that aspect of society having to do with reproduction which, together with other social institutions (like education), constitutes a social formation whose base is the capitalist mode of production. The family will contain within itself what capitalist society essentially is. Thus the social relations in the family will bear the imprint of the commodity form. The capitalist family is a means of private production, the children being their parents' "products": "under conditions of a high degree of individuation characteristic of capitalism, the parents seek to reproduce not their society or their 'home/line/family' but *themselves through* their children" (Harris, 1977:83).

The superstructure is determined "in the last instance" by the economic base, but it nevertheless enjoys a relative autonomy (Althusser, 1971:152). The word "relative" is not intended to suggest "somewhat" but a degree of autonomy in relation to the economic base. For example, kinship structures (and particularly ideas about gender and sex roles) have played an important part in the historical construction of the capitalist division of labor and in the reproduction of labor power. However, ideas about gender did not grow out of capitalist production. In no sense has the capitalist mode of production determined the categories we use to think about sex. Gender and class divisions do not coincide. Capitalism does require a separation of work and home and the relegation of women to the hearth and kitchen, but "this situation developed in a long and uneven process, one element of which was a struggle between male and female workers in which the better organised male craft unions succeeded in overriding the interests of women workers, many of whom themselves were responsible for dependents" (Barrett, 1980:97).

The idea of relative autonomy can also be illustrated by examining the treatment of the state in the writings of historical materialists. The relation between the state and the economic base is conceived dialectically. The process of production and exploitation involves the reproduction of the relations of political domination, and the relations of political domination "are already present in the actual constitution of the relations of production" (Poulantzas, 1978:26). Each is but an "instance" in the development of a single mode of production.

The state emerged as a coercive political institution with the division of society into classes. The character of the state depends on the particular combination of relations and forces of production that constitutes the base of society. The form and mode of operation of the state is assumed to be subordinate to the particular mode of production and to the interests of the class which is dominant in that mode. This theory does not imply that specific groups of capitalists "capture" the state apparatus and self-consciously use it to further their interests. It simply means that there are systematic structural constraints on the state apparatus that tend to yield policies favorable to capital, regardless of the class composition of the state elite. The underlying notion is that managers of the state are dependent on some reasonable level of economic activity in order to adequately finance state operations through tax revenue and maintain public support. Action by the state that would threaten to reduce "business confidence" and stifle investment must be avoided, even if there are state managers ideologically predisposed in favor of tax policies and social programs which might do this (Offe, 1975).

The "logic of capital" manifests itself in state institutions and policies. The state institutes and defends sets of laws, organizations, and policies which guarantee the reproduction of the class which owns the means of production. This will include the preservation of property relations and the maintenance of public order. In the capitalist state, it means preserving private property, maintaining enough law and order so that business can be conducted, ensuring a sufficient supply of cheap labor, protecting markets for goods, and assuming the burden of social costs (e.g. housing) which capitalists find it unprofitable to meet (Hirsch, 1979).

The state thus reflects the form or logic of the dominant mode of production. However, the relation between the state and the mode of production must be dialectically conceived. This means a number of things. The state furnishes the infrastructure of production (e.g. transportation, communication, stable currency) and the conditions for the reproduction of labor (e.g. health care, education). The state thus reproduces capitalist class relations not only by framing "bourgeois law" but also by contributing to the supply of and demand for investment capital, by itself supplying goods and services, and by financing and organizing research and development. Most of these state expenditures primarily benefit large corporations and upper income groups (Barclay, 1981:201). Conversely, the economy provides the state with what it needs in order to survive, namely a healthy and expanding economy from which to extract revenues. And yet, despite this unity, there is also opposition. The state competes with the capitalist class for resources. Capitalists will frequently find that the state is pursuing policies (e.g. in the sphere of foreign relations) which are more directed toward enhancing state power than capitalist accumulation (Block, 1977). Furthermore, the state takes on a "material existence" and an inertia "which are to a certain extent independent of current state policies and class relations" (Therborn, 1978:35). There will also be conflicts within the capitalist class which the state must mediate in such a way as to benefit the entire capitalist class. State policies will not, therefore, always work to the benefit of every capitalist but to the benefit of capitalism in general. Such is the case with education which, as we have seen, is not designed to provide manpower for this or that industry or firm but to provide "a maximum of exchange opportunities to both labour and capital" (Offe and Rouge, 1979:350). In other words, the state's role, through its support for general education, makes it easier for more individuals to enter into capitalist relations of production (i.e. buy and sell labor power) than to remain outside the system altogether.

The dialectical relation between the state and the mode of production means that the state is not a "thing" nor an instrument of this or that group but a relation between social class forces (Therborn, 1978:34). The "presence" of the state—its precise form, its size, its policies and practices—reflects a "moment" in the class struggle. The delivery of goods and services by the state, the provision of welfare benefits, and so on, tends to come in waves as a more or less direct response to threats to the stability of the system created by alienated groups (Piven and Cloward, 1977). For example, a national health insurance scheme, while indeed serving the needs of capital, is less beneficial to capitalists than would be a compulsory private insurance scheme, and is the result of organized working-class pressure (Stephens, 1979:78). The state is part of the class struggle. The state, in turn, has an effect on the course of that struggle because it conditions the way in which classes become organized (Przeworski, 1977:373). The way in which the working classes vote, organize, acquire their leaders, and put forward demands is dependent upon their submission to state regulations and practices.

The state is properly conceived, then, as part of the dialectical working-out of the contradictions of capital. Its role in this process is crucial. For example, the state normally presents itself as serving the interests of society as a whole. During severe economic crises, the state will have to intervene in such a way as to undermine this image of impartiality. This is likely to spark further economic instability and call for yet more state intervention (Wolfe, 1977).

Besides the state and other social relations like the family, the superstructure also includes political doctrines, economic theories, and religious beliefs. These are ideologies, but not in the sense of being illusions. They are ideologies in the sense of being systematically distorted knowledge, distorted in a fashion which is not haphazard but bears a systematic causal relation to the mode of production. Ideologies do accurately represent and account for social experiences, but they also conceal fundamental features of the social world.

> The "real relations" in the sphere of production are ... essentially exploitative and the capitalist appropriates surplus value produced by the labourer. However, the everyday experience of work is lived in terms defined within the sphere of circulation, for *wages* are determined in a labour market and appear simply as the price of labour. In this market, labour and wages are exchanged as equivalents in the same ways as any other act of buying and selling of commodities, giving rise to the notion of a fair wage conceived as a fair price for labour. Thus, the whole conception of a wage, conceals the real relations in which the capitalist extracts a quantity of labour which is not paid for in the wage (Abercrombie, 1980:79).

Economic theories which account for wage levels in terms of the demand for and supply of labor are therefore correct in their analysis, for they accurately describe one level of the capitalist economy. At another level, however, they are ideologies, in that they take the capitalist relations out of their historical context in the production process and make of them natural phenomena based on eternal principles of exchange.

THE LAWS OF CAPITAL ACCUMULATION

Historical materialism is not divided into "statics" and "dynamics." The whole purpose of this research tradition is to lay bare the laws of motion which govern the transition from one mode of production to another. Each mode of production contains within itself the contradictions which will eventually cause its downfall and the transcendence of another.

Capitalism is expansionary. Capitalism cannot survive without expanding, without transforming all means of life into commodities and subordinating all relations to capitalist relations. The self-expansion or accumulation of capital is induced by two kinds of pressure—the competition between capitalists and the struggle between capitalist and worker. The drive to accumulate or expand capital does not therefore result from individual greed. It is the expression of the class struggle in capitalism in which each capitalist must cheapen costs and find new markets in order to survive. In pursuit of this goal, each capitalist tries to transform more and more of life into commodities and incorporate more and more of the population into capitalist relations. As technological innovations are used to improve productivity, more and more value is produced by fewer and fewer workers. If other sources of employment were not provided, demand would not keep pace and commodities would remain unsold. This would lead to the overproduction of goods and a fall in investment, culminating in stagnation. The continuous expansion of markets is thus also fueled in part by the very technological developments which capitalist competition inspires.

Capital accumulation does not mean an increase in the amount of capital. Capital is not a thing and cannot grow like a pile of money. Rather, it means the reproduction of capital on an ever-expanding scale through the transformation of surplus value into new constant and variable capital. In the process, more and more of social life becomes characterized by capitalist social relations. "Mechanization, standardization, overspecialization and parcellization of labor, which in the past determined only the realm of commodity production in actual industry, now penetrates into all sectors of social life" (Mandel, 1975:387). Not only industry, but agriculture, transportation, and service industries are transformed. More and more of the goods consumed become commodities bought and sold on the open market. More and more of the services people need become packaged as items for purchase. More and more of the jobs become proletarianized.

As capitalism advances, its structure gradually changes from the original highly competitive "market model" to one in which capital has become increasingly concentrated and centralized. Concentration refers to the accumulation of capital by individual capitalists (e.g. the growth of giant enterprises) while centralization refers to the reduction in the number of capitalists (e.g. the emergence of trusts, cartels, oligopolies, and monopolies). In the later stages of capitalism, a few, giant interlocked corporations dominate the core of the economy. On the periphery a multitude of small firms compete with each other, largely dependent on trade with giant corporations for their existence (O'Connor, 1973). The large corporations are able to largely determine prices and set conditions for labor as well as governing the rate and direction of research and development. These large corporations cannot be run by a single individual and, as a consequence, the proportion of jobs having nothing to do directly with production increases, thus abetting the trend toward the centralization of authority (Baran and Sweezy, 1966:14–51).

Eventually, giant corporations transcend national boundaries and trade in world markets for raw materials, labor, investments, and consumers. Capitalist social relations eventually comprise a world system consisting of trade among a number of societies which constitute a world division of labor. The core of this system is made up of those national societies in which the labor process employs mainly skilled workers at relatively high wages and is capital intensive. Peripheral countries comprise the international proletariat. They sell their labor power because the world means of production are owned and controlled by core countries. Colonial expansion, foreign investment, and multinational corporations are the concrete manifestations of the growth of this world system. The most important characteristic of a multinational corporation is that it operates on the world system level, taking advantage of the best conditions in each country for the performance of each part of the process of production, planning and managing in one country, producing in another, assembling in yet another, and selling worldwide.

With the advent of a world system of capitalist relations, class relations are formed on a world scale. These class relations form the base which explains patterns of unequal trade, the underdevelopment of Third World countries, and the international migration of capital and labor. The underdevelopment of the peripheral countries is a result of their dependence on the core countries. Conversely, the very development of the core countries requires dependent economies elsewhere in the world. One consequence of the expansion of capital in this way is that capital accumulation (and its attendant crises) takes place on a world scale, with few countries exempt from its booms and busts (Cardoso and Faletta, 1979; Evans, 1979; Wallerstein, 1979). It is this crisis-ridden character of capital accumulation to which we must now turn.

THE CONTRADICTIONS OF CAPITALISM

The development of capitalism is inherently contradictory. The productive forces change and grow continuously. The resistance of the established social relations to adaptation to these ever-changing forces of production constitutes the principal contradiction in any mode of production.

> At a certain stage in their development, the material productive forces of society come into conflict with the existing relations of production, or—what is but a legal expression of the same thing—with the property relations within which they have been at work hitherto. From forms of development of the productive forces, these relations turn into their fetters. Then begins an epoch of social revolution (Marx, 1978:4).

The transition from feudalism to capitalism saw the gradual emancipation of the bourgeoisie from feudal political and legal relations.

> This class then monopolised the ownership and development of a new progressive force of production, capital; progressive in the sense that it represented an expansion of human productive capacity. The feudal relations of production, in particular serfdom and barriers to free economic activity, became a fetter to the further development of the productive forces of society since the development of capital depends on the existence of a pool of free labourers and freedom of economic activity. As the bourgeois forces of production develop, so does the social power of the bourgeoisie since power is derived from property holdings. At a certain point, the bourgeoisie becomes strong enough to throw off feudal relations of production and political domination. The capitalist era and the bourgeois rule are ushered in (Stephens, 1979:5–6).

As capitalism matures, the forces of production become increasingly socialized and the social relations of production become more and more privatized. The socialization of the forces of production means the development of a fully cooperative and interdependent process of production based on a complex division of labor and the interdependence of the producers on a national and (eventually) international level. The process of manufacture socializes while the ownership of the means of production concentrates in fewer and fewer hands. The socialization of the forces of production includes two major developments: first, the herding together of increasing numbers of workers and their growing interdependence on a national scale; second, higher social costs of production (e.g. air pollution, urban crowding, mass transit expenses, welfare benefits). These costs become increasingly socialized but profits from the production process which makes them necessary remain private. This basic contradiction manifests itself in the problem of matching public needs with the demand for private profits and in the debate over the proper role of national and local governments in planning and production.

This underlying, structural contradiction manifests itself in a variety of recurring crises. The most serious of these is probably the tendency of the rate of profit to fall.

> Each individual capitalist must sell his commodities at the market price or below, or suffer a decline in sales to his competitors. To do so, he must continually seek ways to produce a large volume of goods at lower unit costs, for that is what his competitors are doing. This requirement, in turn, engenders yet another; the need for productivity increases. Thus, the individual capitalist *must* compromise, and increase the output per worker through the substitution of labor-saving technologies. Over the economy as a whole, however, this has the long-run consequence of lowering profitability and hence undermining production itself. Periodic crises are thus structured into capitalist production (Appelbaum, 1978:76).

This tendency for the rate of profit to fall is perhaps more accurately described as the tendency of the organic composition of capital to rise. The organic composition of capital is the ratio of constant to variable capital in production. Constant capital is the value of the means of production consumed during the production process; variable capital is the value of the labor power applied during production. A rise in the organic composition of capital means a rise in the value level of constant capital per worker resulting from the constant pressure for technological innovation and cost cutting induced by capitalist competition and by constant pressure from workers for improved conditions, higher wages, and shorter hours.

Surplus value is produced only by variable capital. If the value of constant capital grows at a faster rate than that of variable capital, the point will be reached when no surplus value is being realized.

> Since capitalism is production for profit, once the overall rate of profit (or at least that obtaining in the key economic sectors) drops below some

minimally acceptable level, production ceases. Factories close down and economic crisis ensues. The profit-maximizing strategy of the individual capitalist has resulted in a profitability crisis for the class of capitalists as a whole. This is, for Marx, a structural imperative of capitalist economic production (Appelbaum, 1978:75).

The decline in the rate of profit is a tendency, not an iron law. It sets in motion countertendencies, such as the intensification of the exploitation of labor, the extraction of cheap raw materials from colonies, the use of cheap foreign labor, and the nationalization of unprofitable sectors, all of which function temporarily to sustain the rate of profit. Profit margins can also be maintained by the creation of a "reserve army of labor." Increased productivity, while it tends to lower profits, also creates a state of relative overpopulation, which forces workers to compete with one another, depresses the wage level, and increases profits.

This analysis of the structural contradictions inherent in the capitalist mode of production suggests that the attention given by orthodox social scientists to problems of the market is misplaced. Whether or not competitiveness is maintained at the level of the market for goods and labor, the problem of capital accumulation remains the same—how to increase the rate of exploitation. Whatever the fluctuations in the market for goods, the problem for capitalism is chronic—an insufficiency of surplus value to keep production and accumulation profitable. The study of markets is not without relevance, but it is more important to examine processes at the level of production.

The tendency for the rate of profit to fall is not the only crisis with which capitalism is faced by virtue of the contradictions inherent in it. There is also a tendency for excess productive capacity to develop. Once again, the impetus is the competition which is the essence of capitalism. Each capitalist assumes that, in order to remain competitive and realize a profit, he must constantly seek to expand production. But capitalism protects and perpetuates an unequal distribution of income such that the expanded production cannot be used up by society at large because not enough people have the necessary buying power. The result is a tendency to produce in excess of what the market can absorb and a tendency for a portion of the surplus value to be unrealized.

The tendency toward overproduction can be counteracted in a number of ways. Mass advertising can increase consumption demands. By far the most powerful countertendency to overproduction, however, is the expansionary state, which mops up ever-larger amounts of productive capacity in its military spending, work-projects, and housing and transportation programs, as well as increasing buying power through tax and fiscal policies through its role as an employer and through welfare payments. The expansionary state brings its own crises, however. State spending tends to lower overall productivity because it is not competitive. There is also a tendency for state spending to rise more rapidly than the requirements for the realization of surplus value because state programs, once in place, come to be looked on as an entitlement and the state comes under pressure not to let them lose value. This creates a new crisis, a state "fiscal crisis" in which there is a growing gap between the society's requirements for state expenditures and the capacity of the state to finance these requirements (Block, 1981; Castells, 1978; O'Connor, 1973).

THE EMERGENCE OF CLASS CONSCIOUSNESS

The crises experienced by capitalism both shape and are shaped by the class struggle. The generation of a nascent mode of production within the confines of an existing one creates the dynamic base for growth of unity and consciousness among the class which will eventually overthrow the dominant class. Capitalism creates the material conditions for the transition to socialism. "Free" laborers, brought together in large-scale interdependent enterprises in which control is concentrated in the hands of a few, are the ascendant class. The revolution thus has a material base in the objective contradiction inherent in the capitalist mode of production. The political revolution can be based only on this foundation of economic power. Revolutions do not originate among totally subordinated classes (Skocpol, 1979).

On the other hand, revolutions do not happen just because the structural conditions are appropriate. Revolutions must be made. The subordinate class must become aware of itself as a revolutionary class. In capitalism, the proletariat must become conscious of itself before it can assume its revolutionary role.

> First, workers must recognize that they have interests. Second, they must be able to see their interests as individuals in their interests as members of a class. Third, they must be able to distinguish what Marx considers their main interests as workers from other less important economic interests. Fourth, they must believe that their class interests come prior to their interests as members of a particular nation, religion, race, etc. Fifth, they must truly hate their capitalist exploiters. Sixth, they must have an idea, however vague, that their situation could be qualitatively improved. Seventh, they must believe that they themselves, through some means or other, can help bring about this improvement. Eighth, they must believe that Marx's strategy, or that advocated by Marxist leaders, offers the best means for achieving their aims. And ninth, having arrived at all the foregoing, they must not be afraid to act when the time comes (Ollman, 1972:7–8).

It is not to be supposed that the average worker develops a complex understanding of the class nature of capitalism and the promise of socialism. However, historical materialists do suppose that the overwhelming majority of workers will come to recognize that their interests are opposed to those of capital, and that they should support movements which overthrow the system rather than those which simply repair it. There will be considerable variation in the degree to which workers in different capitalist societies support trade unions and parties of the left. Ethnic and religious loyalties will be one cause of variation in class consciousness (Reich, 1981).

The conditions for the emergence of class consciousness have been the focus of much recent work in historical materialism (Aronowitz, 1973; Gorz, 1967; Hamilton, 1972; Leggett, 1968; Szymanski, 1978). The role of vanguard parties and of the state in the timing of revolution have also come under special scrutiny. Modern revolutions have occurred in countries where old regimes have been undermined by the weak position of that country in international conflicts (Skocpol, 1979:23). Marx believed that the possibility of a peaceful overthrow of capitalism would be determined by the historical tradition and the flexibility of the ruling class of the country in question. Later exponents of historical materialism (e.g. Lenin, Kautsky, Luxemburg) all presented different theories about the transition to socialism. Each theory reflected the historical circumstances of its proponent. Those who tend to see the revolution as peaceful and gradual tend to live in, or are thinking about, advanced capitalist societies. Those who expect a sudden and violent revolution live in or are thinking about regimes which are dominated by military elites or state bureaucracies.

CONCLUSION

Starting with the commodity form, historical materialism extends to comprise a sweeping analysis of social life and its manifestations, from the social relations of the workplace to the ideas and beliefs expressed in religion, law, and politics. On the basis of a realist philosophy, it lays bare the underlying structural dynamics of social forms and processes. The insights yielded by this kind of analysis have been acknowledged, even by its severest critics.

And yet, few research traditions in the social sciences have attracted as much hostility and generated so much debate. And none of the other research traditions I have described has been wracked by so much internal disagreement. Rather than confine our consideration of historical materialism to a few paragraphs, I will devote the final chapter of Part Three to detailing the criticisms of this research tradition which have come from realists and nonrealists alike.

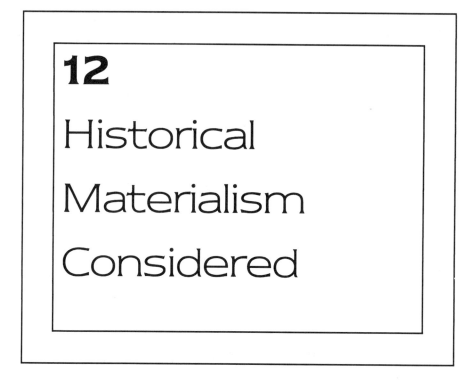

12

Historical Materialism Considered

It is hardly surprising that historical materialism should generate intense debate among sociologists. Its realist foundations contradict both positivist and idealist approaches to sociological problem-formation and resolution. Its claim to subsume sociology (and the other social sciences) within a political economy threatens the very existence of the discipline, and its commitment to praxis introduces political considerations into deliberations which most sociologists would prefer to believe can be treated in an ethically neutral manner.

The response of some sociologists has been to argue that historical materialism has no place in sociology (Bottomore, 1975) or that only selected aspects (e.g. the sociology of knowledge) are worthy of the sociologist's attention (Rossides, 1978:3). This group of sociologists would prefer to strip away the "philosophical" or "ideological" aspects of historical materialism and retain only that which is "purely scientific" (Sztompka, 1979:179). This "scientific" residue consists of the more important of Marx's ideas (e.g. alienation, class) translated into positivist language (e.g. Dahrendorf, 1959).

In this chapter three kinds of criticism of historical materialism will be described. First, there are the criticisms of the empirical assertions of historical materialism. A research tradition is not a substantive theory and contains no propositional statements, but each research tradition does rest on an implicit ontology, a set of assumptions about the nature of the social world and its functioning which those outside the research tradition are free to reject on empirical grounds.

Second, there are criticisms which focus upon the epistemology of historical materialism. Many sociologists are willing to absorb the ideas of historical materialism as to how sociology should be conducted provided these ideas are made compatible with positivist or idealist notions of correct method. Thus we will find sociologists agreeing with some of the empirical claims of historical materialism (e.g. that workers in factories are alienated) but disputing the method of conceptualizing and studying this phenomenon used by historical materialists.

Finally, we must acknowledge that historical materialism "provides a broad paradigm within which different schools flourish and contend" (Gough, 1979:10). The chapter concludes with a summary of the kind of criticism made of the realist version of Marxism I presented in Chapter Eleven by those who acknowledge a debt to Marx, who also seek to distance themselves from positivism and idealism, but who cannot accept that realism is the proper philosophical grounds for Marxian social thought. These critics espouse a Marxism which includes space for the reflexivity of social actors and acknowledges their ability to affect the possible directions in which structure might develop historically. This interpretation of Marxism refuses to see human beings as natural objects subject to the push and pull of underlying structures. Human beings have the potential to comprehend their predicament and can, individually and collectively, strive to avoid, deflect, or transcend these predicaments.

ISSUES OF SUBSTANCE

The Primacy of the Economic

Historical materialism originates in the assumption that man must be in a position to live in order to make history. Social forms and social consciousness are molded by material conditions. This is not technological determinism, because "the forces of production" include much more than materials or machines. However, even the milder proposition that the economic base of a society will, in the long run, determine its political and social forms, has occasioned considerable debate. Most of Marx's critics adopt the position that "it is not legitimate to claim that, because men must eat to live, their mode of life is necessarily determined by the manner in which they produce what they eat" (Giddens, 1973:87). They point out how difficult it has been to formulate either generally or in particular cases "the precise 'determining' force of economic changes, as against other social influences; or, if the primacy of the economic is strongly emphasized, to avoid arriving at a 'technological' interpretation of history" (Bottomore, 1975:68).

The use of the architectural metaphor of "base" and "superstructure" encourages a rather simplistic treatment of noneconomic phenomena. Social relations are either reduced to economic relations or treated as expressions or reflections of economic phenomena. There is a whole world of "civil society"—kinship systems, age structures, sexual segmentation—which is "glimpsed but never analyzed" in historical materialism (Gouldner, 1980:356). There is a certain irony in the fact that, while at the theoretical level historical materialism gives second place to ideas and political consciousness, the very success of Marxist politics depends on a new revolutionary consciousness, and the stability of the new communistic system depends upon the maintenance of this consciousness (Parsons, 1967:123).

The Labor Theory of Value

The labor theory of value is "the first and most fundamental ingredient" of historical materialism (Smelser and Warner, 1976:225). A number of criticisms have been made of this theory. It rests upon the assumption that all kinds of labor (disregarding differences in skills, commitment, and intelligence) can be reduced to a simple average, at least for the purpose of analysis. How is this simple average to be determined? Marx ruled out the possibility that it could be measured simply by observing the worker because levels of skill and technology might not be apparent to us in the number of hours worked.

> Given this formulation, it is difficult to know how to determine simple average labor in commodities other than by observing the ratios at which commodities actually exchange. But the exchange ratio is presumably what is to be explained by refering to the amount of labor (Smelser and Warner, 1976:228).

Either we continue to struggle with an undefinable but crucially important concept, or we define it in such a way that our argument is circular.

Another concept essential to the labor theory of value, that of "socially necessary labor time," is subject to criticism on the same terms. The amount of labor time necessary to produce a good changes as the state of technology improves. Since surplus value is calculated on the basis of a difference between socially necessary labor time required for production and the amount of time actually spent at work, anything that makes it difficult to assess the precise duration of socially necessary time will weaken the theory. The fact that the amount of time considered necessary varies with the state of technological advance only exacerbates these difficulties (Smelser and Warner, 1976:228).

There is a further difficulty with this notion of socially necessary labor time. The workers themselves play some role in determining its duration. How much labor is socially necessary depends partly on what standard of living workers deem appropriate. Socially necessary labor time is thus not something inherent in the labor or production process but the outcome of struggle between capitalist and worker (Gouldner, 1980:211).

Another frequent criticism of the labor theory of value is that it ignores the role of machines in creating wealth and assumes that all value is produced by labor. Machines are treated as dead or past labor. Human labor is not, however, the only source of energy. "Machines can be regarded as mechanical slaves who can be exploited even more than men" (Collins, 1975:426). It is possible to extract increased value in the production process without increasing the exploitation of human beings.

The Class Structure
of Advanced Societies

The work for which those who labor within the research tradition of historical materialism are best known is the analysis of the class structures of advanced societies. Marx, together with Max Weber, is regarded as a founder of the modern sociological study of social inequality (Giddens, 1973). Much of the debate surrounding historical materialism concerns the accuracy of its analysis of the causes and consequences of social inequality.

Most of the critics of historical materialism believe that the two-class model is too simple. Taking their cue from Weber, these critics insist that the analysis of social inequality requires the analytical separation of three dimensions of inequality: "class (market factors, property, technology, income, wealth), status (cultural evaluations expressed in group life, involving such matters as family, religion, race, morality, ethics, consumption, breeding, and general style of life), and party (access to the state, ability to create and enforce law)" (Rossides, 1976:13–14). These several dimensions of inequality, while under the general sway of economic factors, are nevertheless distinct and they vary independently.

The dichotomy between propertied and nonpropertied groups is thus replaced by a series of hierarchies that interact to produce the inequality sociologists refer to as "social stratification." Social classes thus lose their relational and oppositional character and become "social units sharing a composite of statuses in each of the three major dimensions from which they derive a common level of benefits and behavior" (Rossides, 1976:22). That is, the criterion for distinguishing between social classes is the *relative* level of social benefits. Using this criterion, as many as five classes can be discerned.

Parkin (1978:605), no less a critic of historical materialism than Rossides, is less inclined to see classes as aggregates of individuals distinguished by their share of social benefits. While critical of the simplistic nature of the two-class model, he nevertheless wishes to retain the idea of mutual antagonism. His disagreement with historical materialism centers on the choice of criteria by which the line of cleavage is drawn. Power and privilege clearly emanate from the ownership of wealth and capital. Therefore ownership of property is certainly one source of antagonism and an object of conflicting interests. Ownership of the means of production brings with it the ability to exploit and dominate those who must sell their labor power in order to survive. However, the institution of private property is but one method used by the dominant class to restrict access to rewards and privileges. The other method is to use academic and professional qualifications and credentials to exclude the majority from membership. For example, professionalism is a strategy designed to control the supply of entrants to an occupation in order to safeguard or enhance its market value. The skilled manual trades, by virtue of apprenticeship schemes and the closed shop, use a similar strategy. In this case, it is "cultural capital" that provides power and "credentialism" that protects it (Parkin, 1979:46). There seems to be little doubt that, in advanced capitalist societies, the marketplace for skills *is* an important determinant of life chances. Owning property or capital does have certain advantages over owning skills, but nevertheless the ownership of skills is important for class formation. The implication is that one class can exploit another without actually purchasing another's labor power (Stephens, 1979:27).

Historical materialists have always been aware that social hierarchies are multidimensional. The existence of prestige scales and status ladders is acknowledged. However, they have always maintained that these status hierarchies merely reflect economic differences. Others dispute this assumption. They criticize historical materialists for neglecting "the moral element" in inequality. The status hierarchy comprises an autonomous base for feelings of relative impoverishment or advantage (Lockwood, 1981:444). Feelings of relative deprivation—of esteem, worth, honor—can arise independently of and have an effect upon economic deprivations (Runciman, 1966).

This charge that historical materialism fails to give sufficient attention to structures of inequality other than those which derive directly from production relations can be extended to other axes of social differentiation in social life such as age, race, and sex. The "inequalities of age do not have to correspond to the inequalities of social stratification—the old can be either poor or rich...." (Rossides, 1976:30). Ethnic antagonisms also exist alongside class antagonisms, sometimes overlapping but often diverging.

Critics charge that historical materialism has failed to take either age or ethnicity seriously enough, chiefly because neither can be directly related to the logic of productive relations. Age and ethnicity have been treated merely as complicating features, rather than as integral parts of the system. Generational and ethnic conflicts have been treated as attempts on the part of the bourgeoisie to divide and rule the proletariat, or as simply a "displacement" of social antagonisms into more visible spheres (Parkin, 1979:32). The empirical evidence bearing on the thesis that capitalists benefit from racial divisions among the proletariat is at best equivocal (Beck, 1980).

Gender differences also tend to be relegated to secondary importance in the historical materialist research tradition. Gender hierarchies (e.g. patriarchy) comprise forms of exploitation in their own right and possess production relations of their own which exist independently of capitalist production relations. Many aspects of sexual relations are not reducible to class relations (Eisenstein, 1977). The subordination of women is a synthesis of social, cultural, political, and economic components with now one, then another, taking predominance.

Class Struggle

Marx anticipated that the contradictions which manifest themselves in class conflict would worsen with the development of capitalism and that, as a result, the struggle would become more intense. The population would become more polarized as capital became concentrated in fewer hands and as the "immiseration" of the proletariat proceeded. Much of the debate concerning the sociological validity of historical materialism has focused upon the accuracy of these "predictions."

The critics of historical materialism make a number of points:

(1) The separation of ownership and control means that there is no longer a single, homogeneous capitalist class. The ownership and the control of business firms has separated. Stockholders no longer control the operations of the firm (Parsons, 1970:23), and managers are no longer necessarily pursuing their personal self-interest in striving for maximum profits (Parsons, 1967:111).

(2) A new middle class has emerged. The members of this middle class "have not only (historically) been politically conservative, but have also afforded a valuable safety valve for the worker, who can see an immediate means of bettering himself (through upward social mobility) rather than through class conflict leading to revolution" (Crompton and Gubbay, 1978:54).

(3) The category "non-property owners" has become not more homogeneous, but more differentiated. The increasing division of labor in society has produced even finer distinctions between skill levels and between sectors of industry. The proletariat now finds it harder, rather than easier, to see its common interests. For sociological purposes, "the general category 'labor' is far too inclusive to capture the variations in market position and life chances of those who sell their labor services" (Parkin, 1978:605).

(4) The conflict between capital and labor has been eased by the active intervention of the state, due, in large part, to pressure from working class parties and from trade unions. The general regulation of economic activity and the

provision of social services provide a large measure of protection to the working class and have forestalled its "immiseration" (Bottomore, 1979:30). It could be argued that the degree of accommodation which the dominant class has given the social demands of the poor is one reason the United States has not behaved in "a predictable Marxist manner" (Tiryakian, 1975:6).

(5)   Trade unions have been important in providing a sense of security in their own right, quite apart from concessions wrung from the capitalist class. They have played a part in the institutionalization and easing of class conflict. This is especially the case in the United States, where labor leaders have functioned more as labor contractors than as political organizers, "depending more on collective arrangements with employers for the maintenance of their leadership than on a united and militant following" (Piven and Cloward, 1977:101). Unions have also played an important role in setting up elaborate structures to provide job security and economic advancement. Entitlements like seniority rights "serve as forms of property for significant numbers of industrial workers and give them much to lose in the event of a revolution" (Smelser and Warner, 1976:64).

(6)   Many of the trends anticipated in historical materialism have been counteracted by a continuous increase in the standard of living in capitalist countries. Historical materialism has not dealt adequately with the impact of the mass consumption society on political ideas and political action. Through the technological imperatives of a high productivity, high consumption society, more and more workers have come to believe they have a stake in the system (Bottomore, 1979:33). Only very recently have historical materialists begun to study rather than speculate about the way in which both political propaganda and marketing psychology reach down into the private areas of individual life to awaken artificial needs in support of a particular system (Ewen, 1976; Gitlin, 1980).

In light of facts such as these, Parkin (1979:112) proposes that the apocalyptic imagery of historical materialism be replaced with a model which, while retaining the idea of conflict of interest between social classes, does not oblige us to anticipate a revolutionary outcome. He sees the relation between classes in advanced capitalist societies as neither one of harmony and mutual benefit nor one of irresolvable and fatal contradictions.

> Rather, the relationship is understood as one of mutual antagonism and permanent *tension;* that is, a condition of unrelieved distributive struggle that is not necessarily impossible to 'contain'. Class conflict may be without cease, but it is not inevitably fought to a conclusion.

Parkin thus asserts the claims of the Weberian model of class, in which different classes are defined by reference to their mode of collective action and relative market performance rather than by reference to their place in the production process.

Social Change

Historical materialists argue that fundamental social change always takes place through struggle, beginning in the economic sphere and culminating in the political. Other sociologists, no less convinced that societies are always changing, are less willing to believe that change must have its roots in economic contradiction and class conflict.

Critics of the economic determinism of historical materialism argue that the importance of the "economic factor" varies over time and place. They also maintain that ideas and values, being more than simply derivations of material interests, have as powerful an influence on the direction of social change as economic factors.

Max Weber, closer to the idealist tradition than the realist, believed that the master key to understanding the process of change in Western societies was the phenomenon of rationalization:

> ...the spread through law, economy, accounting, technology, and the entire conduct of life of a spirit of functional efficiency and measurement, of an 'economizing' attitude (maximization, optimization, least cost) towards not only material resources but all life. With the inevitability of rationalization, administration takes over, and the complete bureaucratization of all social institutions is inescapable (Bell, 1973:67).

The modern Weberians do not deny that capitalist markets favor the fortunes of capital, but they place much more emphasis than historical materialists on the way in which the rationalized economic enterprise sustains capital. In other words, much more attention is paid to the role of ideas in social change. Theoretical and technological knowledge are the axes around which modern societies are organized. Scientific and technological development drive society forward. In the "post-industrial society" a burgeoning professional and technical class is witness to the displacement of a society in which property has been the basis of power by one in which systematic theoretical knowledge and expertise become the new power bases.

Societal development is thus characterized as the transition from one type of world view to another. The more "modern" society is characterized by the "use of fact and logic in the choice of instrumental behavior for the achievement of various identified goals; increased economic output, improvement in health and life expectancy, a reliable civil service, an appropriately educated population, and the achievement of governable urban areas" (Moore, 1979:1). The modernization process consists of the diffusion of these features throughout the world.

Crises and Contradictions

Historical materialism not only asserts that social change will be caused by changes in the mode of production. It also implies that structural change will only occur through crises and struggle. Its critics see little evidence that capitalism is being rocked by ever-worsening crises or that class conflict is intensifying as a result of the inadequacies of the capitalist system to satisfy all wants. On the contrary, they point to an increasing economic productivity that has upgraded the standard of living of the whole population and given labor a major stake in the economy (Parsons, 1967:125).

Even sympathetic critics have questioned Marx's predictions about the crises of capitalism.

> Marx thought that the contradictory nature of capitalist production would contribute to the system's demise. While we can accept the idea that the social and cooperative character of production is 'contradicted' by the private form of appropriation, it is not at all clear that this contradiction must come to an end, partly because two of the expressions of this contradiction—crises and the falling rate of profit—do not seem to occur as predicted. Profit does not fall as Marx predicted because he underestimated the degree to which increases in labor productivity caused by the introduction of machinery would offset the changing composition of capital caused by the same factor. Crises have been moderated by the development of some macroeconomic planning (Stephens, 1979:46).

One of the "anomalies" with which historical materialism is confronted is that modern capitalism has managed to avert practically all the consequences of the basic contradictions thought to lie at its core without changing its basic character. "Largely through state intervention, modern 'organized' capital has prevented a long-run decline of profit rates, reduced the frequency and gravity of 'realization' crises, reversed the trend toward class polarization, substantially raised living standards of the workers and reduced the class struggle to a harmless form of institutionalized bargaining" (van den Berg, 1980:454). In addition to these initiatives taken by the state, crises have been averted by the rise of transnational corporations paying lower wages and taxes in peripheral countries and creating new markets worldwide in order to maintain high profit rates. Demand and, consequently, profits have been sustained by large-scale borrowing by individual consumers, corporations, and by the state.

As a result of these developments, even those sympathetic to the idea of a science of society oriented to historical materialist principles have been forced to rethink its crisis theory. Habermas (1975) believes that the basic contradiction described in historical materialism has been "displaced" to the political arena as a result of the increasing importance of the state.

The economic intervention of the state developed after it became clear that the spontaneous rules of the market could provoke frequent, major catastrophes for capitalism. Since the turn of the century, the state has functioned as the chief "steering mechanism" of advanced capitalism. It helps achieve financial stability by means of government credits, price guarantees, subsidies, loans, contracts, income-redistribution schemes, welfare and defense spending, and research and development (Sensat, 1979:59).

As a result of this change in the role of the state and as a result of other structural changes within capitalism (e.g. monopolies, transnational corporations), the tendency of the rate of profit to fall is less of a threat to system stability than it was in the nineteenth century (Habermas, 1973:45). These purely economic crises have been replaced, however, by other kinds of crises, each sparked by the expansion of state functions.

As the state assumes a greater role in ensuring continued capital accumulation, it assumes more and more social burdens.

> It bears the costs of imperialistic market strategies and the costs of demand for unproductive commodities (armaments and space travel). It bears the infrastructural costs directly related to production (transportation and communication systems, scientific-technical progress, vocational training). It bears the costs of social consumption indirectly related to production (housing construction, transportation, health care, leisure, education, social security). It bears the costs of social welfare, especially unemployment. And, finally, it bears the externalized costs of environmental strain arising from private production. In the end, these expenditures have to be financed through taxes (Habermas, 1973:61–62).

If the state fails to raise sufficient taxes, a "deficit in administrative rationality" occurs and the system becomes unstable.

A second crisis, "a deficit in legitimation," arises if the state is seen as raising the taxes from the wrong sources, in the wrong ways, for the wrong reasons. The occurrence of a deficit of legitimation is always possible in advanced capitalism because the expectations of all groups are continually being raised above the system's capacity to meet them. The state is thus faced with a dilemma. On the one hand it is forced to expand the categories of individuals and organizations who are unable to meet their needs in the marketplace: it extends entitlements to groups like the disabled, students, and the poor. Thus an increasing number of social choices become politicized. On the other hand,

> the state needs popular support for policies which essentially run counter to the real interests of the mass of the population, since they are designed to *maintain* the system, not to change it fundamentally. Thus it needs to depoliticize decision making by securing a kind of 'mass acclamation', while effectively blocking any real democratic participation, as that could lead the people to call into question the legitimacy of the entire system (van den Berg, 1980:457).

This dilemma occasions frequent and intense debates about the proper extent and direction of state intervention in society.

A third crisis tendency is "motivational." New technocratic modes of state operation tend to undermine traditional motives for economic performance and political participation. The extension of state planning challenges traditional notions of individual freedom and decision making and calls into question the traditional meritocratic association between hard work, merit, and reward.

Habermas thus reverses the historical materialist order of causal relations between economics and politics, giving priority to the political arena in the generation of change-inducing conflict. This view is directly counter to the original dialectical analysis presented by Marx (Boudon, 1980:40). There is no way of telling from Habermas's theory whether the capitalist system might not be able to continue to solve all its problems without fundamental change. "What does it mean to speak of a contradiction when its actual, real-life consequences can take any shape or form, may or may not manifest themselves at any time ... may or may not be observable, and may or not be resolvable!" (van den Berg, 1980:467). The idea of contradiction has been robbed of all its force. For the realist, who subscribes to the notion that there are "laws of motion" within capitalist structures, the "historical necessity" of the new society is shown in the contradictory development of the old society. For Habermas, anxious to acknowledge the role of conscious political action, there is no such necessity (Yaffe, 1973:186).

ISSUES OF EPISTEMOLOGY

The version of historical materialism described in Chapter Eleven uses a distinctly realist epistemology. Criticisms of this epistemology as not being suitable for a social science come from positivists and nonrealist Marxists alike. The nature of positivist and idealist criticisms of realism can be anticipated by consulting the first two parts of this book. By and large, positivists are dismissive of historical materialism because it does not seem to conform to the model of the natural sciences; idealists reject historical materialism on the grounds that it seriously neglects the role of human agency in social life. I will pause only long enough to give some examples of this kind of criticism and devote the bulk of the remainder of this chapter to consider those criticisms of realism which emanate from within that group of scholars who identify themselves as Marxists but who do not accept the argument that historical materialism must rest on realist foundations.

The Dialectic

One of the most distinctive aspects of historical materialism is its use of the dialectical method. But there are many sociologists who argue that this is not a method exclusive to historical materialism. Sociologists working in a variety of research traditions are fond of pointing out that the consequences of human action are frequently the opposite of what was intended. It is not uncommon for these sociologists to style their method of sociological analysis "dialectical."

Schneider (1971) perceives a dialectical "bias" or "bent" in the "entire history of modern sociological thought." In his view, dialectical thinking is not unique to historical materialism, but is found in the work inspired by Spencer, Pareto, and Weber too. This "bias" has yielded some of sociology's most important insight: it suggests that actions can often have results the opposite of what was intended; it suggests that the means people adopt to reach a goal have a tendency to become ends in themselves; and it enhances our sense of irony so that where others might expect to find one thing (e.g. love between close friends) we also expect to find its opposite (e.g. hate). The dialectic is here used as a heuristic tool, no longer part of a distinct metatheory, but as a useful adjunct to positivist theory building (Wardell and Benson, 1978).

That historical materialists have an exclusive concern with the contradictoriness of life is also disputed by Lipset (1975). The idea that social life is ordered by basic contradictions can be incorporated without serious modification into functionalism, where the idea of "structural strain" already plays a prominent role. "Surprising as it may seem to those who would emphasize the theoretical differences among schools of sociology, functionalist analysis shares with Marxist thought Hegel's insight that all social systems inherently contain contradictions, the resolution of which press for social change" (Lipset, 1975:177). Lipset notes that social life provides us with many examples of people being urged to reach goals by prescribed means without being given the necessary resources to do so. The result is "strain" in the system and, possibly, rebellion.

Appearance and Essence

How valid is the distinction realists draw between appearance and underlying structure? Is it really the case that positivists are blind to this distinction? Positivists believe that this is far from being the case (Mayhew, 1981:633). They adopt the position that all science contains concepts which refer to unobservables. It is simply not true that positivists operate on the assumption that an absolute distinction can be drawn between empirical observation and conceptual thought. The difference is one of degree. Some concepts are reached by a greater degree of abstraction than others.

The positivist maintains that no adequate criteria exist by which to distinguish the readily observable from the underlying structure of reality. This can be illustrated from Marx's own work.

> Marx criticised his predecessors for taking the readily observable facts of wages, rent and profits and, thereby, constituting a theory or model of capitalist distribution; thus, they failed to unearth the deeper reality of the structure of exploitation and the extraction of surplus value. Now the facts of intellectual history could be rather differently interpreted. It could be argued that what was most readily observable to the classical economists was that labourers laboured to produce goods whose value was far in excess of the value of the wages which they have received; it

could, therefore, be said that far from having to have the idea of surplus
value and of exploitation unearthed for them, they treated these
seemingly obvious 'facts' as misleading. What seemed to them much less
obvious was the 'correct' explanation of distribution in terms of the
following not-so-readily observable processes: supply and demand; the
necessity of a return to capital sufficient to compensate for the risk, for
entrepreneurial skill and for loss of liquidity; the creation of rent by
variations in the productivity of land and by diminishing returns; the
effect of population processes on the level of real wages; and so on ...
(Cohen, 1980:144–45).

What is considered "mere appearance" and what is considered "essential" or
"real" therefore depends a great deal on the point from which analysis
starts. The metaphor which suggests that a reality always underlies what we
at first apprehend is therefore misleading. Perhaps we will never know
whether the so-called "real" structures actually exist in an invariant and
universal form. We can only treat the assumption of their existence
instrumentally, as a means of gaining reliable knowledge about the world,
and to treat them instrumentally is to treat them in the same manner as the
positivist (Appelbaum, 1979:29).

Social Laws

The proclivity shown by realists to write only of "tendencies" in social
life and their reluctance to formulate universal laws on an abstract level has
led most positivists to discount historical materialism.

The 'historical laws' of Marxian theory are not analytical theoretical laws
comparable to those of the physical sciences. Apart from their specific
vulnerabilities ... they are couched at too concrete a level even to be
considered as analytical uniformities (Parsons, 1967:132).

Positivist sociologists have therefore sought to improve on historical materialism by transforming its statements into formal propositions. Turner
(1978:130), while acknowledging that Marx himself did not intend to
formulate "universal laws," translates the major tenets of historical materialism into an abstract set of propositions about social conflict. There is some
question as to whether Marxists would agree with his conclusion that Marx's
theory focused almost entirely on the causes of violent conflict.

CRITICAL THEORY

Most of the Marxist critics of historical materialism see in it a trend toward
positivism, a kind of Marxist natural science. They reassert the more
humanistic, more voluntaristic aspects of Marx's thought (Anderson,
1980:81). There are some Marxists who believe that historical materialism is

too voluntaristic and places insufficient emphasis on the determinative role of the forces of production, but these comprise a minority of its friendly critics (e.g. Cohen, 1978; Rader, 1979). The majority can be grouped under the heading of "critical theorists." They are united in arguing that realism threatens to render Marxism incapable of *critique*. They are critical theorists in the sense of seeing the purpose of theory as that of pointing out the hiatus between the actual and the possible, between the existing order and a potential future state which man can help bring about. Historical materialism, to the extent that it adopts the view that social actions are determined by underlying structures, is ill-suited to engage in this kind of theorizing.

Critical theory owes a greater debt to Hegel's idealism than does the realist version of historical materialism. One of its earliest exponents, Georg Lukacs, urged Marxists to study not only the objective conditions of action but also the ways in which these conditions were understood and interpreted. In other words, he tried to retrieve a theory of consciousness from Marx's writings. Lukacs (1971:83) located capitalism's "central structural problem" not in the contradiction between the forces of production and the social relations of production but in the phenomenon of reification, the process whereby social phenomena take on the appearance of things.

Marxists influenced by Freud, such as William Reich, Erich Fromm, and Herbert Marcuse, together with members of the Frankfurt School like Theodore Adorno and Max Horkheimer, also sought to develop a Marxist theory of consciousness, a theory which would explain how the values and behavior patterns that serve the interests of the capitalist class had been inculcated by the proletariat (Leiss, 1974:331). Accordingly, they sought to expand the political economy of the mode of production to encompass a "phenomenology of the forms of alienation in daily life: in the family, sexuality, the work situation, cultural activity, verbal and other forms of communication, social interaction, institutions and ideology" (Klare, 1972:6).

This attempt to expand political economy had specific historical causes. The failure of Social Democracy and the rise of Fascism, changes in political consciousness generated by the advent of mass consumerism and the mass media, the impact of technology on more and more areas of social life, the bureaucratization of communism under Stalin and the growth of monopoly capital all posed serious theoretical problems for historical materialism (Jay, 1973). These developments called into question the idea that there are tendencies within capitalism which lead inevitably to its downfall. Clearly, cultural production as well as material production must be the subject of Marxist analysis.

Although the influence of Marx on historical materialism and critical theory is strong, their emphases are different and what they "read into" Marx quite distinct. There is in historical materialism a tendency toward sociological reductionism, a method of analysis in which individual actors are collapsed into social structures. "People are conceived as stepping into already conceived systems, such that they do not create their own motivation or ideological structures (around family, community, or in political groups) nor do they refuse participation or even follow through so enthusiastically that unanticipated effects result" (DiTomaso, 1982:222).

Historical materialism lacks an adequate phenomenology of social action. It takes for granted the facticity of social structures, overlooking the fact that social structures must be perpetuated, modified, or transformed through the medium of meaningful acts and symbolic interaction (Smart, 1976:144). Critical theory, on the other hand, "asserts that in order to have a subject matter at all the social scientist must attempt to understand the intentions and desires of the actors he is observing, as well as the rules and constitutive meanings of their social order" (Fay, 1975:94). Its goal is a method of social analysis which combines the analysis of structures and contradictions with an analysis of felt needs and experienced privations, a theory capable of dealing with both interests and ideology and morality and affectivity.

Critical theorists assume that contradictions are inherent in social structures, but these contradictions do not work themselves out "behind the backs" of human actors. The course of social crises and the nature of their resolution "depends on the practices of social agents, and on how they understand the situation they are part of" (Held, 1980:362).

A much more voluntaristic model of class formation and class struggle emerges from critical theory than from historical materialism.

> Class formations ... arise at the intersection of determination and self-activity: the working class 'made itself as much as it was made'. We cannot put 'class' here and 'class consciousness' there, as two separate entities, the one sequential upon the other, since both must be taken together—the experience of determination, and the 'handling' of this in conscious ways. Nor can we deduce class from a static 'section' (since it is *becoming* over time), nor as a function of the mode of production, since class formations and class consciousness (while subject to determinate pressures) eventuate in an open-ended process of relationships—of struggle with other classes—over time (Thompson, 1978:298).

The critical theorist is much more inclined to see the existence of class depending on the presence of a collective expression of common interests in opposition to those of an antagonistic class, rather than as an objective relation to the means of production, independent of will or attitude.

Social struggle and social change thus have a necessarily subjective component which social theory cannot ignore. Social actors must be treated as free agents "who will not only do what they must but who can respond to appeals and be won over even against their own class interests" (Gouldner, 1980:35). Politics do not automatically fall into line with changes in the mode of production, for people do not necessarily recognize their objective interests. As often as not, the objective conditions for revolution have sparked fascism rather than socialism (Chirot, 1977:254; Parkin, 1979:172).

Antonio Gramsci formulated the concept of hegemony to designate the kind of pervasive influence the ideas of the ruling class could have. Through the use of a network of cultural institutions—schools, churches, newspapers, parties, associations—the capitalist class was able to achieve a kind of "structured consensus" which reduced the scale of coercion necessary to repress the subordinate class (Mueller, 1973:93).

In common with other critical theorists, Gramsci argued that cultural differences between societies or parts of society must be taken seriously because they have important social, political, and economic effects (Anderson, 1976:80). While historical materialism fostered the view that each social formation is but an expression of a certain configuration of underlying elements (the changes in which could be accounted for by laws of transformation), critical theorists adopted a kind of historicism "in which each different social phase of society is seen as operating according to unique and different requirements" (Gouldner, 1980:59). The totality was thus conceived in more Hegelian terms. Capital is not merely one mode of production among others but a unique moment in history with its own essence or form.

Critical theorists see no inevitable transformation of capitalism. Hence their interest in a critique of existing ideologies and their concern to create an awareness of the possibility of a break with the existing structure of domination. Hence, also, their commitment to praxis in which theory and practice define and shape each other, a praxis aimed at the self-emancipation of human subjects.

In summary, then, critical theorists believe that realism reduces the significance of human agency in Marxism to a triviality. They argue, instead, that emancipation must mean self-emancipation, a coming to consciousness of the subjects of history. The study of political economy, to which historical materialism is reduced by realism, treats the mode of production as if it were a thing or natural force happening behind the backs of human beings. A study which expands upon political economy, but which retains Marx's interest in human emancipation, will pay more attention to the complex factors which prevent people from seeing themselves as capable of choosing how to act.

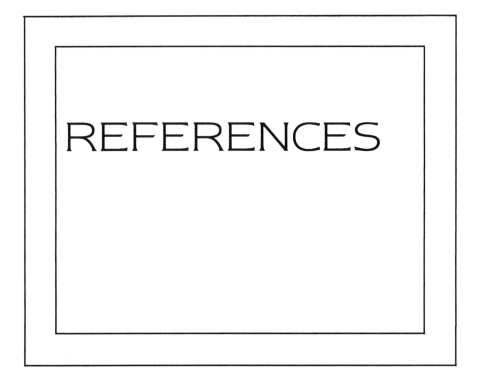

REFERENCES

ABEL, T. 1970. *The foundations of sociological theory*. New York: Random House.

ABERCROMBIE, N. 1980. *Class, structure and knowledge: problems in the sociology of knowledge*. New York: New York University Press.

ABRAHAMSON, M. 1979. A functional theory of organizational stratification. *Social Forces* 58:128–145.

ABRAMSON, E., CUTLER, H. A., KANTZ, R. W., AND MENDELSON, M. 1958. Social power and commitment. *American Sociological Review* 23:15–22.

ACKERMAN, C., AND PARSONS, T. 1966. The Concept of 'social system' as a theoretical device. Pp. 24–42 in G. DiRenzo (ed.), *Concepts, theory, and exploration in the behavioral sciences*. New York: Random House.

ADLER, P., AND ADLER, P. 1980. Symbolic interactionism. Pp. 20–61 in J. Douglas, P. Adler, P. Adler, A. Fontana, C. R. Freeman and J. Kotarba (eds.), *Introduction to the sociologies of everyday life*. Boston: Allyn & Bacon.

ADRIAANSEN, H. 1980. *Talcott Parsons and the conceptual dilemma*. London: Routledge & Kegan Paul.

ALDRICH, H. 1979. *Organizations and environments*. Englewood Cliffs, N.J.: Prentice-Hall.

ALEXANDER, J. 1978. Formal and substantive voluntarism in the work of Talcott Parsons. *American Sociological Review* 43:177–198.

ALTHEIDE, D. 1977. The sociology of Alfred Schutz. Pp. 133–152 in J. Douglas (ed.), *Existential sociology*. New York: Cambridge University Press.

ALTHEIDE, D., AND JOHNSON, J. 1980. *Bureaucratic propaganda*. Boston: Allyn & Bacon.

ALTHUSSER, L. 1971. *Lenin and philosophy and other essays.* New York: Monthly Review Press.

ANDERSON, B., AND CARLOS, M. 1976. What is network theory? Pp. 27–52 in T. Burns and W. Buckley (eds.), *Power and control: social structures and their transformation.* Beverly Hills: Sage.

ANDERSON, J. 1977. Practical reasoning in action. Pp. 174–198 in J. Douglas (ed.), *Existential sociology.* New York: Cambridge University Press.

ANDERSON, P. 1976. *Considerations on western Marxism.* London: New Left Books.
1980. *Arguments within English Marxism.* London: New Left Books.

ANTONIO, R. 1981. The Political Economy of Education. Pp. 46–72 in S. McNall (ed.), *Political economy: a critique of American society.* Glenview, Illinois: Scott, Foresman.

APPELBAUM, R. 1978. Marx's theory of the falling rate of profit. *American Sociological Review* 43:67–80.
1979. Althusser's structuralism. *Insurgent Sociologist* 9:18–33.

ARONOWITZ, S. 1973. *False promises: the shaping of the American working class consciousness.* New York: McGraw-Hill.

ATKINSON, J. M. 1978. *Discovering suicide: studies in the social organization of sudden death.* Pittsburgh: University of Pittsburgh Press.

AVERITT, R. 1968. *The dual economy: the dynamics of American industry structure.* New York: W. W. Norton & Co., Inc.

BALL, D. 1972. Self and identity in the context of deviance: the case of criminal abortion. Pp. 158–186 in R. Scott and J. Douglas (eds.), *Theoretical perspectives on deviance.* New York: Basic Books.

BALL, R. 1979. Sociology and general systems theory. Pp. 115–127 in Scott McNall (ed.), *Theoretical perspectives in sociology.* New York: St. Martin's Press.

BARAN, P., AND SWEEZY, P. 1966. *Monopoly capital.* New York: Monthly Review Press.

BARBANO, F. 1968. Social structures and social functions: the emancipation of structural analysis in sociology. *Inquiry* 11:40–84.

BARCLAY, B. 1981. The economy: who benefits? Pp. 189–216 in S. McNall (ed.), *Political economy: a critique of American society.* Glenview, Illinois: Scott, Foresman.

BARRETT, M. 1980. *Women's oppression today: problems in marxist feminist analysis.* London: New Left Books.

BARRY, B. 1978. *Sociologists, economists, and democracy.* Chicago: University of Chicago Press.

BAUMAN, Z. 1978. *Hermeneutics and social science.* New York: Columbia University Press.

BECK, E. M. 1980. Discrimination and white economic loss: a time series examination of the radical model. *Social Forces* 59:148–168.

BECK, E. M., HORAN, P., AND TOLBERT, C. III. 1978. Stratification in a dual economy: a sectoral model of earnings determination. *American Sociological Review* 43:704–720.

BECKER, H. 1953. Becoming a marijuana user. *American Journal of Sociology* 59:235–242.
1963. *Outsiders.* Glencoe, Illinois: Free Press.
1981. Personal change in adult life. Pp. 307–316 in G. Stone and H. Faberman (eds.), *Social psychology through symbolic interaction* (second edition) New York: John Wiley.

BELL, D. 1973. *The coming of post-industrial society.* New York: Basic Books.

BELLAH, R.   1964. Religious evolution. *American Sociological Review* 29:358–374.
1979. Memorial: Talcott Parsons. *Journal for the Scientific Study of Religion* 18:454–456.

BENN, S.   1976. Rationality and political behavior. Pp. 246–267 in S. Benn and G. W. Mortimore (eds.), *Rationality and the social sciences*. London: Routledge and Kegan Paul.

BENSTON, M.   1969. The political economy of women's liberation. *Monthly Review* 21:13–27.

BENTON, T.   1977. *Philosophical foundations of the three sociologies*. London: Routledge and Kegan Paul.

BERG, A. VAN DEN.   1980. Critical theory: is there still hope? *American Journal of Sociology* 86:449–478.

BERNSTEIN, R.   1978. *The restructuring of social and political theory*. Philadelphia: University of Pennsylvania Press.

BERSHADY, H.   1973. *Ideology and social knowledge*. New York: John Wiley.

BHASKAR, R.   1975. *A realist theory of science*. Leeds: Leeds Books.
1979. *The possibility of naturalism*. Atlantic Highlands, N.J.: Humanities Press.

BIBB, R. AND FORM, W.   1977. The effects of industrial, occupational and sex stratification on wages in blue-collar markets. *Social Forces* 55:974–996.

BIDDLE, B.   1979. *Role theory: expectations, identities and behaviors*. New York: Academic Press.

BLACK, M.   1961. Some questions about Parsons' theories. Pp. 268–288 in M. Black (ed.), *Social theories of Talcott Parsons*. Englewood Cliffs, N.J.: Prentice-Hall.

BLACKBURN, R., AND JONES, G. S.   1972. Louis Althusser and the struggle for marxism. Pp. 365–387 in D. Howard and K. Klare (eds.), *The unknown dimension: european marxism since Lenin*. New York: Basic Books.

BLALOCK, H., AND WILKEN, P.   1979. *Intergroup processes: a micro-macro perspective*. New York: Free Press.

BLAU, P.   1955. *Dynamics of bureaucracy*. Chicago: University of Chicago Press.
1964. *Exchange and power in social life*. New York: John Wiley.
1970. Comment on 'the relevance of psychology to the explanation of social phenomena' by Homans. Pp. 313–339 in R. Borger and F. Cioffi (eds.), *Exploration in the behavioral sciences*. Cambridge: Cambridge University Press.
1977. *Inequality and heterogeneity*. New York: Free Press.
1981. Diverse views of social structure and their common denominator. Pp. 1–26 in P. Blau and R. Merton (eds.), *Continuities in structural inquiry*. Beverly Hills: Sage.

BLAU, P., BLUM, T., AND SCHWARTZ, J.   1982. Heterogeneity and intermarriage. *American Sociological Review* 47:45–61.

BLOCK, F.   1977. The ruling class does not rule: notes on the Marxist theory of the state. *Socialist Revolution* 33:6–28.
1981. The fiscal crisis of the capitalist state. *Annual Review of Sociology* 7:1–27.

BLUMER, H.   1969. *Symbolic interactionism*. Englewood Cliffs, N.J.: Prentice-Hall.
1975. Exchange on Turner's 'Parsons as a symbolic interactionist'. *Sociological Inquiry* 45:59–62.
1977. Comment on Lewis 'the classic American pragmatists as forerunners of symbolic interactionism'. *Sociological Quarterly* 18: 285–289.

BOGGS, C.   1976. *Gramsci's marxism*. London: Pluto Press.

BONACICH, E.   1979. The past, present and future of split labor market theory. Pp. 17–64 in C. Marret and C. Leggons (eds.), *Research in race and ethnic relations*. Greenwich: JAI Press.

BOTT, E.   1957. *Family and social network*. London: Tavistock Publications.

BOTTOMORE, T.   1975. *Marxist sociology*. New York: Holmes & Meier.
1979. *Political sociology*. New York: Harper & Row, Pub.

BOUDON, R.   1975. Three basic paradigms of macrosociology: functionalism, neo-marxism and interactionist analysis. *Theory and Decision* 6: 381–406.

1980. *The crisis in sociology.* New York: Columbia University Press.

BOWLES, S., AND GINTIS, H.   1975. The problem with human capital theory—a marxian critique. *American Economic Review* 65:74–82.

1976. *Schooling in capitalist America.* New York: Basic Books.

BRAVERMAN, H.   1974. *Labor and monopoly capital.* New York: Monthly Review Press.

BRITTAN, A.   1973. *Meanings and situations.* London: Routledge and Kegan Paul.

BUCKLEY, W.   1967. *Sociology and modern systems theory.* Englewood Cliffs, N.J.: Prentice-Hall.

BURAWOY, M.   1979. *Manufacturing consent.* Chicago: University of Chicago Press.

BURGER, T.   1977. Talcott Parsons, the problem of order, and analytic sociology. *American Journal of Sociology* 83:320–324.

BURGESS, R., AND BUSHELL, D. JR.   1969. A behavioral view of some sociological concepts. Pp. 273–290 in R. Burgess and D. Bushell, Jr. (eds.), *Behavioral sociology.* New York: Columbia University Press.

BURR, W., LEIGH, G., DAY, R., AND CONSTANTINE, J.   1979. Symbolic interaction and the family. Pp. 42–111 in W. Burr, R. Hill, F. I. Nye, and I. Reiss (eds.), *Contemporary theories about the family.* Volume Two: General Theories/Theoretical Orientations. New York: Free Press.

BURRIS, V.   1979. The structuralist influence in Marxist theory and research. *Insurgent Sociologist* 9:4–17.

BURT, R.   1980. Models of network structure. *Annual Review of Sociology* 6:79–141.

CARCHEDI, G.   1977. *On the economic identification of social classes.* London: Routledge and Kegan Paul.

CARDOSO, F., AND FALETTA, E.   1979. *Dependency and development in Latin America.* Berkeley: University of California Press.

CASTELLS, M.   1978. *City, class and power.* New York: St. Martin's Press.

CAVAN, S.   1966. *Liquor license: an ethnography of bar behavior.* Chicago: University of Chicago Press.

CHADWICK-JONES, J. K.   1976. *Social exchange theory.* New York: Academic Press.

CHARON, J.   1979. *Symbolic interactionism.* Englewood Cliffs, N.J.: Prentice-Hall.

CHEAL, D.   1980. Rule-governed behavior. *Philosophy of Social Sciences* 10:39–49.

CHIROT, D.   1977. *Social change in the twentieth century.* New York: Harcourt Brace Jovanovich.

CICOUREL, A.   1964. *Method and measurement in sociology.* Glencoe, Illinois: Free Press.

1968. *The social organization of juvenile justice.* New York: John Wiley.

1972. Delinquency and the attribution of responsibility. Pp. 142–159 in R. Scott and J. Douglas (eds.), *Theoretical perspectives on deviance.* New York: Basic Books.

1974. *Cognitive sociology.* New York: Free Press.

COHEN, B.   1980. *Developing sociological knowledge.* Englewood Cliffs, N.J.: Prentice-Hall.

COHEN, G. A.   1979. *Karl Marx's theory of history.* Princeton: Princeton University Press.

COHEN, P.   1968. *Modern social theory.* London: Heinemman.

1980. Is Positivism Dead? *Sociological Review* 28:141–176.

COLEMAN, J.   1975a. Legitimate and illegitimate use of power. Pp. 221–236 in L. Coser (ed.), *The idea of social structure.* New York: Free Press.

1975b. Social structure and the theory of action. Pp. 76–93 in P. Blau (ed.), *Approaches to the study of social structure.* New York: Free Press.

COLLINS, R.   1975. *Conflict sociology.* New York: Academic Press.

COOK, K., AND EMERSON, R.   1978. Power, equity, and commitment in exchange. *American Sociological Review*, 43:721–739.

COSER, L.   1975a. Merton's use of the European tradition. Pp. 85–102 in L. Coser (ed.), *The idea of social structure: papers in honor of Robert K. Merton*. New York: Free Press.

1975b. Two methods in search of a substance. *American Sociological Review* 40: 691–700.

1977. *Masters of sociological thought* (second edition) New York: Harcourt Brace Jovanovich.

COULTER, J.   1979. *The social construction of mind: studies in ethnomethodology and linguistic philosophy*. Totowa, N.J.: Rowman and Littlefield.

CROMPTON, R., AND GUBBAY, J.   1978. *Economy and class structure*. New York: St. Martin's Press.

CULLEN, J., AND NOVICK, S.   1979. The Davis-Moore theory of stratification: a further examination and extension. *American Journal of Sociology* 84:1424–1437.

CUZZORT, R., AND KING, E.   1980. *Twentieth century social thought* (third edition). New York: Holt, Rinehart and Winston.

DANDEKER, C., AND SCOTT, J.   1979. The structure of sociological theory and knowledge. *Journal for the Theory of Social Behavior* 9:303–325.

DAHRENDORF, R.   1959. *Class and class conflict in an industrial society*. London: Routledge and Kegan Paul.

DAVIS, F.   1959. The cab-driver and his fare: facets of a fleeting relationship. *American Journal of Sociology* 65:150–165.

DAVIS, K., AND MOORE, W.   1945. Some principles of stratification. *American Sociological Review* 10:242–249.

DAWE, A.   1973. The underworld of Erving Goffman. *British Journal of Sociology* 24: 246–253.

1978. Theories of social action. Pp. 362–417 in T. Bottomore and R. Nisbet (eds.), *A History of sociological analysis*. New York: Basic Books.

DEMERATH, N. J., III.   1967. Synecdoche and structural-functionalism. Pp. 499–518 in N. J. Demerath III and R. Petersen (eds.), *System, change and conflict*. New York: Free Press.

DEUTSCHER, I.   1973. *What we say/what we do: sentiments and acts*. Glenview, Illinois: Scott, Foresman.

DEVEREUX, E.   1961. Parsons' sociological theory. Pp. 1–63 in M. Black (ed.), *The social theories of Talcott Parsons*. Englewood Cliffs, N.J.: Prentice-Hall.

DiTOMASO, N.   1982. 'Sociological reductionism' from Parsons to Althusser: linking action and structure in social theory. *American Sociological Review* 47: 14–28.

DOUGLAS, J.   1967. *The social meanings of suicide*. Princeton: Princeton University Press.

DOUGLAS, J.   1980. Introduction to the sociologies of everyday life. Pp. 1–19 in J. Douglas, P. Adler, A. Fontana, C. R. Freeman, and J. Kotarba (eds.), *Introduction to the sociologies of everyday life*. Boston: Allyn & Bacon.

DREEBEN, R.   1976. The organizational structure of schools and school systems. Pp. 857–873 in J. Loubser, R. Baum, A. Effrat, and V. M. Lidz (eds.), *Explorations in general theory in social science: essays in honor of Talcott Parsons*. (Volume Two) New York: Free Press.

DURKHEIM, E.   1938. *The rules of sociological method*. Chicago: University of Chicago Press.

1960 a. *Montesquieu and Rousseau.* Ann Arbor: University of Michigan Press.

1960 b. *The division of labor in society.* Glencoe, Illinois: Free Press.

EDWARDS, R.   1979. *Contested terrain.* New York: Basic Books.

EISENSTEIN, Z.   1977. Capitalist patriarchy and the case for socialist feminism. *Insurgent Sociologist* 7: 2–18.

EMERSON, J.   1970. Nothing unusual is happening. Pp. 208–222 in T. Shibutani (ed.), *Human nature and collective behavior.* Englewood Cliffs, N.J.: Prentice-Hall.

EMERSON, R.   1969. Operant psychology and exchange theory. Pp. 379–405 in R. Burgess and D. Bushell, Jr. (eds.), *Behavioral sociology.* New York: Columbia University Press.

1976. Social exchange theory. *Annual Review of Sociology* 2:335–362.

1981. Social exchange theory. Pp. 30–65 in M. Rosenberg and R. Turner (eds.), *Social psychology.* New York: Basic Books.

EMERSON, R.   1969. *Judging delinquents: context and process in juvenile court.* Chicago: Aldine.

EMERY, F., AND TRIST, E.   1972. *Toward a social ecology.* Harmandsworth: Penguin.

ERICKSON, B.   1981. Secret societies and social structure. *Social Forces* 60:188–210.

ERIKSON, K.   1966. *Wayward puritans.* New York: John Wiley.

ETZIONI, A.   1968. *The active society.* New York: Free Press.

EVANS, P.   1979. *Dependent development.* Princeton: Princeton University Press.

EWEN, S.   1976. *Captains of consciousness.* New York: McGraw-Hill.

FAY, B.   1975. *Social theory and social practice.* London: Allen and Unwin.

FINE, G.   1981. Friends, impression management, and preadolescent behavior. Pp. 257–272 in G. Stone and H. Faberman (eds.), *Social psychology through symbolic interactionism* (second edition). New York: John Wiley.

FISCHER, C., JACKSON, R., STUEVE, C. A., GERSON, K., JONES, L., AND BALDASSARE, M.   1979. *Networks and places: social relations in an urban setting.* New York: Free Press.

FRANK, A. G.   1974. Functionalism and dialectics. Pp. 342–352 in R. S. Denisoff, and O. Callahan, and M. Levine (eds.), *Theories and paradigms in contemporary sociology.* Itasca, Illinois: F. E. Peacock.

FREEMAN, C. R.   1980. Phenomenological sociology and ethnomethodology. Pp. 113–154 in J. Douglas, P. Adler, P. Adler, A. Fontana, C. R. Freeman, and J. Kotarba (eds.), *Introduction to the sociologies of everyday life.* Boston: Allyn & Bacon.

FREUD, S.   1954. *The interpretation of dreams.* London: Allen and Unwin.

FRIEDRICHS, R.   1970. *A sociology of sociology.* New York: Free Press.

GALASKIEWICZ, J.   1979. *Exchange networks and community politics.* Beverly Hills: Sage.

GANNON, T., AND FRIEDHEIM, E.   1982. 'Structuralism' or structure: comment on Mayhew. *Social Forces* 60:877–882.

GAMBLE, A., AND WALTON, P.   1976. *Capitalism in crisis.* London: MacMillan.

GANS, H.   1972. The positive functions of poverty. *American Journal of Sociology* 78:275–289.

GARFINKEL, H.   1967. *Studies in ethnomethodology.* Englewood Cliffs, N.J.:Prentice-Hall.

GELLNER, E.   1975. Ethnomethodology: The re-enchantment industry or the Californian way of subjectivity. *Philosophy of Social Sciences* 5: 431–450.

GERAS, N.   1973. Marx and the critique of political economy. Pp. 284–305 in R. Blackburn (ed.), *Ideology in social science.* New York: Vintage.

GIDDENS, A.   1973. *The class structure of advanced societies.* London: Hutchinson.
1976. *New rules of sociological method.* London: Hutchinson.
1977. *Studies in social and political theory.* New York: Basic Books.
1981. Time and space in social theory. Pp. 3–14 in S. McNall and G. Howe (eds.), *Current perspectives in social theory.* Greenwich, Conn: JAI Press, Inc.
GITLIN, T.   1980. *The whole world is watching.* Berkeley: University of California Press.
GLASER, B., AND STRAUSS, A.   1965. *Awareness of dying.* Chicago: Aldine.
1967. *The discovery of grounded theory.* Chicago: Aldine.
GLASSNER, B.   1980. *Essential interactionism: on the intelligibility of prejudice.* Boston: Routledge and Kegan Paul.
GLEESON, D., AND ERBEN, M.   1976. Meaning in context: notes towards a critique of ethnomethodology. *British Journal of Sociology* 27:474–483.
GLUCKSMANN, M.   1974. *Structuralist analysis in contemporary social thought.* London: Routledge and Kegan Paul.
GOFFMAN, E.   1967. *Interaction ritual.* Garden City: Anchor Books.
1971. *Relations in public.* New York: Harper Colophon Books.
1974. *Frame analysis.* New York: Harper Colophon Books.
GOLDTHORPE, J.   1973. A revolution in sociology? *Sociology* 7:449–462.
GOODE, W.   1973. Exchange Theory. *Journal of Comparative Family Studies* 4: 171–175.
1978. *The celebration of heroes.* Berkeley: University of California Press.
GORDON, D.   1972. *Theories of poverty and unemployment.* Lexington: D. C. Heath.
GORMAN, R.   1977. *The dual vision: Alfred Schutz and the myth of phenomenological social science.* Boston: Routledge and Kegan Paul.
GORZ, A.   1967. *Strategy for labor.* Boston: Beacon Press.
GOUGH, I.   1979. *The political economy of the welfare state.* London: Macmillan.
GOULDNER, A.   1970. *The coming crisis in western sociology.* New York: Basic Books.
1980. *The two Marxisms.* New York: Seabury.
GRANDOVETTER, M.   1974. *Getting a job: a study of contacts and careers.* Cambridge: Harvard University Press.
GUSFIELD, J.   1981. *The culture of public problems: drinking, driving and the symbolic order.* Chicago: University of Chicago Press.
HABERMAS, J.   1971. *Knowledge and human interests.* Boston: Beacon Press.
1973. *Theory and practice.* Boston: Beacon Press.
1975. *Legitimation crisis.* Boston: Beacon Press.
HAMILTON, R.   1972. *Class and politics in the United States.* New York: John Wiley.
HARRE, R.   1972. *The Philosophies of Science.* Oxford: Oxford University Press.
1980. *Social being: a theory for social psychology.* Totowa, N.J.: Rowman and Littlefield.
HARRIS, C. C.   1977. Changing conceptions of the relation between family and societal form in western society. Pp. 74–89 in R. Scase (ed.), *Industrial society: class, cleavage and control.* New York: St. Martin's Press.
HEAP, J.   1980. Description in ethnomethodology. *Human Studies* 3:87–106.
HEATH, A.   1976. *Rational choice and exchange theory.* Cambridge: Cambridge University Press.
HEILBRONER, R.   1980. *Marxism, for and against.* New York: W. W. Norton & Co., Inc.
HELD, D.   1980. *Introduction to critical theory.* Berkeley: University of California Press.
HEESE, M.   1978. Theory and value in the social sciences. Pp. 1–16 in C. Hookway and P. Pettit (eds.), *Action and interpretation: studies in the philosophy of the social sciences.* Cambridge: Cambridge University Press.

HEWITT, J. 1976. *Self and society: a symbolic interactionist social psychology.* Boston: Allyn & Bacon.

HEYDEBRAND, W. 1977. Organizational contradictions in public bureaucracies. *Sociological Quarterly* 18:83–107.

HIRSCH, J. 1979. The state apparatus and social reproduction: elements of a theory of the bourgeois state. Pp. 57–107 in J. Holloway and S. Picciotto (eds.), *State and capital: a marxist debate.* Austin: University of Texas Press.

HOMANS, G. 1974. *Social behavior: its elementary forms* (revised edition). New York: Harcourt Brace Jovanovich.

HOPKINS, T. 1978. World-system analysis: methodological issues. Pp. 199–218 in B. H. Kaplan (ed.), *Social change in the capitalist world economy.* Beverly Hills: Sage.

HORAN, P. 1978. Is status attainment research atheoretical? *American Sociological Review* 43:534–541.

HORWITZ, A. 1977. Social networks and pathways of psychiatric treatment. *Social Forces* 56:86–105.

JALEE, P. 1977. *How capitalism works.* New York: Monthly Review Press.

JAY, M. 1973. *The dialectical imagination: a history of the Frankfurt school and the institute of social research, 1923–1950.* Boston: Little, Brown.

JOHNSON, H. 1973. The generalized symbolic media in Parsons' theory. *Sociology and Social Research* 57:208–221.

KADUSHIN. C. 1981. Notes on expectations of reward in n-person networks. Pp. 235–254 in P. Blau and R. Merton (eds.), *Continuities in structural inquiry.* Beverly Hills: Sage.

KALLEBERG, A., AND SORENSON, A. 1979. The sociology of labor markers. *Annual Review of Sociology* 5: 351–379.

KALLEBERG, A., WALLACE, M., AND ALTHAUSER, R. 1981. Economic segmentation, worker power, and income inequality. *American Journal of Sociology* 87: 651–683.

KANTER, R. 1972. Symbolic interactionism and politics in systematic perspective. *Sociological Inquiry* 42: 77–92.

1977. *Men and women of the corporation.* New York: Basic Books.

1980. *A tale of 'o': on being different in an organization.* New York: Harper & Row, Pub.

KATZ, F. 1976. *Structuralism in sociology.* Albany: State University of New York Press.

KEAT, R. 1981. *The politics of social theory.* Chicago: Chicago University Press.

KEAT, R., AND URRY, J. 1975. *Social theory as science.* Boston: Routledge and Kegan Paul.

KESSLER, S., AND MCKENNA, W. 1978. *Gender: an ethnomethodological approach.* New York: John Wiley.

KLARE, K. 1972. The critique of everyday life, the New Left, and the unrecognizable Marxism. Pp. 3–33 in D. Howard and K. Klare (eds.), *The unknown dimension: european Marxism since Lenin.* New York: Basic Books.

KOHN, M., AND SCHOOLER, C. 1973. Occupational experience and psychological functioning: an assessment of reciprocal effects. *American Sociological Review* 38: 97–118.

KOLAKOWSKI, L. 1978. *Main currents of Marxism: its rise, growth and dissolution* (Volume One). Oxford: Clarendon Press.

KUHN, M., AND MCPARTLAND, T. 1954. An empirical investigation of self-attitudes. *American Journal of Sociology* 19:68–76.

KUHN, T. 1962. *The structure of scientific revolutions.* Chicago: University of Chicago Press.

KUHN, T.   1974. Second thoughts on paradigms. Pp. 458–482 in F. Suppe (ed.), *The structure of scientific theories.* Urbana: University of Illinois Press.

KUNKEL, J.   1969. Some behavioral aspects of social change and economic development. Pp. 321–366 in R. Burgess and D. Bushell (eds.), *Behavioral sociology.* New York: Columbia University Press.

LAKATOS, I.   1970. Falsification and the methodology of scientific research programmes. Pp. 91–195 in I. Lakatos and A. Musgrave (eds.), *Criticism and the growth of knowledge.* Cambridge: Cambridge University Press.

LAUDAN, L.   1977. *Progress and its problems: towards a theory of scientific growth.* Berkeley: University of California Press.

LAUER, R., AND HANDEL, W.   1977. *Social Psychology: the theory and application of symbolic interactionism.* Boston: Houghton Mifflin.

LAUMANN, E., GALASKIEWICZ, J., AND MARSDEN, P.   1978. Community structures as interorganizational linkages. *Annual Review of Sociology* 4:455–484.

LAW, J., AND LODGE, P.   1978. Structure as process and environmental constraint. *Theory and Society* 5: 373–386.

LEE, G.   1979. The effect of social networks on the family. Pp. 27–56 in W. Burr, R. Hill, F. I. Nye, and I. Reiss (eds.), *Contemporary theories about the family.* (Volume One). Research-Based Theories. New York: Free Press.

LEGGETT, J.   1968. *Class, race and labor.* New York: Oxford University Press.

LEINHARDT, S.   1977. Social networks: a developing paradigm. Pp xiii–xxxiv in S. Leinhardt (ed.), *Social Networks.* New York: Academic Press.

LEISS, W.   1974. Critical theory and its future. *Political Theory* 2:330–349.

LEITER, K.   1980. *A primer on ethnomethodology.* New York: Oxford University Press.

LEVINE, A., AND WRIGHT, E. O.   1980. Rationality and the class struggle. *New Left Review* 123:47–68.

LEVI-STRAUSS, C.   1963. *Structural anthropology.* New York: Basic Books.

LEVITAN, T.   1975. Deviants as active participants in the labeling process: the visibly handicapped. *Social Problems* 22:548–557.

LEWIS, J. D., AND SMITH, R.   1980. *American sociology and pragmatism: Mead, Chicago sociology, and symbolic interactionism.* Chicago: University of Chicago Press.

LICHTMAN, R.   1970. Symbolic-interactionism and symbolic reality: some Marxist queries. *Berkeley Journal of Sociology* 15:75–94.

LIEBERMAN, S.   1956. The effects of changes in roles on the attitudes of role occupants. *Human Relations* 9:385–402.

LIGHT, J., AND MULLINS, N.   1979. A primer on block modeling procedure. Pp. 85–118 in P. Holland and S. Leinhardt (eds.), *Perspectives in social network research.* New York: Academic Press.

LIPSET, S. M.   1975. Social structure and social change. Pp. 172–209 in P. Blau (ed.), *Approaches to the study of social structure.* New York: Free Press.

LOCKWOOD, D.   1967. Some remarks on 'the social system'. Pp. 281–292 in N.J. Demerath III and R. Peterson (eds.), *System, change and conflict.* New York: Free Press.
    1981. The weakest link in the chain? some comments on the Marxist theory of action. Pp. 435–481 in R. Simpson and I. Simpson (eds.), *Research in the sociology of work.* Greenwich: Conn.: JAI Press, Inc.

LOFLAND, J.   1976. *Doing social life.* New York: John Wiley.
    1980. Early Goffman: style, structure, substance and soul. Pp. 24–51 in J. Ditton (ed.), *The view from Goffman.* New York: St. Martin's Press.

LOFLAND, L.   1973. *A world of strangers.* New York: Basic Books.

LOPREATO, J.   1971. The concept of equilibrium. Pp. 309–343 in H. Turk and R. Simpson (eds.), *Institutions and social exchange: the sociologies of Talcott Parsons and George Homans.* Indianapolis: Bobbs-Merrill.

LOUBSER, J. 1976. General introduction. Pp. 1–23 in J. Loubser, R. Baum, A. Effrar, and V. M. Lidz (eds.), *Explorations in general theory in social science: essays in honor of Talcott Parsons* (Volume One). New York: Free Press.

LUKACS, G. 1971. *History and class consciousness.* Cambridge: MIT Press.

MAINES, D. 1977. Social organization and social structure in symbolic interactionist thought. *Annual Review of Sociology* 3:235–259.

——— 1981. Recent developments in symbolic interaction. Pp. 461–486 in G. Stone and H. Faberman (eds.), *Social psychology through symbolic interaction* (second edition). New York: John Wiley.

MANDEL, E. 1975. *Late capitalism.* London: New Left Books.

MANNING, P. 1976. Decline of civility: a comment on Erving Goffman's sociology. *Canadian Review of Sociology and Anthropology* 13:13–25.

MARSH, J., AND STAFFORD, F. 1967. The effect of values on pecuniary behavior. *American Sociological Review* 32:740–754.

MARTINDALE, D. 1981. *The nature and types of sociological theory* (second edition). Boston: Houghton Mifflin.

MARTINS, H. 1972. The Kuhnian 'revolution' and its implications for sociology. Pp. 13–58 in T. J. Nossiter, A. H. Hanson and S. Rokkan (eds.), *Imagination and Precision in the social sciences.* London: Faber and Faber.

MARX, K. 1962. *Capital* (Volume Three). Moscow: Progress Publishers.

——— 1973. *Grundrisse.* New York: Vintage.

——— 1978. Preface to a contribution to the critique of political economy. Pp. 3–5 in R. Tucker (ed.), *The Marx-Engels reader.* New York: W. W. Norton & Co., Inc.

MATTHEWS, S. 1978. *The social world of old women: management of self-identity.* Beverly Hills: Sage.

MATZA, D. 1969. *Becoming Deviant.* Englewood Cliffs, N.J.: Prentice-Hall.

MAYHEW, B. 1980. Structuralism versus individualism: part I, shadowboxing in the dark. *Social Forces* 59:335–375.

——— 1981. Structuralism versus individualism: part II, ideology and other obfuscations. *Social Forces* 59:627–648.

MAYHEW, B., AND SCHOLLAERT, P. 1980. The concentration of wealth: a sociological model. *Sociological Focus* 13:1–35.

MCHUGH, P. 1968. *Defining the situation: the organization of meaning in social interaction.* Indianapolis: Bobbs-Merrill.

MCLAIN, R., AND WEIGERT, A. 1979. Toward a phenomenological sociology of the family: a programmatic essay. Pp. 160–205 in W. Burr, R. Hill, F. I. Nye, and I. Reiss (eds.), *Contemporary theories about the family.* Volume Two: General Theories/Theoretical Orientations. New York: Free Press.

MCNALL, S., AND JOHNSON, J. 1975. The new conservatives: ethnomethodologists, phenomenologists and symbolic interactionists. *Insurgent Sociologist* 5: 49–65.

MCSWEENEY, B. 1973. Meaning, context and situation. *Archives Europeenes de Sociologie* 14:137–153.

MEAD, G. H. 1934. *Mind, self and society.* Chicago: University of Chicago Press.

MEEK, R. 1967. *Economics and ideology and other essays.* London: Chapman and Hall.

MEHAN, H. 1979. *Learning lessons: social organization in the classroom.* Cambridge: Harvard University Press.

MEHAN, H., AND WOOD, H. 1975. *The reality of ethnomethodology.* New York: John Wiley.

MERTON, R. 1968. *Social theory and social structure.* New York: Free Press.

——— 1981. Remarks on theoretical pluralism. Pp. i–vii in P. Blau and R. Merton (eds.), *Continuities in structural inquiry.* Beverly Hills: Sage.

MILLS, C. W. 1978. Situated actions and vocabularies of motives. Pp. 301–307 in J. Manis and B. Meltzer (eds.), *Symbolic interaction* (third edition). Boston: Allyn & Bacon.

MITCHELL, J. C.   1969. *Social networks and urban situations*. Manchester: Manchester University Press.

MOLM, L., AND WIGGINS, J.   1979. A behavioral analysis of the dynamics of social exchange. *Social Forces* 57:1157–1179.

MOON, J. D.   1975. The logic of political inquiry. Pp. 131–228 in F. Greenstein and N. Polsky (eds.), *Handbook of political science*. Volume One: Political Science, Scope and Theory. Reading: Addison Wesley.

MOORE, W.   1978. Functionalism. Pp. 321–361 in T. Bottomore and R. Nisbet (eds.), *A history of sociological analysis*. New York: Basic Books.

1979. *World Modernization: the limits of convergence*. New York: Elsevier.

MUELLER, C.   1973. *The politics of communication*. New York: Oxford University Press.

MULKAY, M.   1979. *Science and the sociology of knowledge*. London: Allen and Unwin.

MUNCH, R.   1981. Talcott Parsons and the theory of action. I: the structure of the Kantian core. *American Journal of Sociology* 86:709–739.

1982. Talcott Parsons and the theory of action. II: the continuities of development. *American Journal of Sociology* 87:771–826.

NADEL, S. F.   1957. *Theory of social structure*. Glencoe, Illinois: Free Press.

NISBET, R.   1974. *The sociology of Emile Durkheim*. New York: Oxford University Press.

NOBLE, D.   1979. Social choice in machine design: the case of automatically controlled machine tools. Pp. 18–50 in A. Zimbalist (ed.), *Case studies in the labor process*. New York: Monthly Review Press.

O'CONNOR, J.   1973. *The fiscal crisis of the state*. New York: St. Martin's Press.

OFFE, C.   1975. The theory of the capitalist state and the problem of policy formation. Pp. 125–144 in L. Lindberg, R. Alford, C. Crouch, and C. Offe (eds.), *Stress and contradiction in modern capitalism*. Lexington: Lexington Books.

OFFE, C., AND RONGE, V.   1979. Theses on the theory of the state. Pp. 345–356 in J. W. Freiberg (ed.), *Critical sociology: european perspectives*. New York: Irvington Publishers.

O'KEEFE, D.   1979. Ethnomethodology. *Journal of the Theory of Social Behavior* 9: 187–220.

OLLMAN, B.   1972. Toward class consciousness next time: Marx and the working class. *Politics and Society* 3:1–24.

1976. *Alienation: Marx's conception of man in capitalist society* (second edition). Cambridge: Cambridge University Press.

1979. *Social and sexual revolution: essays on Marx and Reich*. Boston: South End Press.

PARKIN, F.   1978. Social Stratification. Pp. 599–632 in T. Bottomore and R. Nisbet (eds.), *A history of sociological analysis*. New York: Basic Books.

1979. *Marxism and class theory: a bourgeois critique*. New York: Columbia University Press.

PARSONS, T.   1937. *The structure of social action*. New York: McGraw-Hill.

1949. The social structure of the family. Pp. 173–201 in R. Anshen (ed.), *The family*. New York: Harper and Brothers.

1954. *Essays in sociological theory* (revised edition). Glencoe, Illinois: Free Press.

1960. *Structure and process in modern societies*. Glencoe, Illinois: Free Press.

1961. An outline of the social system. Pp. 30–79 in T. Parsons, E. Shils, K. Naegele, and J. Pitts (eds.), *Theories of society* (Volume One). Glencoe, Illinois: Free Press.

1966. *Societies: evolutionary and comparative perspectives*. Englewood Cliffs, N.J.: Prentice-Hall.

1967. *Sociological theory and modern society*. New York: Free Press.

1970. Equality and inequality in modern society, or social stratification revisited. *Sociological Inquiry* 40:13–72.

1971. *The system of modern societies.* Englewood Cliffs, N.J.: Prentice-Hall.

1975. The present status of 'structural-functional' theory in sociology. Pp. 67–83 in L. Coser (ed.). *The idea of social structure.* New York: Free Press.

1977. *Social systems and the evolution of action theory.* New York: Free Press.

PARSONS, T., AND PLATT, G.   1973. *The American university.* Cambridge: Harvard University Press.

PHILLIPSON, M.   1972. Theory, methodology and conceptualization. Pp. 77–118 in P. Filmer, M. Phillipson, D. Silverman, and D. Walsh (eds.), *New directions in sociological theory.* London: Collier-MacMillan.

PIVEN, F., AND CLOWARD, R.   1977. *Poor people's movements.* New York: Pantheon Books.

POULANTZAS, N.   1978. *State, power, socialism.* London: New Left Books.

PRZEWORSKI, A.   1977. Proletariat into a class: the process of class formation from Karl Katusky's *The Class Struggle* to recent controversies. *Politics and Society* 7: 343–402.

PSATHAS, G.   1973. Introduction. Pp. 1–21 in G. Psathas (ed.), *Phenomenological sociology: issues and applications.* New York: John Wiley.

1980. Approaches to the Study of the World of Everyday Life. *Human Studies* 3:3–17.

RADER, M.   1979. *Marx's interpretation of history.* Oxford: Oxford University Press.

RADNITSKY, G.   1970. *Contemporary schools of metascience* (revised and enlarged edition). New York: Humanities Press.

1972. Toward a theory of research which is neither logical reconstruction nor psychology or sociology of science. *Quality and Quantity*, 6:193–238.

REICH, M.   1981. *Racial inequality: a political economic analysis.* Princeton: Princeton University Press.

REX, J.   1974. *Sociology and the demystification of the modern world.* London: Routledge and Kegan Paul.

ROCHE, M.   1973. *Phenomenology, language and the social sciences.* London: Routledge and Kegan Paul.

ROCHER, G.   1975. *Talcott Parsons and American sociology.* New York: Barnes and Noble.

ROCK, P.   1979. *The making of symbolic interactionism.* Totowa, N.J.: Rowan and Littlefield.

ROSDOLSKY, R.   1977. *The making of Marx's 'Capital'.* London: Pluto Press.

ROSENBERG, M.   1981. The self concept: social product and social force. Pp. 593–624 in M. Rosenberg and R. Turner (eds.), *Social psychology.* New York: Basic Books.

ROSSI, I.   1981. Transformational structuralism: Levi-Strauss' definition of social structure. Pp. 27–50 in P. Blau and R. Merton (eds.), *Continuities in structural inquiry.* Beverly Hills: Sage.

ROSSIDES, D.   1976. *The American class system.* Boston: Houghton Mifflin.

1978. *The history and nature of sociological theory.* Boston: Houghton Mifflin.

RUNCIMAN, W.   1966. *Relative deprivation and social justice.* Berkeley: University of California Press.

SALAMAN, G.   1979. *Work organizations: resistance and control.* New York: Longman.

SAYER, D.   1979. *Marx's method.* Atlantic Highlands: Humanities Press.

SCHNEIDER, L.   1971. The dialectic in sociology. *American Sociological Review* 36: 667–678.

SCHUR, E.   1980. *The politics of deviance: stigma contests and the use of power.* Englewood Cliffs, N.J.: Prentice-Hall.

SCHUTZ, A.   1962. *The problem of social reality.* The Hague: Martinus Nijhoff.
1970. *On phenomenology and social relations.* Chicago: University of Chicago Press.
SCOTT, R.   1972. A proposed framework for analyzing deviance as a property of social order. Pp. 9–36 in R. Scott and J. Douglas (eds.), *Thoretical perspectives on deviance.* New York: Basic Books.
SENNETT, R.   1974. *The fall of public man.* New York: Vintage Books.
SENSAT, J.   1979. *Habermas and Marxism: an appraisal.* Beverly Hills: Sage.
SHAPERE, D.   1977. Scientific theories and their domains. Pp. 518–565 in F. Suppe (ed.), *The structure of scientific theories* (second edition). Urbana: University of Illinois Press.
SHIBUTANI, T.   1961. *Society and personality.* Englewood Cliffs, N.J.: Prentice-Hall.
SHIBUTANI, T., AND KWAN, K.   1965. *Ethnic stratification: a comparative approach.* New York: MacMillan.
SHOTT, S.   1979. Emotion and social life: a symbolic interactionist analysis. *American Journal of Sociology* 84: 1317–1334.
SIMMEL, G.   1950. *The sociology of Georg Simmel.* Glencoe, Illinois: Free Press.
SKOCPOL, T.   1979. *States and social revolutions.* Cambridge: Cambridge University Press.
SLABBERT, F. VAN ZYL.   1976. Functional methodology in the theory of action. Pp. 46–58 in J. Loubser, R. Baum, A. Effrat, and V. M. Lidz (eds.), *Explorations in general theory in social science: essays in honor of Talcott Parsons* (Volume One). New York: Free Press.
SMART, B.   1976. *Sociology, phenomenology and Marxian analysis.* London: Routledge and Kegan Paul.
SMELSER, N.   1959. *Social change in the industrial revolution.* Chicago: University of Chicago Press.
1963. *The sociology of economic life.* Englewood Cliffs, N.J.: Prentice-Hall.
1968. *Essays in sociological explanation.* Englewood Cliffs, N. J.: Prentice-Hall.
1971. Stability, instability, and the analysis of political corruption." Pp. 7–29 in B. Barber and A. Inkeles (eds.), *Stability and social change.* Boston: Little, Brown.
SMELSER, N., AND WARNER, S.   1971. *Sociological theory: a contemporary view.* New York: General Learning Press.
SMITH, A.   1973. *The concept of social change: a critique of the functionalist theory of social change.* London: Routledge and Kegan Paul.
SONQUIST, J., AND KOENIG, T.   1976. Examining corporate interconnections through interlocking directorates. Pp. 53–84 in T. Burns and W. Buckley (eds.), *Power and control: social structures and their transformation.* Beverly Hills: Sage.
SPANGLER, E., GORDON, M., AND PIPKIN, R.   1978. Token women: an empirical test of Kanter's hypothesis. *American Journal of Sociology* 84:160–170.
STEPHENS, J.   1979. *The transformation of capitalism in socialism.* London: Macmillan.
STINCHCOMBE, A.   1968. *Constructing social theories.* New York: Harcourt Brace Jovanovich.
1975. Merton's theory of social structure. Pp. 11–34 in L. Coser (ed.), *The idea of social structure.* New York: Free Press.
1978. *Theoretical methods in social history.* New York: Academic Press.
STONE, G.   1962. Appearance and the self. Pp. 86–118 in A. Rose (ed.), *Human behavior and social process.* Boston: Houghton Mifflin.
STRAUSS, A.   1978. *Negotiations.* San Francisco: Jossey Bass.

STRYKER, S.   1978. Symbolic interactionism as an approach to family relations. Pp. 323–332 in J. Manis and B. Meltzer (eds.), *Symbolic interaction* (third edition). Boston: Allyn & Bacon.

1980. *Symbolic interactionism.* Menlo Park: Benjamin/Cummings Publishing Co.

1981. Symbolic interactionism: themes and variations. Pp. 3–29 in M. Rosenberg and R. Turner (eds.), *Social psychology.* New York: Basic Books.

SUDNOW, D.   1965. Normal crimes: sociological features of the penal code in a public defender office. *Social Problems* 12:255–275.

SUMNER, C.   1979. *Reading ideology.* New York: Academic Press.

SWANSON, G.   1971. Frameworks for comparative research: structural anthropology and the theory of action. Pp. 141–202 in I. Vallier (ed.), *Comparative methods in sociology.* Berkeley: University of California Press.

SZACKI, J.   1979. *History of sociological thought.* Westport: Greenwood Press.

SZTOMPKA, P.   1974. *System and function.* New York: Academic Press.

1979. *Sociological dilemmas: toward a dialectical paradigm.* New York: Academic Press.

SZYMANSKI, A.   1978. *The capitalist state and the politics of class.* Cambridge: Winthrop Publishers.

TALLMAN, I., AND IHINGER-TALLMAN, M.   1979. Values, distributive justice and social change. *American Sociological Review* 44:216–235.

TAYLOR, C.   1977. Interpretation and the sciences of man. Pp. 101–131 in F. Dallmayr and T. McCarthy (eds.), *Understanding and social inquiry.* Notre Dame: University of Notre Dame Press.

THERBORN, G.   1978. *What does the ruling class do when it rules?* London: New Left Books.

THOMAS, D., FRANKS, D., AND CALONICO, J.   1972. Role-taking and power in social psychology. *American Sociological Review* 37:605–614.

THOMAS, P.   1976. Marx and Science. *Political Studies* 24:1–23.

THOMPSON, E. P.   1978. *The poverty of theory.* London: Merlin Press.

TIRYAKIAN, E.   1975. Neither Marx, nor Durkheim ... perhaps Weber. *American Journal of Sociology* 81:1–33.

TOBY, J.   1976. Inadequacy, instrumental activism, and the adolescent subculture. Pp. 407–414 in J. Loubser, R. Baum, A. Ettrar, and V. Lidz (eds.), *Exploration in general theory in social science: essays in honor of Talcott Parsons* (Volume One). New York: Free Press.

TURK, A.   1967. On the Parsonian approach to theory construction. *Sociological Quarterly* 8:37–50.

TURNER, J.   1978. *The structure of sociological theory* (revised edition). Homewood, Illinois: Dorsey Press.

TURNER, J., AND MARYANSKI, A.   1979. *Functionalism.* Menlo Park: Benjamin/Cummings Publishing Co.

TURNER, R.   1962. Role-taking: process versus conformity. Pp. 20–40 in A. Rose (ed.), *Human behavior and social processes.* Boston: Houghton Mifflin.

1968. The self-conception in social interaction. Pp. 93–106 in C. Gordon and K. Gergen (eds.), *The self in social interaction* (Volume One). New York: John Wiley.

TURNER, S.   1977. Blau's theory of differentiation: is it explanatory? *Sociological Quarterly* 18: 17–32.

1980. *Sociological explanation as translation.* New York: Cambridge University Press.

USEEM, B.   1980. Solidarity model, breakdown model, and the Boston anti-busing movement. *American Sociological Review* 45:357–369.

WAGNER, H.   1963. Types of sociological theory. *American Sociological Review* 28: 735–742.

1973. The scope of phenomenological sociology. Pp. 61–90 in G. Psathas (ed.), *Phenomenological sociology: issues and applications.* New York: John Wiley.

WALDMAN, S.   1972. *Foundations of political action: an exchange theory of politics.* Boston: Little, Brown.

WALLERSTEIN, I.   1979. *The capitalist world economy.* Cambridge: Cambridge University Press.

WALSH, D.   1972. Sociology and the social world. Pp. 15–36 in P. Filmer, M. Phillipson, D. Silverman, and D. Walsh (eds.), *New directions in sociological theory.* London: Collier/Macmillan.

WALSTER, E., BERSHEID, E., AND WALSTER, G. W.   1976. New directions in equity research. Pp. 1–42 in L. Berkowitz (ed.), *Equity theory: toward a general theory of social interaction.* New York: Academic Press.

WARDELL, M., AND BENSON, J. K.   1978. A dialectical view: foundation for an alternative sociological method. Pp. 232–248 in S. McNall (ed.), *Theoretical perspectives in sociology.* New York: St. Martin's Press.

WEBER, M.   1964. *The theory of social and economic organization.* Glencoe, Illinois: Free Press.

WEIGERT, A.   1981. *The Sociology of everyday life.* New York: Longman.

WEINSTEIN, E., AND TANUR, J.   1978. Meanings, purposes and structural resources in social interaction. Pp. 138–147 in J. Manis and B. Meltzer (eds.), *Symbolic interactions* (third edition). Boston: Allyn & Bacon.

WELLMAN, B.   1979. The community question: the intimate networks of East Yorkers. *American Journal of Sociology* 84:1201–1231.

1980. A guide to network analysis. Working Paper No. 1A, Structure Analysis Programme, University of Toronto, Toronto, Canada.

1981. Network analysis from method and metaphor to theory and substance. Working Paper 1B, Structural Analysis Programme, University of Toronto, Toronto, Canada.

WHITE, H.   1970. *Chains of opportunity.* Cambridge, Mass: Harvard University Press.

WHITE, H., BOORMAN, S., AND BREIGER, R.   1976. Social structure from multiple networks. *American Journal of Sociology* 81:730–780.

WIEDER, L.   1974. *Language and social reality.* The Hague: Mouton.

WILSON, T.   1970. Normative and interpretive paradigms in sociology. Pp. 57–79 in J. Douglas (ed.), *Understanding everyday life.* London: Routledge and Kegan Paul.

WINCH, R.   1963. *The modern family.* New York: Holt, Rinehart and Winston.

1977. *Familial organization.* New York: Free Press.

WINTON, C.   1974. *Theory and measurement in sociology.* Cambridge, Mass.: Schenkman.

WOLFE, A.   1977. *The Limits of legitimacy.* New York: Free Press.

WRIGHT, C.   1975. Social structure and mass communications behavior. Pp. 379–416 in L. Coser (ed.), *The Idea of social structure.* New York: Free Press.

WRIGHT, E.   1978. *Class, crisis and the state.* London: New Left Books.

1979. Value controversy and social research. *New Left Review* 116:53–82.

1980a. *Class structure and income determination.* New York: Academic Press.

1980b. Class and occupation. *Theory and Society* 9:177–201.

WRONG, D.   1970. The oversocialized conception of man in modern sociology. Pp. 29–40 in G. Stone and H. Faberman (eds.), *Social psychology through symbolic interaction.* Boston: Ginn Blaisdell.

1979. *Power: its forms, bases and uses.* New York: Harper and Row, Pub.

YAFFE, D. 1973. The Marxian theory of crisis, capital and the state. *Economy and Society* 2:186–232.

ZEITLIN, I. 1973. *Rethinking sociology.* Englewood Cliffs, N.J.: Prentice-Hall.

ZIMMERMAN, D. 1974. Preface. Pp. 9–26 in D. L. Wieder, *Language and social reality.* The Hague: Mouton.

ZIMMERMAN, D., AND POLLNER, M. 1971. The everyday world as a phenomenon. Pp. 80–104 in J. Douglas (ed.), *Understanding everyday life.* London: Routledge and Kegan Paul.

ACKNOWLEDGMENTS

Permission to reprint the following quotes is hereby gratefully acknowledged:

P. 8   Michael Mulkay, *Science and the Sociology of Knowledge*. London: Allen and Unwin. Copyright © 1979 Allen and Unwin.

Pp. 30, 31   Hubert Blalock and Paul Wilken, *Intergroup Processes: A Micro-Macro Perspective*. New York: Free Press. Copyright © 1979 Free Press.

Pp. 40, 70   Emile Durkheim, *The Division of Labor in Society*, translated by George Simpson. New York: Free Press. Copyright © 1933 The Macmillan Company.

P. 65   Robert Merton, *Social Theory and Structure*, enlarged edition. New York: Free Press. Copyright © 1968 Free Press.

P. 71   Wilbert Moore, "Functionalism," in Tom Bottomore and Robert Nisbet (eds.) *A History of Sociological Analysis*. New York: Basic Books, and London: Heinemann Educational Books. Copyright © 1978 Basic Books and Heinemann Educational Books.

P. 84   Charles Ackerman and Talcott Parsons, "The Concept of 'Social System' as a Theoretical Device" in *Concepts, Theory and Explanation in the Behavioral Sciences*. New York: Random House. Copyright © 1966 Random House.

Pp. 88, 210   Talcott Parsons, *Sociological Theory and Modern Society*. New York: Free Press. Copyright © 1967 Free Press.

P. 92   Richard Munch, "Talcott Parsons and the Theory of Action. II: The Continuity of Development," *American Journal of Sociology*, 87 (1982), pp 771-826. Copyright © 1982 The University of Chicago Press.

Pp. 93, 94   Talcott Parsons, *Essays in Sociological Theory*, rev. ed. New York: Free Press. Copyright © 1954, 1949 Free Press.

P. 100   Dennis Wrong, *Power: Its Forms, Bases, and Uses*. New York: Harper & Row. Copyright © 1979 Harper & Row and Basil Blackwell, Ltd.

P. 111   Paul Rock, *The Making of Symbolic Interactionism*, Totowa. NJ: Rowman and Littlefield. Copyright © 1979 Rowman and Littlefield.

Pp. 115, 210   Percy Cohen, "Is Positivism Dead?" *Sociological Review*, 28 (1980), pp. 141-76. Copyright © 1980 Routledge & Keegan Paul Ltd.

P. 116   Thomas P. Wilson, "Normative and Interpretive Paradigms in Sociology," in Jack Douglas (ed.), *Understanding Everyday Life*. New York: Aldin Publishing Co. Copyright © 1970 Aldine Publishing Co. and Routledge & Keegan Paul Ltd.

P. 143   Raymond McLain and Andrew Weigert, "Toward a Phenomenological Sociology of the Family," in *Contemporary Theories about the Family, Volume Two: General Theories/Theoretical Orientations.* Wesley Burr, Reuben Hill, F. Ivan Nye, and Ira Reiss, eds. New York: Free Press. Copyright © 1979 Free Press.

P. 147   C. Robert Freeman, "Phenomenological Sociology and Ethnomethodology," in Jack Douglas (ed.), *Introduction to the Sociologies of Everyday Life.* Boston: Allyn and Bacon. Copyright © 1980 Allyn and Bacon.

P. 155   D. Lawrence Wieder, *Language and Social Reality.* The Hague: Mouton. Copyright © 1974 Mouton Publishers.

P. 158   Suzanne Kessler and Wendy McKenna, *Gender: An Ethnomethodological Approach.* New York: John Wiley and Sons. Copyright © 1978 by John Wiley and Sons.

P. 164   John Anderson, "Practical Reasoning in Action" in Jack Douglas (ed.) *Existential Sociology.* New York: Cambridge University Press. Copyright © 1977 Cambridge University Press.

P. 165   Denis Gleeson and Michale Erben, "Meaning in Context: Notes Toward a Critique of Ethnomethodology," *British Journal of Sociology,* 27 (1976), pp. 474-83. Copyright © 1976 Routledge and Kegan Paul Ltd.

P. 169   C. C. Harris, "Changing Conceptions of the Relation between Family and Societal Forms in Western Society, in R. Scase (ed.), *Industrial Society: Class, Cleavage and Control.* New York: St. Martin's Press. Copyright © 1977 St. Martin's Press.

P. 171   Russell Keat and John Urry, *Social Theory as Science.* Boston: Routledge & Keegan Paul Ltd. Copyright © 1975 John Urry and R. N. Keat.

P. 174   Paul Thomas, "Marx and Science," *Political Studies,* 24 (1976), pp 1-23. Copyright © 1976 Oxford University Press.

P. 180   Leszek Kolakowski, *Main Currents of Marxism: Its Rise, Growth and Dissolution.* Oxford: The Clarendon Press. Copyright © 1978 The Clarendon Press.

P. 191   Nicholas Abercrombie, *Class, Structure and Knowledge: Problems in the Sociology of Knowledge.* New York: New York University Press. Copyright © 1980 Nicholas Abercrombie.

Pp. 193, 206   John D. Stephens, *The Transition from Capitalism to Socialism.* London: Macmillan Press Ltd. Copyright © 1979 John D. Stephens.

Pp. 194, 195   Richard Appelbaum, "Marx's Theory of the Falling Rate of Profit: Toward a Dialectical Analysis of Structural Social Change," *American Sociological Review,* 43 (1978), p. 75. Copyright © 1978 The American Sociological Association.

233   Acknowledgments

P. 205   Daniel Bell, *The Coming of Post-Industrial Society.* New York: Basic Books. Copyright © 1973 by Daniel Bell.

P. 207   Axel van den Berg, "Critical Theory: Is There Still Hope?" *American Journal of Sociology,* 86 (1980), pp. 449-478. Copyright © 1980 The University of Chicago Press.

P. 207   Jurgen Habermas, *Theory and Practice.* Boston: Beacon Press. Copyright © 1973 Beacon Press.

Name

Index

Subject Index